MASTERING THE METAL

MASTERING THE METAL

THE STORY OF JAMES WATSON AND EDDIE BRAVO

ZACK MOORE

WITH EDDIE BRAVO AND JAMES WATSON

Post Hill
PRESS

A POST HILL PRESS BOOK

Mastering the Metal:
The Story of James Watson and Eddie Bravo
© 2023 by Zack Moore with Eddie Bravo and James Watson
All Rights Reserved

ISBN: 978-1-63758-580-1
ISBN (eBook): 978-1-63758-581-8

Cover design by Conroy Accord
Cover art illustration by Hannah Vandermolen

This is a work of nonfiction. All people, locations, events, and situation are portrayed to the best of the author's memory.

Post Hill Press
New York • Nashville
permutedpress.com

Published in the United States of America
1 2 3 4 5 6 7 8 9 10

To Jamie, Luca, Mateo, and 10th Planet family.
—ZACK

To the 17 fans of my music worldwide,
y'all are my favorite people.
—EDDIE

To my sweetheart.
—JAMES

CONTENTS

Chapter 1: The Introduction (Zack) 1

Chapter 2: The Music (Zack) 30

Chapter 3: Let There Be Rock (James) 43

Chapter 4: Little Rock, Arkansas (James) 53

Chapter 5: Meeting James Watson (Zack) 63

Chapter 6: Edgar Cano (James) 75

Chapter 7: James Discovers Rock 'n' Roll (James) 90

Chapter 8: Santa Ana High School (James) 105

Chapter 9: Training Partners (Zack) 114

Chapter 10: Resistance (James) 134

Chapter 11: The Rap Game (Zack) 149

Chapter 12: James Moves To Hollywood (James) 164

Chapter 13: Blackened Kill Symphony (James) 177

Chapter 14: I'm Alive (James) 191

Chapter 15: Laurel Canyon and Religion (Zack) 201

Chapter 16: The Definition of Quality (Zack) 210

Chapter 17: The System (Zack) 237

Chapter 18: The Master (Zack) 253

Endnotes. 277

Acknowledgments. 278

CHAPTER 1

THE INTRODUCTION
(ZACK)

Thursday, January 27th, 2022

"Could you please put a mask on?" asked the Avis rental car employee.

"My friend just told you that there are bed bugs on your bus. Let's stay focused," I replied.

"We are still on airport property, sir."

"Please just give me the car that's reserved for Zack Moore."

Welcome to Los Angeles, California.

A place where people from all around the world flock to be seen is being run by a fear so heavy that many are willingly covering their faces and consciously voting for more mandates, while they try to force the rest of us to take part in a lie they can't let go of.

Cover my mouth.

Stick it in me.

Tell me what to do.

Govern me harder.

On some level, you can't blame the businesses or employees in this climate. There's real tyranny going on here. This is not Texas. It's a tale of two distinct cultures in America, a split that can feel like it may never be resolved.

California businesses have a reasonable fear of potential consequences if they don't comply completely. It doesn't take coming to California to know that things are a bit odd here.

The only people in Texas that seem to still hold onto masks are the politicized administrators in charge of the big city public schools.

Hospitals don't have a choice since the feds are forcing them to comply. The employees at Austin-Bergstrom International Airport don't bother you for not wearing a mask. It isn't until you get on the plane that things get weird.

Masks were never necessary, so the forced masking we've seen happen across America is just forced expression. They are a forced acknowledgment that we're all taking part in this thing that we're not supposed to tell the truth about and a form of religious garb for Godless people who think they're too smart for religion.

Their desire to force participation in their new religion is a complete violation of our First Amendment and our personal sovereignty.

Even worse are the corrupt politicians forcing nonfunctioning medical products with thousands of associated potential health consequences from corrupt companies on the public. It's a darker, and more obviously corrupt, form of forced expression.

States now decide which laws they do and don't want to follow. Some states are determining you don't have the rights granted to you by the Constitution with their attempts at forced expression as a condition of employment, education, or health care. California is one of those states.

New York is too. I went to my first Yankees game as a three-year-old. I taught myself to read by analyzing box scores in the local newspapers the morning after games, frustrated when a game ended too late to make the next morning's paper. Yet during the 2021 season, I would have been relegated to the "unvaccinated" section of

2

the stadium. Taking a product that was rushed to market became a requirement to take part in life.

This trip to Los Angeles was a trip back in time, a reminder of "The Science" of early June 2020, when we were told masks worked as Antifa riots broke out. This left-wing militant group had been wearing masks since 2017 to conceal their identities. It was a normalization of their preferred attire.

Of course, Americans were told masks didn't stop transmission when their perceived usefulness could have been used to open up small businesses in March, April, and May of 2020.

Masks "worked" once they facilitated political events for a political movement whose supporters wanted to unseat a president they perceived to be the worst thing that ever happened to the country because their television told them so.

We were also told that "racial justice protests" couldn't spread Covid. That was fun.

Traveling has taken on a new feel. I'm traveling in America, but aspects of it will make me feel like I'm in a foreign land.

Michael Plaster, an Austin native who moved out to Los Angeles a decade ago to pursue filmmaking dreams, flew in with me.

I'm a New Jersey native who moved to Austin after a childhood of visits and dreams of one day becoming a Texan. The dreams officially came true the day I looked down at a license four years ago with that beautiful five-letter word TEXAS in the top left corner, and my cauliflower ears below.

Plaster is Eddie Bravo's primary documentarian, the videographer behind the "Mastering the System" series on the 10th Planet website, and a founder-slash-owner of The Grappling Network, a video platform with distribution across various online streaming services.

He was the first to properly explain to me how Chinese Communist Party (CCP) money could influence our industries like it had Hollywood.

The Grappling Network hopes to become the background noise at bars across the country as Americans hop off the traditional ball sports wave. The popularity of the three major American sports has been threatened by those sports leagues, and everyone in the media that covers them, going along with the totalitarian and divisive mainstream narrative. It's to the chagrin of the average fan who expects sports to be an escape from their daily slog.

Sports are intended to be an inspiring experience by watching examples of the heights of human potential, but recently it has frequently turned into an extension of the politics that audiences head to sports to avoid. Fighting has become a nice replacement for a lot of fans, something real. A sport with athletes who are not completely beholden to a big sneaker deal that is built on questionable labor practices—athletes who still have real opinions, rather than what you hear at pro-ball sports press conferences.

Legacy news networks, Hollywood, American-based multi-national corporations (whether Silicon Valley, the apparel industry, or professional sports leagues), academic institutions from universities down to elementary schools, and establishment politicians are all part of the narrative.

Once you've seen it, you see it everywhere. They all have the same opinions.

Pro-lockdown, pro-riot, pro-mask, pro-vaccine mandate, and so on. We know all of their opinions now. They've made sure to tell us.

Each company is always working and positioning itself via public statements to maximize their future environmental, social, and governance (ESG) score, a worldwide social credit score standard for corporations.

ESG is a set of standards for a company's behavior used by "socially conscious investors" to screen potential investments.

In a tweet from March 2, 2022, mathematician, author, and social critic James A. Lindsay says the ESG score exists for three reasons:

1. A sword, to implement divide-and-conquer and box out competition.
2. A shield, to look morally virtuous while doing it.
3. To install arbitrary power, diversity, equity, and inclusion (DEI), ESG, and other political officers and to enforce compliance with its arbitrary standards.

The point of the ESG is to give people like Klaus Schwab of the World Economic Forum infinite power over everything and everyone. Politicians just come out and say it now: the goal is a new world order.

It exists to enforce market actors to fall in line for global money while pretending to serve some incoherent vision of a "greater good." Do so and you too shall profit.

It doesn't matter if your food product is filled with cancer causing chemicals or your new pill kills people, your company hash-tagged "Black Lives Matter" on Twitter.

The propaganda push hasn't stopped since March 2020.

In the non-digital world, we get constant reminders of these politics every time we see a perfectly healthy twenty-something with a mask, the Democrat MAGA hat, on outside during a bright, sunny day. Walking alone.

Politics are everywhere now. They've become unavoidable. My intention isn't to be political, but to not acknowledge the environment we exist in at this moment in history is to not tell the story of what we're living through. The nature of reality itself is now a political conversation. There is no explaining where we are in early 2022 without discussing the experience of the Covid cold war.

We can't forget this. We can't forget who did this to us. We can't let history be rewritten.

Of course, to be Eddie Bravo is to be impacted by this.

We've all been impacted.

Plaster and I hopped in my rental car and set our GPS in the direction of 10th Planet Headquarters in downtown Los Angeles.

This was my second trip to train at 10th Planet Headquarters and my first to Eddie's nightly 8:45 p.m. competition class. We stopped at Starbucks for post-flight caffeine and something light to eat. From the drive-thru, we could see the sparkling new SoFi Stadium where the Super Bowl was played two weeks later on February 13th, 2022.

I didn't know this at the time. I hadn't watched a game all season.

Previously, my focus as a writer was on the world of NFL salary caps and player contracts: how teams spent their money and determining, then communicating, which spending patterns seemed to have the most success.

It was *Moneyball* for football. I was working to see what was being undervalued and what kind of decisions created the greatest return on investment, thus increasing an organization's probability of securing a Super Bowl championship.

This pursuit was guided by a dream, a goal of becoming an NFL agent or working in an NFL front office, the career path I saw forward with my experiences around the game as a college football player.

Now I don't care for any of it.

Taking the exit off Interstate 110 and pulling into downtown Los Angeles, Plaster pointed out a building on the corner that was delayed for a few years while Donald Trump was president because his administration had reworked trade deals that slowed the flow of Chinese money in American building projects.

Joe Biden's administration turned that faucet back on. "The Big Guy" probably got his 10 percent somewhere along the money trail too.

All of it just feels like more evidence of my "conspiracy theory" that Covid-19 is a war between a largely unsuspecting, unknowing global citizenry and the Chinese Communist Party, World Economic Forum, and BlackRock types with the established elements of the world's political and corporate classes, especially here in America.

From Nancy Pelosi to the Mitt Romney-types around the world, from Nike to Adidas, from *The Wall Street Journal* to the

New York Times, from the Celtics to the Lakers—they're all bought and paid for.

Their goals are diametrically opposed to the people's goals: lockdowns, silencing dissent on social media in the name of safety, endless arguments over masks to provoke and distract citizens from dealing with more pressing issues, Black Lives Matter, and Antifa-fostered riots, mail-in voting, and so on.

They sold out and consistently attack our nation's most foundational principles: speech, guns, due process.

You can tell who the bad guys are because they tell you they are every time they push woke politics. It became pretty simple in 2020. The woke politics are a signal for us to distrust.

There are vaccine mandates that push every potential dissenter out of entire industries, including our military and health care. It's all done for products that are only efficacious in providing profit for the connected, establishment class of America.

Pfizer paid the largest criminal fine in United States history for false advertising; yet people are supposed to just blindly trust them because Hunter Biden's dad and a bunch of other good-for-nothing lifetime politicos said so.

The list of things that benefited this one agenda is long, and they have attacked the rights of those who oppose them in any way, large or small. That is cancel culture: the effort to render people this group disagrees with as unfit and unable to produce and acquire resources in their given field.

Where the old school communists would kill you, these communists create circumstances where you will be unable to survive, and they hope you'll finish the job for them via suicide or overdose (two American problems that haven't gotten better over the last two years).

Vaccine mandates are the next step in cancel culture, making your silent dissent, or simple critical thinking, punishable. It's an attempt at taking personal autonomy away from you and your children with the help of the pharmaceutical industry that created the opioid epidemic we are now living, and dying, through.

At the time of this trip, Canadians can't go to a grocery store without a vaccine passport. Going to a restaurant can also require a vaccine passport in Los Angeles.

I get shocked looks for my maskless face in convenience stores and am forced to wear a mask to legally buy cannabis, a hilarious irony.

The week leading into Super Bowl Sunday saw a vote to extend the State of Emergency for California, while the state prepared to host seventy thousand at SoFi Stadium.

Our moral betters, including the CCP's favorite American athlete LeBron James, were seen maskless all game in a city where the peasants can't get a drive-thru coffee without one.

Ellen DeGeneres enjoyed the fresh air in the stands, while audience members in her studio have been masked.

Los Angeles Mayor Eric Garcetti was seen at the game not following his own orders.

Gavin Newsom made a maskless appearance at the 49ers vs. Rams NFC championship game the weekend I visited. Garcetti was maskless in a photo with Magic Johnson, then he publicly claimed that he was holding his breath while his mask was off.

Hilarious.

None of this is supposed to make sense. Letting the citizens know that you don't have to follow the rules that you make and enforce like a tyrant is the point. That's all.

Making people do things that make no sense makes them more likely to do things that make no sense, like taking your shoes off at the airport.

Confusion, demoralization, and distractions are key.

The creep is key.

The crises to justify the creep and the creep comes like the slow intensification of the squeeze on a good rear naked choke: "Ten percent, twenty percent, forty percent...seventy percent...tap or nap."

The Introduction

To speak about this time is to speak of politics. The early 1940s are remembered for the last World War, so too shall be this time.

To exist is to be affected, the degrees vary based on where you live, who your surround yourself with, and what you do for work.

It's a line of demarcation in our lives, an experience that changed all of us in some way. We saw elements of a near-death experience at the outset with our lack of knowledge of what virus might be coming to our shores, followed by the fear of recognizing the lengths that corrupt entities were willing to go to in order to see an agenda win out.

Being Eddie during a time where the mob was looking for scalps makes for an interesting experience. He has generally kept a low profile as the previous two years illustrated to him the beauty in the simplicity of his life with his wife, son, friends, black belts, and team. He's not trying to convince anyone of his beliefs anymore; he's just going to exist with the good people he has around him.

If you can't figure it out now, he's not going to be the one to convince you. He's detached from the emotion of it, free from caring what others think and continuing to build a life where he can't be impacted by what those others think.

Early in the Covid event, or Event 201 as the Johns Hopkins Center for Health Security, the World Economic Forum, and the Bill and Melinda Gates Foundation called their October 18, 2019 planning meeting, Eddie was frustrated with Moonheads who were going along with the narrative.

Moonheads are what we call the black belt business owners who run each of the one hundred-plus 10th Planet Jiu Jitsu schools around the world. This is the organization a thirty-three-year-old Eddie Bravo founded immediately following his submission victory over Royler Gracie at ADCC (Abu Dhabi Combat Club) in 2003. Each school is called a Moon.

10th Planet Austin, under the leadership of Curtis Hembroff and Gabe Tuttle, had broken into smaller units to continue the training momentum that we had all worked very hard to build as individuals in our own journey, as a team, and as a community.

Guys and girls were training at satellite locations but also training in small groups in the gym the whole time. I trained with Eddie's brown belt, Manny Chavez, who would become our Moonhead at a new Round Rock location in September 2020. It felt like we were practicing our religion in some country that had banned our religion. We were sparring in the garage, trying to stay quiet.

Thankfully, the neighbors were cool.

Some other 10th Planet schools had no plans of reopening yet and weren't doing all they could to serve their community. Our role is to be the space where people come to forget about their problems and improve themselves; their space for therapy.

And people had a lot of problems they needed to forget about.

The government was threatening Eddie's livelihood, plus the careers of many people he cared about. Eddie was left wondering if some of his black belts truly listened and learned what he was teaching, to not believe things just because someone else said them, but to look into it and find out for yourself.

This was a stressful time, and guys like us were already at our wits' end. The story the mainstream establishment was telling during this time has, over time, been proven to be a lie in every meaningful way. But for us, there were too many holes in the story already; we knew too much. And over time, a "crazy conspiracy theorist" like Eddie Bravo would be proven prescient.

A major moment for me was UFC President Dana White's press conference after the UFC was the first major sport to return to action in May 2020. This was months before the other sports would.

After the UFC Fight Night on May 13th that was headlined by the Glover Teixeira TKO victory over Anthony Smith, a reporter asked Dana White how he felt about a *New York Times* article that was critical of the UFC's execution of their return to fights with event UFC 249. As White pointed out, this writer had never written about the

UFC before, but now he was going to impose his politics on the situation, which was getting him a lot of attention.

Clicks.

A huge factor of the Covid-19 response was politicized journalists maximizing their clicks throughout the event by flooding the market with takes that would evoke the maximum level of fear for the virus or maximum fear for the social consequences of disobeying the authorities they agreed with.

Mainstream journalists would openly mock the Covid-associated deaths of people who didn't support Covid lockdowns with the same unquestioning ferocity that they did.

An interim lightweight championship match between Justin Gaethje and Tony Ferguson headlined UFC 249. Tony had already won an interim title in October 2017, but was stripped of it due to a freak knee injury.

After Tony earned that belt, Eddie put his own black belt around Tony's waist. This was the black belt he received from Jean Jacques Machado upon his own return from that fateful ADCC, a great sign of respect for a student.

White responded to the reporter's question by saying, "Oh, fuck that guy.... I don't give a shit what that guy thinks, what he has to say, or what he writes. Good for him. He's pulling good traffic."

The reporter began, "Do you not worry about..."

White shut him down by saying, "I don't give a fuck."

"Fair enough..."

"Don't give a fuck," White repeated with an intense stare.

It was metal.

In mid-May 2020, 10th Planet Austin reopened to the public. There were no masks, no changes other than us using the back door to enter. We added a liability waiver that everyone needed to sign upon their first visit to the school.

We celebrated our return with a belting ceremony where I earned my purple belt, which comes after white and blue, but before brown and black. It provided me an opportunity to step up to a bigger role as a leader—a step closer to being a made man.

From my perspective, a blue belt seems to be earned when you have illustrated that you've made a lifestyle commitment to the sport. Purple belts are said to be reserved for blue belts who have illustrated a commitment that has them on the path towards black. You have proven yourself to be more than capable.

Brown belt seems to be for those that hit that next level of technical understanding. Brown belts are purple belts, but better in all the important ways, while black is a total mastery of the mental and physical side of the sport. Black belts are the kind of coaches Eddie can trust to properly program the students with all of the best that the system has to offer and fill the leadership role that the belt represents.

The black belt is a huge stamp of approval. Coaches don't want to give those out to people who might sully the reputation of that black belt for everyone else in the system and those in the know. Your coaches are going to have to trust that you're going to stay committed to the path, you're going to stay sharp, and you're going to stay committed in your focus on the evolution of the sport.

After promotions, my coach Curtis returned home to Alaska with his wife Priscilla for a year to try and serve his Kenaitze Indian Tribe, a longtime goal of his, to bring back what he had learned outside his tribe to serve his people. He left all of us to carry forward what he started.

Four years prior, in late 2015, Curtis had come out from Los Angeles and planted our 10th Planet flag in the middle of Texas and quickly built a formidable team with multiple schools—a remarkable leader. Originally, 10th Planet Austin was across the street from where we are now, housed in the Joe Rogan-affiliated Onnit Gym.

As we got back into the gym regularly, I began to see that everyone there had a similar perspective. We weren't sure what was happening, but we were done listening. We knew the things we were told by our society's formerly trusted institutions were not true.

With everything else going on, our gym environment was the only place that felt real. I'm sure that was lifesaving for a lot of people, at our gym and at others that did the same.

Since that first day back in May 2020, our school has doubled in size, added that Round Rock location, and is in the process of adding two to three more locations in the next two years. We attracted more people to our tribe, more people who know that you must be willing to die if you want to live.

These were people who found training important enough to move their lives from California or New York to come train with us, people who trusted the 10th Planet name and what we were building in Austin.

"The Summer of Love" hadn't kicked off yet, so while I watched White's response and thought the media's reckoning was right around the corner, a long series of distractions and ways to prolong the "pandemic" had slowed that reckoning down.

As we began to realize that Texas, Georgia, and other states that had reopened for two, and then three, weeks with no wave of the dead bodies that the CCP-influenced and allied corporate media in America promised us, the establishment's narrative took damage.

But George Floyd's death and the subsequent riots provided not just a distraction, but a Covid case bump through the summer to help carry Covid fear to the mail-in ballot election through case counting. And there was a lot of fraudulent "counting" going on that year.

On June 1, 10th Planet Long Beach was burned down and destroyed. Everything was lost and one of our Moons would no longer be operating, leaving a community without their home or ability to train.

Every business that was burned down on that block was black- or brown-owned.

Every 10th Planet school was affected by what has happened between 2020 and 2022. Our 10th Planet Montreal location was raided for doing Jiu Jitsu in January 2022.

The only way out of this thing is through creating tribes of people you can trust to build communities and businesses together. Otherwise, you're always at risk of being spit out by a system that not only doesn't care about you, but also has the gall to pretend it cares with all their nice-sounding, bumper sticker slogans.

Michael and I pulled around the back of 10th Planet Headquarters, parked, and rolled up our first joint of the trip. It's the proper way to do Jiu Jitsu, opening up your creativity and your ability to tap into the flow state.

We were 0.3 miles from where the Lakers play in one direction and 0.5 miles from Skid Row in the other direction.

As we smoked, Charles Rials showed up. Originally, I was slated to stay on his couch for a few days, but I opted for a hotel as my old neck injury flared up the Saturday before my flight. I'd never met him, yet he offered me a place to stay. Such is the way of our tribe.

It's comforting to know you can go to a whole lot of somewheres in this world and find people with decent values who you can inherently trust to a reasonable point. Jiu Jitsu gyms are becoming travel destinations and community centers for people looking to work hard and grow. That has value that can't be measured with numbers.

If you want to find some good people, find a good fight gym.

Passing the joint between the three of us, Charles began to tell me his story as a fifteen-year-old foster kid who left to try and make it on his own, which he has. Martial arts and the military have always been a great path for young men who otherwise might not have had the opportunity to find the right mentors for them. This is a story that comes up for me time after time. Hundreds of conversations like this educate me on the human experience.

On a later trip, during a moment such as this, Charles showed us the news clip regarding the stepfather who beat him so badly that he was put in foster care two different times. The newscaster tells us that stepfather, "Mr. Cecil," was beaten to death with a wooden dowel by a Mexican gangbanger he hired to do his lawn.

THE INTRODUCTION

It was a surreal experience hearing Charles recount the way this man treated him and learning about his ultimate karmic demise.

We stomped out the joint and walked in the back door. The front window of the dojo was still covered with a black privacy sheet so that people walking by on the street side couldn't see inside.

I saw Eddie briefly in February 2021 as he was in Austin for a Who's Number One event with FloGrappling. Eddie, myself, and a few others had what we call a "team safety meeting" in the parking lot where we got a glimpse at what he was thinking about at the time.

We were on a similar wavelength then, both talking about how everything we saw around us at the gym and around our people was real, while the narratives that were formed on these social media sites and online weren't even happening in a real physical space. They aren't real—not the opinions, sometimes not even the people. They are robots or might as well be robots. Non-player characters, NPCs for short.

Algorithms decide what is popular. Code decides what is seen as a successfully shared thought. The best idea doesn't win. The preferred idea is propagated.

Fake world narratives inside the fake world of cyberspace.

As you can imagine, if you get Eddie rolling, he puts on a show. His public persona is who he is.

He's deeply metaphorical, thinking for the sake of thinking. He plays with ideas just to see how it helps the rest of his thoughts sit in his mind. Above all else, he's just looking for a good laugh.

The last time I saw Eddie for an extended period like this was in September 2019. He came to Austin for a Thursday morning appearance on Infowars with Alex Jones, a Friday night Tin Foil Hat comedy show with Sam Tripoli, Reed Marshal Becker, and Xavier Guerrero, and then a Saturday morning seminar at 10th Planet Austin.

Appear on the news on Thursday morning. Comedian on Friday night. World-class martial artist on Saturday morning.

The world is waiting for his grand reappearance on *The Joe Rogan Experience*, but he's been giving the public bits and pieces of where his head is at through the *Tin Foil Hat* podcast with his compatriots Tripoli and XG. In April 2022, he launched his own podcast named *Look Into It* on Rokfin.

Here I was in town, ready to hear the rants that so many wanted to hear.

I changed in the locker room, came out onto the mat, and warmed up as brown belt Danny Gutierrez finished teaching his all-levels class.

We went in for the brief right-hand slap with the hug, which serves as the handshake for friends in the Jiu Jitsu community, as his class ended.

Eddie walked in, came on the mat, took his seat on his knees, and went into his review of the Courtney Love documentary he was watching before the next class started. It's complete with all the intelligence connections and conspiratorial angles. We're on the same page.

I'd spent the previous six months thinking about the music scene in Laurel Canyon during the late 1960s and how dark forces have captured the entertainment industry.

Most people learn of Eddie through his appearances on *The Joe Rogan Experience*; it's how I did. Because of this, his 10th Planet schools are filled with people who know what he is about and what he stands for. People seek out 10th Planet for the Jiu Jitsu, but it's also a culture that has been built through the broadcasting of these conversations. It would make sense, Eddie and Joe met on the mats at Jean Jacques Machado's Jiu Jitsu school.

10th Planet represents a chance for someone like me to be part of a society of like-minded people. These are curious types obsessed with seeking out whatever information will better help them understand the world around them and how to solve a problem.

About 75 percent of people who inquire about training at 10th Planet Austin first heard of it through Joe Rogan or Eddie Bravo.

My introduction to Joe's podcast was episode number 208 with "Freeway Rick" Ross. My friend Derek King, a high school football teammate and college football training partner during winter and summer breaks, was the one who turned me onto it. He is someone who I'll be seeing on this trip to Los Angeles.

Regardless of the illegality of what he did, listening to "The Real Rick Ross" tell a story of making hundreds of millions of dollars selling crack cocaine in Los Angeles in the 1980s, while being illiterate, and then teaching himself to read in prison to get himself out was a deeply inspiring tale.

It also alerted me to a conspiracy theory I hadn't known about at the time, which was the fact that the CIA was involved in drug trafficking operations that helped spark and sustain the crack epidemic. They purposefully destroyed black, urban communities in cities like the one I'm in right now the same way these CIA types would destroy white, rural communities in the 2000s with the opiate epidemic.

No matter how big he gets, at the heart of Joe's podcast success is a willingness, ability, and knowledge base that allows him to dive into topics that legacy corporate media outlets would never cover. In fact, the biggest reason why he's successful is just the personality type that would lend him to honestly discussing topics like "Freeway Rick" Ross's life story.

People are always in search of the most real shit, and free-flowing podcast conversations have become the most real form of media most have ever consumed.

A guest comes in and, in this case, a comedian, one of the more articulate and open professional communicators available, helps guide that person down a path of telling us who they are, what they've learned, and the lessons they want to leave behind. The more a podcast feels like people just hanging out, the more real it is. Listeners can feel more of a kinship to the producer, recognizing and appreciating the unscripted vulnerability of the format.

Joe's podcast introduced me to Eddie, the UFC, and the sport of Jiu Jitsu, which I had almost no knowledge of when I started listening in 2012. I learned about Eddie's matches against Royler, his Eddie Bravo Invitational (EBI) tournaments, his style of thinking, and his sense of humor, which was in line with mine. It was these podcast episodes that attracted me to 10th Planet—for the Jiu Jitsu and the people that were surely there.

It's always been Eddie's ability to be himself without judgment that might be his most inspiring trait. He doesn't take himself too seriously in one of the most macho industries that someone could be in: fighting.

No one is 100 percent sure if his flat earth theories are a personal belief or trolling intended to get you to reconsider your perspective on NASA, an organization founded by Nazi scientists.

The Eddie Bravo Invitational ran from June 2014 through June 2018 before Eddie took a few years off from it to put on Combat Jiu Jitsu tournaments. Combat Jiu Jitsu Worlds' uses open palm strikes once one competitor is off his feet with his butt or back on the ground. It's a nice cross between Jiu Jitsu and MMA for those looking to progress towards MMA or simply make their Jiu Jitsu more efficient.

In March 2022, EBI returned for the welterweight (170-pound) tournament. Alan Sanchez of 10th Planet San Mateo would win, making three straight Combat Jiu Jitsu and EBI wins for 10th Planet.

Keith Krikorian of 10th Planet San Diego earned the Combat Jiu Jitsu Worlds featherweight (145-pound) title in December 2021, while Ryan Aitken of 10th Planet Atlanta earned the middleweight (185-pound) title in October of that year.

Garry Tonon and Gordon Ryan won nine of the first sixteen EBI tournaments. Their coach, John Danaher with his Danaher Death Squad, saw his students win eleven of the twelve tournaments they entered in that four-year window. The one they lost was EBI 10 where Danaher's student Eddie Cummings lost to 10th Planet Oceanside's Geo Martinez in overtime.

In March 2022, Sanchez beat the Danaher-trained Oliver Taza in overtime in the tournament's final match.

Eddie's podcasts and events, plus the successes of Tonon and Ryan, both New Jersey guys, inspired me to join my first gym in June

Jean Jacques Machado, Eddie Bravo, and Victor Davila—the co-founder of EBI and CJJW.

2016, Silver Fox BJJ in Saddle Brook, New Jersey. The professor of Silver Fox BJJ is Karel Pravec, a Renzo Gracie-black belt, and his school is a Renzo Gracie affiliate. Danaher's team trained in Renzo's blue basement across the river in Manhattan.

There wasn't a 10th Planet near me when I started in 2016. I know because that's the first thing I looked up, but moving to Austin would put me where I am now.

During the Covid period, Danaher's team, the Danaher Death Squad, moved from New York City to Puerto Rico, then the team split up and both teams moved to Austin to open separate schools. Danaher runs New Wave Jiu Jitsu out of the Roka facility and Renzo Gracie in North Austin, while the B Team entered a space just around the corner from us that used to house Royler Gracie-affiliate Gracie Humaita Austin.

The B Team guys train with us during our Sunday open mats: Craig Jones, Nicky Rodriguez, Jacob Rodriguez, Damien Anderson, Nicky Ryan, Izaak Michell, and Ethan Crelinsten.

Ethan broke 10th Planet's streak at EBI Promotions with a win over 10th Planet Seattle owner Nathan Orchard in the final round of the Combat Jiu Jitsu Worlds 155-pound tournament in June 2022, Ethan would beat Damien Anderson in the semifinals, while Nathan would beat Keith Krikorian.

Gracie Humaita black belt Tim Kennedy would soon open a gym in Cedar Park, Texas, while ADCC Champion Xande Ribeiro is running Six Blades Jiu Jitsu in North Austin.

These new gyms are added to a community that already has Brazilian Fight Factory, home of the Tackett Brothers and Kody Steele, plus Village Of Wolves (V.O.W.) BJJ, another killer gym that partners with our friends at Black Sheep Boxing to coach their MMA fighters in Jiu Jitsu.

A decade earlier, there were just six gyms in the whole city. It's now the place to be for Jiu Jitsu, and soon MMA.

Curtis and Gabe added a third Eddie Bravo-black belt to the 10th Planet Austin staff with rubber guard expert Ben Eddy. They added a full staff and schedule for our striking program, plus an in-house MMA team led by UFC veteran Andrew Craig. We even have a strength and conditioning program led by TacFit's Esik Melland.

I spent the morning of my flight to Los Angeles at 10th Planet Austin, working at the gym, chatting with John, Garry, and his main training partners Yuting Hong and Nick Pierorazio. Their team had been training in our MMA cage since November, preparing for Garry's One Championship world title fight on March 11.

The two biggest Jiu Jitsu scenes in America, New York City and Southern California, met in Austin, on our block, and we were there to catch the wave. We get to be a part of history as Austin becomes a hub for fighting, technology, and comedy, a distinctly unique trio that adds to the existing live music scene.

In many ways, Austin is now the Los Angeles of the 1950s and 1960s as it becomes the destination, the place to be. Austin is where the future feels like it is being created.

The moves of Joe Rogan and Elon Musk from California to Austin were catalysts for the buzz that has surrounded the city since the summer of 2020. Texas was already growing, the Covid event increased that growth rate.

Gordon Ryan was a young protégé who came into the No-Gi scene and proved Eddie's belief that you didn't have to practice in a Gi to be the best in the world. There was a crazy belief that you did, despite the wildly different circumstances of being shirtless or wearing a rash guard with shorts in No Gi versus wearing the thick, heavy fabric of the Gi, complete with a jacket and long pants.

Gordon reached the next level of financial success as a professional grappler because of the excitement his No-Gi grappling brought to what was the boring reality of Gi grappling. Eddie knew that Jiu Jitsu in the Gi would never excite enough of the public to garner the progression of economic success for the sport.

Together, Gordon and Eddie helped to prove Eddie's thesis correct. It was a historical bond through the Eddie Bravo Invitational tournaments. Gordon would eventually win seemingly every meaningful tournament in the sport and become a very wealthy man in a kind of working-class sport.

In September 2022, Gordon headlined ADCC with a Super Fight victory over ADCC legend Andre Galvao. The event helped push grappling further into the mainstream. Eddie's affiliation was well represented with seven athletes in the seven brackets at the event.

The old myth that you needed to be good in a Gi to be good at No Gi was upheld by personal and business interests, held up by black belts who didn't want to have to teach a different game to their students, especially not something they didn't primarily learn themselves having come up through the ranks in the Gi.

In many ways, there's a desire for comfort.

The Gi provided a way for them to have an advantage over any college wrestler or athletic brute who walked in the door. It was something for them to grip onto that their opponent wouldn't understand to decrease the coach's probability of getting smashed in front of their students.

Schools selling Gis at $160 to $200 a pop didn't want people to get away with wearing something much cheaper: shorts and a T-shirt or a rash guard, something you might already own or could buy elsewhere.

Most Gi schools still only offer two, at most three, No-Gi classes per week as a means of appeasing the student's desire for No Gi just enough to retain them.

Austin has become an entirely No-Gi scene and is, without question, the mecca for grappling right now. Eddie's old dreams, today's realities.

Eddie's podcasts with Joe Rogan grew and grew from Eddie's first appearance on episode number thirteen during a comedy trip to North Carolina together to Eddie's most recent appearance in May 2020 on the last Fight Companion episode with Brendan Schaub and Bryan Callen, a series which would regularly garner ten million-plus listeners. These episodes helped grow the sport, alerting the world to the great martial artists that Joe and Eddie would enthusiastically discuss.

Stepping on the mats with the opportunity to train with our team at HQ made me forget about that neck pain. Here I was with the opportunity to write a book with Eddie, so I better do what I came to do in the first place when I came to 10th Planet: train.

And I better not suck.

We went through our warm-up series, moving through the various movements towards submission to get our bodies loose before forty-five minutes of hard drilling, followed by five eight-minute sparring rounds.

When we got to drilling, I was on fire.

My drilling style comes from my sports background. I play through the whistle, so where others complete the drill, passing their opponent's guard and settling into side control or another pin, then stopping the drill as the pass has been secured, I progress to there and keep going through until Eddie stops us. Where others drill until someone wins the position, I drill through. We keep going.

At one point during the night, I used one of the support poles in the middle of the mats to scale my feet up the side as a means of further securing the pressure necessary to complete a head and arm triangle choke on my partner. It was dope.

Hard rounds. Completely spent.

You're constantly judging your progress based on who you're tapping, who's not tapping you, who was tapping you, but isn't tapping you anymore, who you stalemate with, and so on. This is a decent night against some of HQ's best grapplers.

I had an encouraging eight-minute round with Calvin Curtin, a top brown belt in our system. He then smashed me a few nights later. He has been a brown belt for about a year longer than I've been a purple belt. We're about the same size.

That's how it goes. You're scrapping every day to make up the ground between you and all of the other Calvins out there. There is no off-season to the training.

The garage that serves as the locker room's back wall has the night's cold air blowing underneath it. There are three open showers on the right wall as you walk in, plus a toilet and a urinal in an enclosed room complete with a sink.

There's no towel service at this gym.

I walked out of that locker room to the preparation sounds of a jam session. Eddie was in the middle on the acoustic guitar with lead vocals. Gracie Jiu-Jitsu Laguna Hills owner and black belt Dr. Arman "Hammer" Fathi was on the piano doing backup vocals while Charles set on a cajón, a Peruvian box-shaped percussion instrument, that served as the beat to their songs. Thomas Herndon, a blue belt and tenured professor of economics who splits time between Headquarters and 10th Planet New York City, was sitting on a chiropractic table that Arman sometimes adjusts athletes on.

We were sitting in front of the gym, which has become the back since Covid. Black screens cover the front windows. This is just how

Credit: Michael Plaster

Eddie in a post-practice jam session at 10th Planet Headquarters.

it is now. Since fighting and Jiu Jitsu have hit the mainstream with the UFC's ESPN contract, many of the schools these fighters train with have survived these last two years through acts of rebellion.

We're underground. We're outlaws.

The Introduction

I find myself surrounded by people who are comfortable with struggle due to the nature of what we do in our training and have crafted personal philosophies based on their own experiences with struggle. No matter where I go with this sport, the kind of person you meet has some very similar characteristics.

I walked past the mats on my left, towards the jam session. The wall to my right was covered with magazine articles from the 2000s, when Eddie was becoming well known in the fight world. The scene was readying my mind to capture every moment I could.

Reaching the back, I leaned on a pole with a smirk, watching the scene unfold as the band launched into their first song.

Ccccccc-n-n
Ccccccccccc-n-n

Cause we just got done
Practicing Killing
It's the end of the world
We're just smoking and chillin'

Cause we just got done
Practicing Killing
It's the end of the world
We're just smoking and chillin'

You know they did it
I told you they would do it
They put the whole world on lockdown you idiot
They won't admit it, a scamdemic
They put the whole world on lockdown you idiot
You know they did it
I told you they would do it
They put the whole world on lockdown you idiot
You know they did it, the scamdemic
They put the whole world on lockdown you idiot

Ccccccc-n-n
Ccccccccccc-n-n

Stay home, be a hero
Save some liiiiives
Stay home, be a hero
Pass the fuck out with your kids and your wife, Yeah
Stay home, be a hero
Save some liiiiiiiiiiiiiives
Stay home, be a hero
Pass the fuck out with your kids and your wife, Yeah

I told you they would do it
I told you they would do it

Now you want a gun
I told you they would do it
And now you want a gun
I told you they would do it
Cause we just got done
Practicing killinnnn'

This is the real reason I came, to talk about Eddie's origin story as a musician. To learn about the way he mastered the metal and in mastering the metal, he could, and would, become who he has become. The process is the progress.

"Practicing Killing" is one of my favorite songs, bringing me back to the oddest and likely the scariest time in many of our lives.

While I'd been addicted to opiates at one time, I conquered addiction the same way I got into it, by making decisions. Addiction is a series of wrong decisions that lead you somewhere, dealing with my three herniated discs or not. Getting out of any hole that you've dug yourself into is a series of the right, correct decisions.

We can understand that. Personal problems are something you have control over. What happened during those Covid times was something you could have felt you had no control over if you had been demoralized enough. But truly, the strategy for conquering any problem is always the same: your decisions.

There's almost always a way out, a right move to be made. Choose the right option, make the right decision.

The Introduction

Scenes of March 2020 went through my head as I listened to the lyrics: long walks with my girlfriend and her two boys, walks that bonded us together stronger as we had hours to talk about what was on our minds.

At the time, we weren't entirely sure what was going on. There seemed like there might be a collective good faith effort of "two weeks to stop the spread," but there were the press conferences that involved bad-faithed corporate journalists questioning if President Donald J. Trump was a racist for calling the virus that came from China the China virus.

Arguments over what to call the reportedly viral iceberg that we were about to run our ship into seemed to be like a waste of time and resources if we were truly at risk. It was the first clue that everything wasn't as it seemed.

The second was Alex Jones explaining what had happened and predicting what would happen on Sam Tripoli's podcast. Jones had an intellectually sound argument based on what I already knew. He also has a far higher batting average on the truth than his biggest, most powerful, establishment detractors do.

After that, it was off to the races for me. Something on a global scale was happening, and I needed to figure out what that was since not knowing seemed like it could put us in a really difficult position if we weren't truly prepared for what might be happening.

If you aren't getting the right information, then you're putting yourself at risk. Keeping track of the narrative was the key to unraveling the lie. Watching the "truth" change, watching goalposts move, and seeing debate silenced was what tipped you off to something darker happening below the surface.

Unraveling the lie was the key to protecting your mental health from the tyranny, so was abandoning environments that didn't serve you and avoiding mandates for things you never needed.

In late March, entrepreneur Aaron Ginn wrote a data-based article on Medium.com that illustrated, using health department data from South Korea and Italy, that a huge number of people would test positive for Covid and the dead would largely be senior citizens with multiple comorbidities. After just over twenty-four hours on the site and views in excess of two million, Medium took the article down for fear of "misinformation" under the guise of Ginn being a non-medical expert.

It didn't matter that he was using data from national health departments or that his reasonable conclusions were based in that data. What mattered was that we were not to be told that Covid-19 was not something to fear because plans had been established that no one was going to get in the way of.

Then, of course, was the onslaught of censorship, including censorship of YouTube videos as innocuous as telling people to go outside and get some sun because vitamin D is very important for your immune system to help fight off viruses.

Censorship might be why this book exists. If everything can get swept off the Internet, then you need something physical to tell your story. You can no longer just blindly trust, you must make things harder on these modern book burners.

To hear Eddie play this song in early 2022 as the narrative fails and Canadian truckers take to Ottawa to cause a ruckus against those who imposed that narrative is to take a breath and realize that we're about to make it to the other side, at least the other side of this current "crisis."

Many of the mandates in Canada dropped after those truckers did their freedom convoy.

To be grateful to be where we are is the key takeaway from the entire experience. The lesson is to be grateful for those around us. Be grateful for those whose love and trust have given us the courage to love and trust, both ourselves and them.

Like Eddie said, these things we can't hold, but concern ourselves with, aren't real. What's real is what's around us, what we live with.

Without Eddie, Curtis, and the brave people around me, who would I be?

And how do we make more people like them, so other people like me have people like them around?

Their jam session went on for about an hour. Around 12:10 a.m., Plaster and I said our goodbyes to the crew. We headed off to get what is likely the best and biggest eight-dollar burrito the city may have to offer, especially at one in the morning.

I dropped Plaster back at his apartment near Headquarters and then headed off to Pasadena to lay my head down at the cheapest decent hotel I could find.

The next day, I met the guy I came to see, the guy who Eddie promised me was the real star of the show.

CHAPTER 2
....

THE MUSIC
(ZACK)

Look north up any street in Pasadena to marvel at some of the best views in the country.

The last time I saw mountains pitted up against a city like this was a road trip to Boulder, standing in the Pearl Street Mall with architecture that isn't all that different from what you might see in Boston, but with a far different backdrop.

Southern California's beautiful mountains can be forgotten by those of us who remember it for its beaches.

My first walk of the day was to the gas station for Swisher Sweets.

On this trip, I spent a not insignificant amount of time rolling blunts on the desk of my Sheraton Hotel room. The day before my return to Austin, I bought the pipe that serves as my souvenir for this experience.

It's a second to breathe. A respite. A reset.

That's much of what a good smoke is. That's what a walk on a sunny day is, surrounded by natural reminders of our world's potential for beauty.

That moment to step outside and focus solely on the slow burn of the thing in front of you is part of the cigarette addiction. Taking that moment to reset, with the added stimulant that is nicotine, is the benefit.

The ritual is the benefit.

I woke up late, but that was okay. I was ready for the day's meeting with a friend who I'd been texting for four months, James Watson. He was Eddie's longtime musical partner during their younger years, starting all the way back when Eddie was still in high school.

I was here to get the story.

California is a remarkable and beautiful place. That can't be denied. Mountains and beaches as gorgeous as they get and scenic views that sneak up on you as you traverse the landscape. Santa Monica's backdrop of mountains behind the pier captures it all, which is what makes it one of the most easily identifiable scenes in America.

I can lose sight of the positives of this place sometimes. Maybe my viewpoint is a little jaded. My community at 10th Planet Austin is filled with people who will tell you they have just escaped California: refugees.

If someone is joining for a drop-in at 10th Planet Austin and says they're visiting from California, my next comment is "so you're thinking about moving here?"

That's met with a laugh and some version of "how'd you know?"

There's a lot to be thankful to California for. It's provided the entire country with a place and source of inspiration, a dream to aspire to, and a version of yourself to hope to become. "Young man goes west" is a theme of this and many other American stories. It's a beautiful consequence of that Manifest Destiny attitude. As Americans, seeking something more is in our bloodline.

James came west from Arkansas to California, and I moved west for the version of myself I was aspiring to. We didn't know who we would become or how, but we moved west to try.

California has pushed the country in the right direction on cannabis, marijuana, pot, whatever you want to call it. Joe and Eddie played their part too, helping people realize the introspective, relaxed, flow state result of Joe's very public smoke sessions, especially in the early years of the podcast.

Eddie has long been known as the marijuana proponent in Jiu Jitsu, which the traditionalists in the sport always looked down on.

Together, they normalized the pre-workout ritual that many fighters partake in. The 10th Planet parking lots are filled with people smoking their last bit of weed before the night's class.

A cultural shift. Stoned warriors.

"The zone" people discuss in sports is where you've removed yourself from the equation, you're unconscious and completely locked into your performance as a by-product of your prior training and programming. Flow state.

I found that zone distinctly a few times in football.

It was achieved during the last two games of my senior year in high school. Another time was at a county all-star football game the summer before heading off to college, and then another was during a spring scrimmage while playing for the University of Rhode Island.

I remember feeling like I got to decide how the game would go those days, the results were pre-ordained and in my favor.

I tore up some ankle ligaments halfway through that scrimmage at Rhode Island while running from the back side slot across the middle of the field in an attempt to get in front of the back side line-backer to block for a screen pass to the other side of the formation.

It was the same area of the field where I broke a foot four years earlier, just before my junior year of high school football. Damn injuries.

I played through that fall season of my junior year at URI, but I'd never be the same player again as the ankle injury, surgery, and recovery process rendered my lateral movement, my most valu-able skill set besides my hands, less effective for the rest of my collegiate career.

In this sport of Jiu Jitsu, and likely because of my training, I've found that zen flow state far more frequently. The pacing of

10-Round Tuesdays helps bring it about. Some days you just have it, you're firing on all cylinders, you're loose.

These Tuesday rolling sessions are a kind of pinnacle of our training week, a testament to our training. I frequently don't take the rest time in between the rounds, prodding my next partner to get started the second we choose each other.

Slap, bump, roll. The rounds are six minutes, with forty-five seconds of rest in between, repeated for a total of ten rounds. It's an almost seventy-minute marathon—seventy minutes of scraps.

We do that every week. The Jiu Jitsu version of the runner's high that we feel after one of these sessions is a flood of dopamine that no drug will ever be able to give me, so to be able to be there, capable of that flow state, is the highest order principle that now guides my life-style choices.

It's a second chance at being an athlete, and I've found myself with coaches that will put me in a position to succeed in a competition or a self-defense scenario if I just keep showing up.

I can do that: consistency. Trust the process.

Trust your programming.

James met Eddie when James was twenty-four, Eddie sixteen. Eight years separated the guitar player from Arkansas and the drummer-slash-producer from Santa Ana, California.

Edgar Bravo, Eddie as he would be later known, was a young Mexican kid with a father and a stepfather who were never there for him. Zero for two on the dad front. James arrived at a very important time becoming a much needed positive influence.

Eddie couldn't decide if he wanted to be a professional football player or a rock star, but he knew he wasn't going to play in no bull-shit USFL, "I'm going to the NFL dog. Fuck that."

Both football and music seemed like a potential way forward, a path toward attention, adulation, and meaning. Eventually, rock music became the most likely path.

As a general concept, the rock star hasn't been around long. Eddie was born in 1970, James in 1962. Someone who could command an

A nine-year-old Edgar Bravo on his Pee Wee football team.

audience that could fill a football or baseball stadium was a new phenomenon; a level of idolatry that few could have ever experienced in human history was now becoming the domain of a few select rock and roll bands.

Technological advancements were the cause of the change. Distributors were now capable of mass-producing audio tracks, putting their products in more hands and ears as the playing of that music was becoming more accessible and personal.

Music has been a communal activity through time. To the Greeks, music became an important feature of religious festivals, marriage and funeral rites, and banquet gatherings.

Large, collective, unifying communal experiences through music, which this era of rock brought about, are of value to people. As Dr. Jordan Peterson notes, the unity music brings is a religious experience: all of us in the same place at the same time listening to something meaningful that everyone in the crowd shares together.

Worldwide supply chains distributing music to the masses served to make this religious experience something you could become attuned with at home, then come to the concert for the full experience.

Texas Hill Country's live music scene is part of what attracted my family to Austin. For a week every February, from eight to eighteen, my father, myself, and eventually my little sister would visit friend, and author, Russ Hall. Together, we would travel to bars in the area to listen to music made by other friends like Mike Blakely, Johnny Gringo, and John Arthur Martinez.

Blakely is also a successful Western writer and a historian, having even written books with Willie Nelson and Kenny Rogers.

My mom would spend summers traveling to live music on the Jersey Shore, which she does in Texas now. She still sees those same artists, and their friends, frequently.

Our entire family currently resides up and down Interstate 35, which runs through the middle of Texas through Dallas, Waco, Austin, and San Antonio, connecting America from Duluth, Minnesota through Laredo, Texas.

When I was a kid, I wondered why some of the extremely talented musicians I saw weren't more famous, asking my dad why we didn't hear them on the radio.

Instead, they were living in the way the traveling musician had always lived, the path of sharing that thing you love for the love of it, not because you're promised some level of worldwide adulation and recognition on the other side of it. The dream is being able to play, keeping that ride going, and living off your art like they do.

I thought the dream was being on the radio with the fame and adulation that comes with it.

The dream could be doing the thing you love at night and on the weekend. And when you're not doing that, you're working and making money to stay in that pursuit, stay doing the thing you love like how so many are with Jiu Jitsu, trying to figure out a way to make the art you love your profession. The dream is that one day you'll have honed your abilities well enough to quit that other job, if you so choose.

Your arrival is the daily destination. It's the opportunity to do what you love, not your first radio play. Loving your art enough to keep doing it no matter what challenge tries to stand in your way.

This music is a service for those of us who listen, but also for the musicians who yearn to play to an audience, to share what they've created in the art form they most love.

Money is a by-product, not the destination. It's about being a source of entertainment and, potentially, joy for those around you. It's about name recognition with the people around you, rather than worrying about recognition from people thousands of miles away.

Through this most personal art, music was something done within the community, building and bringing people together during important events. No DJ was there to press play; someone needed to be able to make the music happen. Through this, distinct, geographical styles came about.

My Frank Sinatra– and Jay-Z–influenced home city's culture was distinctly different than the place I'd eventually move to, a city that played its role in the development of Gary Clark Jr., Janis Joplin, Willie Nelson, and Stevie Ray Vaughan.

Music represents the difference between places and cultures, like what Jiu Jitsu enthusiast Anthony Bourdain taught us about food.

Making music that could be played through the various generations of personal audio players and headphones increased the power of the bands that got pushed to a level that would have been hard to predict before it happened.

New recording distribution included the open blue ocean of television. A small handful of networks were looking for programming that would attract and addict people to their new platform. On February 9, 1964, the Beatles were seen by seventy-three million viewers during their famed first appearance on *The Ed Sullivan Show* on CBS. The other two networks were ABC and NBC.

In August 1965, Sullivan would introduce them to the stage at the Beatles' Shea Stadium concert, the first stadium rock concert.

The objective of music is to create an emotional response using words, instruments, and sounds. You're taking an emotion you are feeling, then communicating that into vibrations that are exported to others, transmitting sound and that emotion—sending out a frequency.

This was once done exclusively via face-to-face interaction, but now it's largely done via recording. Sometimes it will even be captured via a video on a social media platform and shared immediately with millions. Recording means the listener can play those sounds back as much as they want, constantly capable of recreating the emotion they're seeking. Something I frequently find myself doing in an attempt to catch the wave.

When the Beatles were on *The Ed Sullivan Show*, children and adults were abuzz, wondering where they could find the album that made them feel how they felt when they watched the performance. There was excitement, curiosity, and the indelible groove of a good song with a new sound. Albums would then become one's most sacred and closest held possession, a powerful reminder of meaning. Art.

As Hunter S. Thompson once said,

> *Music has always been a matter of Energy to me, a question of Fuel. Sentimental people call it Inspiration, but what they really mean is Fuel. I have always needed Fuel. I am a serious consumer. On some nights I still believe that a car with the gas needle on empty can run about fifty more miles if you have the right music very loud on the radio.*

I was in the car driving the forty-five minutes across the city towards Long Beach to pick up James for an afternoon together before our group meeting on Sunday where Eddie and James gave me the whole saga, together.

I turned on a Spotify playlist compiled by "mike."—my new favorite, and independent, artist. He put together a playlist of his tracks, entitled "mike. new wave.", in the order he wants the listener to consume them. I'm not sure what genre it would be classified as because it's a sound that is all his own.

After his All-American caliber pitching career at Duke came to an end with a blown out elbow, Mike Seander became Mike Stud, the college rapper who made his first viral hit with the GarageBand computer program. Mike hailed from Cranston, Rhode Island, the hometown of many of my college friends. Still today, he's Duke's single season record holder for lowest ERA, which happened during his freshman season back in 2007, a 1.61 ERA in twenty-eight appearances.

The Rhody native puts out great social content and a podcast with a style of communication that reminds me of listening to friends. In one of those episodes, he mentioned that over the last few years he felt like he "cracked the code" on music.

Of all the art forms, none have as much personal experience and engagement with us as music.

Driving with your windows down while blasting a soundtrack to your life is an essential American scene for the romantic.

Your playlist for windows-down-driving weather and writing at midnight is going to be different. The soundtrack music behind a scene in a movie lets you know we're reaching an important moment and whether we should feel the tension of physical danger or romantic heartbreak. You're not going to cruise down the highway listening to the strings of some soundtrack score.

Yoga music is different than max-out-deadlift music.

For mike., cracking the code on music might have meant, to him, that he finally understood all that he was trying to capture in terms of a vibe or, what he calls, a wave. We're trying to create waves we can ride forward. Trying to capture and bottle the positive energy we can use to fuel us forward, something that we've all felt in the songs that speak the most to us. The stuff that gets us going. The songs we put on repeat. Art we connect with.

THE MUSIC

Music can be utilized as a meditative avenue, a tool for finding the balance to maximize our ability to focus on the task in front of us.

If loud sounds can shatter glass, then what do the vibrations and frequencies of music do to us?

Music pushes past the conscious and into the subconscious, making your feelings known, yet doing so in a way that isn't always direct in the sense of cause and effect. The music doesn't tell you what to think—good art tends to avoid that temptation. It helps you make it known to yourself how something feels like only you could know how.

That's why when someone doesn't like a song we like, we get that brief feeling of hurt that borders on offense. Musical choice is deeply personal, sometimes more personal than we even know. Art involves the consumer in as much that their experiences flavor the consumption and experience of that art.

For Eddie, his attraction to speed metal as a kid was a testament to the anger and insecurity that a tumultuous family environment embedded in him. Watching him listen to his and James's old speed metal tracks together, I saw the watery film of nostalgia overtake his eyes in recognition of how much the chaos in the songs was driven by his insecurity and anger.

Plato believed that music was capable of influencing the very virtue of human character by way of the common harmonic nature shared by the soul, music, and the universe.

Pythagoras found that the same arithmetic proportions in music were also found in nature, which is what he believed gave music its influence over the soul.

Music is a direct transmission of emotional energy, capable of imitating the bodily movements associated with emotions, causing us to move, sometimes in a way that we couldn't stop if we tried.

Music can set the mood. It is more powerful and memorable than just words. It can be a vehicle for remembering every lyric for a song you haven't heard in a decade. No one can do that with any three-to-four-minute speech, no matter how powerful.

Music is capable of providing catharsis, helping individuals who could be in states of extreme enthusiasm, pity, or fear return to a more balanced state.

The ears are the gates to the soul. Be careful what you allow in there.

Consider what we do with music: we sing along. We chant the words the artist put in the song, and we chant along to the instruments that accompany those words. Consider where most people most frequently heard music through the last few hundreds or thousands of years: they heard it in church. Listening to and chanting the word of God, which sounds like a good idea, no matter my or your valid personal issues with organized religion.

If good music is akin to gospel, then bad music could logically move someone towards weakness or evil. Bad music with the wrong values could manipulate people towards the wrong things.

Eddie's entire life has been about creating music. His warm-up system is about this, greasing the groove and getting us prepared for a night of training. He reminds us of the pathways that we should always be working on, thinking about, and studying. The music producer has composed flows that move from first engagement to the submission.

He made the systematic expression of the sport into a dance, helping us find the rhythm of his game, letting it spread through his association, and getting programmed into us as muscle memory to become our own. As it spread, coaches he trained and trusted tested it, learned more, reported back, and improved that warm-up system with Eddie, without anyone caring about who gets the credit.

Eddie could add in a back control or guard passing system created by someone he doesn't even need to like. He doesn't care where it comes from. He only cares about what works. No ego, no emotion. It's about creating the best systems for every phase of the game.

Surprisingly, people can sometimes care where something comes from, causing an unwillingness to admit just how well something may work.

Rhythm and harmony are in all physical expression. Once you know the moves, it's all a dance.

In baseball, the pitcher has a way he does his wind up, knowing from his toes to his shoulders how his body moves through the grooves it has created through years of dedicated practice. Using this muscle memory, he loads onto his back leg to uncork the pitch. The batter moves his center of gravity in a rhythmic way to coil his weight on to his back leg and explode with a swing as he throws his hands with the bat head behind it to try to launch the pitcher's offering. Fielders gently move their feet in the lead up to the pitch, flowing into a position on every play, ready to move in whatever direction is necessary.

Basketball is all rhythm, a dance that you can produce with the ball in your hands. Rhythm being most pronounced at the foul line as every shooter has his little routine that puts him in the proper place to take that shot.

In football, the beat of the quarterback's drop as he hits his final step, finds his receiver, and executes the pass is based on rhythm. That receiver's three steps to his slant route where he lines up his defender, creates leverage by getting himself lined up on the inside half of his opponent's body, jukes his final step with a head fake to the outside of the field, and then breaks inside for the route is all based in years of working on that rhythm with a beat in his head. He's inhaling and exhaling as he runs, finding that right amount of shake to it.

A lot is made of Rickson Gracie's breath work and for good reason. This rhythm of the game that Eddie has passed on to us has made thousands of grapplers move like him, using their breath as a means of achieving the looseness and flow that is necessary to execute the free-flowing, submission-focused style of fighting that Eddie has produced. On a night where I'm rolling well, everything is aligned and I'm free to perform.

I was just outside Long Beach, Lakewood to be exact, pulling into a typical working-class neighborhood in a sprawling metroplex. One thing about Los Angeles that I can't deny is that the streets seem clean, at least in areas that aren't overrun by homeless encampments. Pasadena had workers out in the warm morning sun and the drive over was as beautiful as I could reasonably ask for in a county of ten million-plus.

I pulled up in front of a house that is pure Americana: a three-bedroom built in 1952 on about a tenth of an acre. We've seen houses like this on our television many times.

There is a front walk, gates on the outside of the glass door, and a big living room window to the right of that door, facing the street. The driveway is set to the right side of the property. It is well manicured with beautiful green grass.

My blue bubble text went through with the swoosh, letting our man know I had arrived.

I parked the car, walked around the back, and made my way up the front walk.

CHAPTER 3

. . . .

LET THERE BE ROCK
(JAMES)

I may have been born in 1962, but my story doesn't start there. My story, the James Watson story, starts with the music.

Let there be rock.

One name bears the closest resemblance to what could be constituted as a founder of rock and roll because, of course, no one "founded" rock and roll. Instead, various genres and styles of music molded and evolved toward what would become known as rock and roll. A combination of factors and influences eventually resulted in a sound that needed to be defined with its own genre of music.

In 1923, Sam Phillips was born in Florence, Alabama, across the Tennessee River and four miles from Muscle Shoals, which would host its own musical revolution through FAME Studios in the 1950s. Muscle Shoals Rhythm Section, the group of session musicians the studio would use with their artists' recording sessions, would leave FAME to start the famed Muscle Shoals Sound Studio in 1969.

This band, also known as "The Swampers," would work with legends.

They spanned the history of the sound as they recorded, produced, or engineered classic hits by Aretha Franklin, the Rolling Stones, Bob Dylan, and Lynyrd Skynyrd.

Muscle Shoals and their Swampers even got lyrical recognition on Skynyrd's "Sweet Home Alabama."

In the 1940s, before the area became famous for the Muscle Shoals Sound, Phillips worked as a DJ and radio engineer for station WLAY (AM). The station's "open format" of broadcasting music by both white and black musicians would inspire him later.

During this time, major record companies were working to get themselves out of the "race music" business as they had deemed it unprofitable. Race music was a euphemism for music that was made by black artists and intended for black audiences. The success of this music, which would later be called rhythm and blues, or R&B, on jukeboxes and local radio showed that the market was there. Of course, they would be back later when it turned out that *a lot* of people wanted to listen to this music if it was put in front of them.

Phillips would move to Memphis in 1945 to become an announcer and sound engineer for WREC, a local radio station.

The BBC notes that the term "rock 'n' roll" derives from the literal "rocking and rolling" of the ship on the sea, a phrase used by seventeenth-century sailors.[1] By the 1920s, the term had become a popular metaphor for either dancing or sex, so Trixie Smith wrote a 1922 blues ballad titled, "My Man Rocks Me (With One Steady Roll)."

Alan Freed, the Cleveland-based DJ who would help spread and popularize this style of music that combined the country music of white America with the R&B of black America, began to use the term in the early 1950s, which would convert the use of the term into the musical mainstream.

The origin of the term isn't without reason. The art of rock and roll music is primal.

Dancing. Sweating. Freedom in the flow. The enjoyment of the moment.

Sex.

It happened at the right moment in time. Social standards were relaxing and America was becoming the post-World War II America it would become. Freed wouldn't have been able to promote this kind of music so successfully to the world that existed twenty years prior, during the Great Depression. The entire vibration of rock and roll wasn't set for that time; it was set for the time it came.

Technology played a role. A lessening of prejudice did as well, although the foundation of rock and roll proved that prejudice still remained as the new medium of television meant the audience knew the race of the performers. Despite the fact that radio billboard charts illustrated the country's love of black music, the television studios and corporations wanted white faces. The music would often be "covered" in more ways than one.

In 1950, 96 percent of homes in the United States had a radio. That same year, Phillips opened the Memphis Recording Service, which would later become Sun Studio, a studio that is still operating today and advertises itself as "The Birthplace of Rock 'n' roll."

When it was opened, the slogan was "We Record Anything— Anywhere—Anytime."

According to the tale of Sam Phillips by way of Pulitzer Prize-winning historian Louis Menand in his 2015 article for the *New Yorker*, "Phillips's dream, the reason he set up the studio, was to have a place where any aspiring musician could come in to try out." Phillips would offer some of his musical expertise built over his time in radio to give suggestions and encouragement, then record what he liked. For a fee, musicians could cut their own record.

The kind of unpolished music the corporations had deemed unprofitable was what Phillips liked. He hated formulas, believing music to be about self-expression. While the pop sound of the time was smooth and harmonic, he preferred imperfection for the way it made music sound alive, authentic, and attainable.

While his actions were forward thinking, Phillips wasn't in the business for the socially conscious aspects of the music. He would later say, "If I could find a white man who had the Negro sound and the Negro feel, I could make a billion dollars."

Green, silver, and gold are everyone's favorite colors. People don't care what color you are if you're making them money or giving them money.

Much of the essence of rock and roll is the feeling of "I could do that," which I'd feel all those years later. It's what gave high school garage bands the courage to try it on their own. Inspiration produced by the uninhibited, spontaneous, and fun feeling that the music created when done right was another reason to give it a go.

Word spread, so musicians no one else would record started turning up at the Memphis Recording Service. Music historian Peter Guralnick considered "Rocket 88" by Jackie Brenston and His Delta Cats to be the first rock and roll song of all time. The Delta Cats were a band led by then nineteen-year-old Ike Turner, who also wrote the song. The song would reach the top of the Best Selling R&B Records chart on June 9, 1951, staying there for three weeks.

They had recorded that song with the band at the studio. It was then released by Chess Records from Chicago in 1951, one of two small independent labels Phillips would work with, the other being Modern Records in Los Angeles.

He would soon find the record companies untrustworthy, of course, as they would look to poach his clients. He'd start Sun Records in 1952.

Billboard started charting songs in 1940. By the end of the decade, the charts were categorized three ways: pop, country-and-Western, and rhythm and blues, the new term to replace "race music."

This charting system was predicated on a segregated market. *Billboard* knew when a song was a "rhythm and blues" hit and not a pop hit because sales were segregated; rhythm and blues hits came from record stores that catered to a black clientele. On-air plays were reported by radio stations that programmed for black listeners, while jukebox requests were totaled from venues with black customers.

Black artists could have pop hits, but it remained largely segregated.

Before the 1940s, the radio airwaves were dominated by CBS, NBC, and Mutual, but an FCC policy would break up this oligopoly, making licensing numbers go from eight hundred in 1940 to more than two thousand in 1949. Those new radio stations meant that people were beginning to have access to more localized programming.

Per Louis Menand, "by 1940, there were close to half a million jukeboxes in the United States, so radio DJ and jukebox plays were charted in *Billboard*: they were market indicators. A song that was played a lot could be predicted to sell a lot, so distributors and retailers took notice."[2]

While major record companies had gotten out of the distribution of R&B, independent labels filled the gap. Rock and roll became possible with the realization that not everyone buying or listening to the R&B records these labels put out was black. A new market segment could be formed and supported.

Per Menand, in 1952, when Phillips started his studio, 40 percent of R&B record buyers at the Dolphin Record Store in Los Angeles were white. The year before, Freed was astonished to see white teenagers eagerly buying R&B records at a local record shop, so he followed his "quality music" program with an R&B show. In 1954, he would move to WINS in New York City, soon becoming one of the first to call the R&B listened to by white kids "rock and roll," which helped reposition the product.

Menand wrote "in 1948, less than two per cent of American households had a television set. By 1955, more than two-thirds did." Most television viewers got three or four channels, so the audiences for them were huge. Prime time was dominated by variety shows like *The Ed Sullivan Show*. The rock and roll phenomenon was partially created by television, which led to the search for the white face that would make it mainstream.

Sponsors avoided "mixed-race shows," not wanting to alienate viewers or advertisers. The same excuse is used for censorship today.

Despite this, the success of black musicians illustrated the grass-roots potential. In post-war era America, a new demographic was emerging, one who was the target for music marketers: teenagers. And these teenagers were listening to the same music as people who looked different than them, going to the same performances, and illustrating the unifying power of the art.

Elvis Presley would be the one to break through and make rock and roll mainstream. He walked into Sun Records in the summer of 1953 at the age of eighteen to make a record for his mother, paying four dollars to record two songs. He was in the right place at the right time; his sound with a white face was what the networks wanted.

The press claimed he was unclassifiable in conventional terms. "He has a white voice, sings with a Negro rhythm, which borrows in mood and emphasis from country styles."

Presley's 1956 performance on *The Milton Berle Show* would net forty million viewers with his hip-shaking performance. This kind of viewership had the power to make stars and heroes. Being able to reach forty million sets of eyes, ears, and minds was an unimaginable scale at any point in history up to that point.

Television. Mass communication. A powerful tool. A powerful weapon.

For good or for evil.

Elvis' style of "a white man signing black" excited listeners of all backgrounds. His first hit "That's All Right" would make regional charts before he'd make a splash nationally a year or so later. His success led to white performers and producers imitating R&B songs, rather than recasting them in a pop style.

R&B was still seen as "race music," which is why the name shift had to occur. *Billboard* classified rock and roll for the pop charts with pop essentially meaning typically white, non-country-and-Western music.

Black musicians would benefit from the popularity of the sound with Chuck Berry's May 1955 song for Chess Records named "Maybellene" hitting number one on the R&B chart and number five on the pop chart. Little Richard's "Tutti Frutti" was released a few months later, hitting number seventeen on the pop chart by January 1956, which was when the twenty-one-year-old Presley began appearing on television regularly.

Menand found that over the three years from 1954 to 1957, the number of black performers on the pop retail chart jumped from 3 percent to 30 percent. The radio was still colorblind.

Presley and Pat Boone would quickly cover "Tutti Frutti," profiting off imitating black art and calling it white.

We can't completely racialize the story though. As an example, Presley's "Hound Dog" was originally released by a black R&B singer named Willie Mae "Big Mama" Thornton in 1953, but was written by a couple of Jewish teenagers living in Los Angeles named Jerry Leiber and Mike Stoller. They were on commission from producer Johnny Otis, who was recording Thornton for Peacock Records.

Music in the corporate sense has always had many cooks in the kitchen.

"In 1956, seventy-six per cent of top R. & B. songs also made the pop chart; in 1957, eighty-seven per cent made the pop chart; in 1958, it was ninety-four per cent. The marginal market had become the main market, and majors had got into the act," wrote Menand.[3]

Art was changing our culture, so naturally the corporations wanted their piece. White listeners were listening to music they weren't supposed to listen to, music that wasn't marketed to them, so the industry had to scramble to meet demand.

Rock and roll was the first major genre of music marketed to young people. The main marketing tactic prior was down racial lines. Marketing towards young people meant marketing towards all young people, not just white or black. The energetic performances, catchy melodies, and often insightful lyrics appealed to all. It was exciting, an art that was theirs, something the adults and squares didn't understand or take part in.

They had their own way to play it as well, thanks to new technology that meant they didn't have to listen to the family phonograph in the living room. Jukeboxes at their favorite hangout was one way, but the 45-rpm record—the single—and the cheap record players that were both developed and marketed by RCA starting in 1949 meant teenagers would play "their" music alone in their rooms.[4]

This was music becoming a more singular, isolated behavior, rather than something that people generally took part in with others, which likely increased the personal nature of it.

In 1954, the transistor radio came on the market, meaning kids could listen to their favorite radio DJ anywhere. This included lunchrooms and schoolyards across the country and world, making the singular activity communal in that sense. They were now capable of listening to the music they enjoyed anywhere. Rock and roll fit perfectly into this new teen culture that came about after World War II.

By 1958, Phillips was the first to record Elvis, B.B. King, and Johnny Cash.

I couldn't tell you the whole story though. I wasn't there. This was just what I've been told.

I'm always just a little skeptical of a story that I can't prove myself.

But that's about where I enter the story. James Watson, born April 16, 1962, about eighteen months before John F. Kennedy would be assassinated amid extremely questionable circumstances that allegedly involve our nation's intelligence community.

His death would completely reshape the history of this country.

Change the trajectory, deviate from the timeline.

All leading towards an intelligence community whose power would grow and grow, seemingly unchecked.

Kennedy was an advocate for peace and, judging by the time since, some people profit too much from war to ever give it up. Four and a half years after his death, another advocate of peace named

Martin Luther King, Jr. would lose his life in equally questionable circumstances.

Consider the tale of "Freeway Rick" Ross from that first Rogan podcast Zack listened to and the Iran-Contra cocaine running operation the CIA was running through Mena, Arkansas when Bill Clinton was governor and a former director of the CIA, George H.W. Bush, was vice president. Tom Cruise even starred in a movie about the CIA's drug running project, playing the role of Barry Seal in *American Made*.

Joe Biden would then introduce a 1994 Crime Bill, which banned "assault weapons," as a way to deal with the record wave of violent crime sparked by the crack cocaine epidemic that the other "Presidential" Presidents helped facilitate. Sentencing guidelines for crack cocaine versus regular cocaine were overtly racist, intended to lock up black Americans at a far higher rate than whites in this "War on Drugs."

Consider the story of Frank Lucas, as told by the film *American Gangster*. The Vietnam War had plenty of heroin drug running going on there too, snuck back in the caskets of dead servicemen.

Consider the Taliban outlawing heroin production in Afghanistan 1999 heading into 2000, 9/11 being alleged to have been committed by Saudi Arabian nationals, and then a twenty-year war with a nation Osama Bin Laden wasn't even living in. During that time, Afghanistan grew to produce 80-plus percent of the world's opium per the United Nations Office on Drugs and Crime.

Per the BBC, "Heroin made from opium grown in Afghanistan makes up 95% of the market in Europe" as of 2021.[5] Only 1 percent of the US supply comes from Afghanistan. Most of the US supply comes from our neighbors in Mexico.

Over the last two decades, an American opiate epidemic (that was sparked by the FDA giving Purdue Pharma a label that said their prescription heroin wasn't addictive) turned into a California wildfire. Hulu's docudrama *Dopesick* tells the whole story.

As a friend of mine says, "I'm just saying you should look into it."

I was born in Little Rock, Arkansas.

Two and a half hours by car east of Mena, one hour north of Johnny Cash's hometown of Kingsland, Arkansas, and two hours southwest of Memphis.

It's right in the heart of where this new style of music came out of both in time and space.

As a friend of mine says "It is better before you should hear (?)"

CHAPTER 4

LITTLE ROCK, ARKANSAS
(JAMES)

When you hear the first few licks from a guitar player, you can guess who he is. In the modern day, Gary Clark Jr. has a deep bass tone. Jimi Hendrix took the distortion that Chuck Berry had invented, and then got it a little more distorted than the typical country lick.

Music was first recorded in the late 1860s, but one of the earliest things I've ever heard is the nasty, noisy acoustic of Robert Johnson. Pull it up on your Spotify, listen to a lick, and you'll hear Johnson, but you'll also hear almost every country, bluesy lick you've heard since. The riff that would play when *Chappelle's Show* would leave for commercial in the early 2000s was surely inspired by it.

Everyone pays their respects and many have been influenced since. Eric Clapton, a man who some refer to as God, states that Johnson was "the most important blues singer that ever lived." Bob Dylan cited Johnson's lyrics and musicianship as key influences.

Johnson spent some of his early childhood years in Memphis where he would find his love for blues and popular music. Having any education at all in the big city placed him apart from most of his contemporaries.

He eventually relocated with his mother to a plantation in Arkansas where they would live as sharecroppers. At seventeen, he married the sixteen-year-old Virginia Travis. Soon after, she died in childbirth with her surviving relatives blaming Robert's decision to sing secular songs, known as "selling your soul to the Devil," for her death.

James (left) with his father and siblings, Gail (left), Mark (middle), and Lynda (right).

Church was the first place I would hear music, as I'm sure it was for many. My mother made me go there every Sunday in Little Rock.

Johnson changed his name to Johnson after his mother told him that Noah Johnson was his father, not Charles Dodds, with whom she was married and had ten children.

Dodds was a relatively prosperous landowner and furniture maker in Hazlehurst, Mississippi, but he would be run from the area by a lynch mob following a dispute with John and Joseph Marchetti, two Italian Hazlehurst businessmen. Legend has it that Joseph and Charles shared the same mistress.

Dodds left in the middle of the night, disguised as a woman, and resettled in Memphis under the name Charles Spencer.

This was two years before Julia Dodds, Robert's mother, moved with Robert to Memphis. Noah Johnson fathered Robert during that time between.

These licks we hear from a guitar player aren't just sounds. They're personalities and emotions playing through the instrument. Johnson's nasty, noisy sound was of the acoustic variety. Gibson Guitars didn't bring Les Paul in to electrify the guitar until fifteen years after Johnson's two recording sessions in San Antonio (1936) and Dallas (1937).

Johnson didn't marry again after Virginia's death. When he traveled around the country as far as Texas and New York City, even into Canada, he stayed with members of a large extended family or female friends. He formed long-term relationships with women in the various cities he would frequent or he stayed with whatever woman he could seduce from his perch on stage.

He moved frequently between Memphis and Helena, Arkansas, plus smaller towns of the Mississippi Delta. These female hosts were largely ignorant of his life elsewhere. He used at least eight different surnames to help him keep his different lives to himself.

Just over a year following his final recording session, Johnson passed away at twenty-seven years of age. A mysterious death with its own legend, Johnson may have been murdered by the jealous husband of a woman he had been flirting with over the few weeks he had been playing at a country dance hall about fifteen miles from Greenwood, Mississippi.

Rumor is that the woman gave him a bottle of whiskey poisoned by her husband, but fellow blues musician Sonny Boy Williamson knocked it out of his hand, telling him to never drink from a bottle he hadn't personally seen opened. To that, Johnson replied, "Don't ever knock a bottle out of my hand."

He was offered another bottle, accepted it, and began feeling ill the evening after, eventually succumbing to the poison a couple days later. Musicologist Robert "Mack" McCormick claimed to have gotten a confession, but he never revealed the man's name.

Rock and roll.

The less exciting story is that Johnson may have died of congenital syphilis.

Johnson's style would become known as Delta Blues, representing the Mississippi Delta region. It is an art form of heartbreak, anger, fear, and craving to be truly free in a segregated south, fresh off slavery, but practicing sharecropping. You can hear the angst and dirt of the music coming out of the cotton fields.

This is the spirit of the blues, the definitive and authoritative expression of pain. You can't manufacture the sounds that Robert Johnson was able to create with a guitar.

My birth would come a decade following the release of the Les Paul model Goldtop that Gibson would first put out in 1952. This was eleven years following Paul first approaching Gibson with his idea of a solid body electric guitar.

In the time between, in January 1948, Paul would almost lose his arm to amputation following a shattered right arm and elbow in a near fatal automobile accident on an icy Route 66 just west of Davenport, Oklahoma. He was traveling back from Wisconsin to Los Angeles after visiting family with his wife Mary Ford.

Doctors at Oklahoma City's Wesley Hospital told him they would be unable to rebuild his elbow, so he was flown to Los Angeles, where his arm was set at an angle that allowed him to cradle and pick up the guitar. The music mattered that much.

The years of my youth were the years of experimentation with this new sound. The electrification of the music allowed for this new rock and roll style to begin to flourish with people experimenting and able to play to larger and larger audiences.

My family thought my growing love of rock and roll was corny, as it was considered "white" music, but my attraction was sparked by the very music that my sisters turned me onto.

With the electrification of the guitar, it went from a background, acoustic instrument to an emotion-stirring one that was situated at the front of the band.

As a young kid, I wanted to become a comic book illustrator for Marvel, enamored by stories of main characters with superhuman powers. My family bought some encyclopedias. I tore out the blank pages because I loved drawing my own comics. Growing up poor, I got money by doing yard work for my grandparents to get the latest version of Hulk or Daredevil from the drug store on the corner. These mom-and-pop stores would sell comics for ten or fifteen cents. In mint condition, they could be worth hundreds, maybe thousands of dollars now.

Luke Cage came out as I was discovering rock and roll. He was one of my favorites. Nothing like the Netflix show, although I do like the modern-day version. On Netflix, he's beating up other black people who are pimping, drug dealing, and using the "nigga" version of the word, something I've always disagreed with having grown up during a time where that *n*-word ended with an *r* and every letter in between was filled with hate.

There was none of that in the Luke Cage versions I bought.

Growing up in the 1960s, my mom was the first black office clerk to work in an aluminum factory. This meant nothing to me until I got into my forties. She worked every day to support our family with no excuses.

My dad, from a drinking family, never kept a steady job. He was a master transmission technician and could do wonders on almost any vehicle. He was known as a "shade tree mechanic" and pretty much kept work through a steady line of cars from people he had worked on and word of mouth. Some people couldn't afford a regular mechanic, while others, truth be told, didn't like the prices or dealings with white folks.

This was Arkansas where, when I was a kid, the KKK still had parades and where it was clearly known that you don't go to this place or that city because those peckerwoods would string you up.

Tales of real-life lynching and face-to-face hate were only a grandparent away.

Depending on which friend I was with growing up, one would say, "Y'all rich," which puzzled me.

We grew up on pretty much the same two or three meals a week. Boiled squash, greens that were possibly bought roadside, along with black-eyed peas or corn on the cob. On a good week, we'd get pork and beans with fried chicken. I get hungry just thinking about that!

As years grew by, the good weeks would add a few more items like green peas. During a bad month, things were taken away.

My dad was a really, really good fisherman. He kept fish on the table along with the southern essential of Kool-Aid.

On real low cash weeks, we had to depend on our grandparents to chip in on food. I loved their cooking. That is one of the times I found out that we were not poor.

You never know you're poor until you meet someone who has a lot more. Growing up on my block, we were all lower-middle class to poor people. Nothing shocked my best friend Larry and me more than when we would meet other kids that thought we were rich or had a lot more than they did.

Larry himself was handicapped, one arm and one leg were shorter than the other. His example taught me grace no matter your physical situation.

While in third or fourth grade, a good friend of mine dropped by, saw my dad, and asked, "Is that your uncle?"

I said, "No, my dad."

He was blown away that I had a father at home.

All of my life, my parents stayed together, as they are now in heaven. They died a week apart from each other in 2017. My father went first from pulmonary disease due to a lifetime of smoking, then my mother's departure was due to her dementia.

Both are horrible ways to go. My younger brother Mark would be especially shattered by it, as he spent their last days caring for them. They were our rock.

More than a few of my friends stopped by my house for no other reason than to get a meal during those grade school days because they had nothing at their homes the night before.

I knew that we certainly lived check to check, but only when I went over to some of my grade school friends' houses did I even find out what a food stamp was.

By the time I hit middle school, I became such a comic book freak. The type of clothes that I wore or if my afro was trimmed right meant nothing to me compared to the new Thor or Wolverine comic book coming out. Luckily, my two foxy sisters were able to save me from diving into the dark hole of "nerdom" with music.

We listened to all of the classic soul music: the Temptations, the Jackson 5, James Brown, Gladys Knight and the Pips. I became attracted to the lead guitar break in the songs, noticing that often-times the guitar solo would have a little distortion in it.

Heavy metal, the genre I eventually fell in love with, would be known for its heavy distortion of the guitar. And those heavy metal guitar solos would be much longer than the lead guitar breaks in the songs I fell in love with in my youth.

Charles was one of my grade school friends and the first friend I would really discuss music with. We would talk about the latest soul or R&B song that was out. I would say that I love that sound or that part of the song, and it would always be the guitar solo. I'd look at a certain band on the dance show *Soul Train* and say, "Man, I like what that dude was playing," and Charles would notice it was always the guitarist I was talking about, not just the bassline.

In the sixth grade, Charles sat in front of me in class. One day he turned around and said, "You know what? You should probably listen to rock music."

I said, "Rock music? What's that?"

He was like, "You don't know what rock music is?"

"I mean, I've heard about it, but is that like Sly and the Family Stone?"

"You're close. This is like a lot of music that white people listen to."

"Like *American Bandstand*?"

"Well...kind of, but not one hundred percent."

So Charles gives me an 8-track; that's how long ago it was. It had Deep Purple, Emerson, Lake and Palmer, and Alice Cooper. Charles was far ahead of me because his father listened to Jimi Hendrix. The Hammond organ that Keith Emerson played reminded me of church music; I was into that.

While I had known about the guitar, Charles was the man who turned me onto the guitar in my favorite genre and the place where it would really flourish as an instrument.

Much is dependent on what your parents listened to, what songs those who were closest to you played within your earshot.

Charles's dad was really cool. He was in the army, traveling around. Hendrix and Janis Joplin, that was what he listened to, and he would let Charles borrow his albums.

We would become best friends.

Later that same night, Charles called when a midnight special came on that would have rock 'n' roll bands on to perform.

My dad went crazy on me when the call came through that late at night, but my love affair with rock had begun. I'd eventually take a picture of a midnight special years later that featured KISS, trying to capture the moment in time as it buzzed by through the television.

I was a fanatic, trying to capture something that was here and gone without the playback we have today.

"What do you think about the stuff I gave you," he'd ask soon after giving me the 8-track. I liked it, so he said, "Oh, you should listen to this radio station that comes on late at night called Beaker Street."

It was acid rock in some sense, but most technically it was old school, progressive rock. You know, Bachman-Turner Overdrive. It was hard driven rock, and I thought it was great.

Charles is my friend who broke into a music store with a guy who was pretty much a criminal so that he could get a synthesizer. Charles also got the cheapest guitar in the world for me.

I couldn't believe Charles didn't take me.

He said, "Oh, James, that's not you."

That's who I became with friends like Charles. I became "that good guy over there."

"Oh, little James, his mom takes him to church all the time. Good guy, good guy."

I was shocked that another black guy my age actually liked rock and roll music as my family thought "white" music was corny compared to the soul and R&B that I grew up on.

Eventually, I would spend every dime I had buying rock magazines and albums.

Charles was a brave, tough guy. He was streetwise and brave enough to (finally) go to rock concerts with me when we were older, even though we obviously would be surrounded by white kids, and Arkansas is, and was, for sure the Deep South.

Charles was taller and more muscular than me, but who wasn't? He was quick-witted, intelligent, and could talk his way in and out of anything. He seemed so smooth with females. Some people laugh when they hear that because he wasn't a soul brother type. He came off more as an intellectual. Still does.

What many didn't know is that he was really into street life. He was the second guy I ever saw smoke weed. He could somehow talk street hoodlums older than us into buying us liquor and, lucky for me, talk various girls into fooling around with this shy kid called Bowie.

Bowie was my lifelong nickname from my family, but I was always James to him.

A year or two after meeting Charles, I was in art class with my good friend Robert when this fat ass white guy, who was usually cool with me, noticed a white girl he had a crush on being super friendly with Robert and me. Robert was a very intelligent guy. Not many kids could draw the Avengers as well as me, and I knew almost every Styx and Aerosmith album.

So this lard ass was telling us, "I'm a kick y'all nigger ass with a tire iron if you keep trying to sweeten her up."

She was appalled. Of course.

I grabbed a little clay cutting knife and Robert gave him the old slap on each ear smack just before our teacher came by to break up the ruckus.

People today who feel like everything is racist give me the same uneasy feelings that the widespread use of the *n*-word, in either form, give me. I grew up in the middle of some real face-to-face racism. One of my earliest memories was of the Japanese internment camps, right here in America, so I know that true oppression and hardship don't only happen to one race of people either.

While I was getting into rock and roll, a young Mexican kid in downtown Los Angeles would be falling in love with the same music.

Especially KISS.

CHAPTER 5

MEETING JAMES WATSON
(ZACK)

Friday, January 28th

James was in the passenger's seat next to me. We took the thirty-minute drive towards Huntington Beach, having an extension of the ongoing conversation that we'd been having through texts.

I didn't notice the 90-plus percent outdoor mask compliance throughout most of Los Angeles County—at least not on this day. Huntington Beach is California's ground zero in the rebellion against Covid restrictions.

As Mark Twain said, "Travel is fatal to prejudice, bigotry, and narrow-mindedness." So often travel will be about expanding your understanding of how life can be lived.

At a time when the world went mad, I was lucky enough to be in Austin, Texas, the place where everyone who could flee, fled to. I was training in a place where things felt normal, I was in maybe the one place in the world that could keep me relatively sane as I watched the nonsense unfold.

Life has been much different elsewhere. It gave me anxiety to see so many masks on people outside, seeing the way that it became a religious phenomenon.

As James told me, a lot of people see it as a way of being polite. He's not wrong. If you have a certain perspective, it would seem like the polite thing to do, even if you knew the mask did nothing. Being polite has its place.

But I can't stand it or take part.

Taking part in lies has led me down the wrong paths. It can pull you further away from who you are supposed to be—further into being someone you don't want to live with 24/7/365, whether you know it or not.

It leads to self-medication on drugs, alcohol, food, social media, or sex that will eventually spiral out of control, wasting your time and potential. The repercussions of these last few years on the public will be evident in increased suicides, violence, and overdoses.

People's lives were upended by lies and deceit. Real consequences were suffered.

Every few weeks there will be a new news story about someone facing consequences for not taking part in the lies.

One week it's a story about a Connecticut school nurse who would be suspended from her job for being "transphobic" for revealing that the school is letting kids hide the steps they are taking to "transition into a new gender" from their parents. Another week it will be a story about an award-winning New York City public school teacher who is kicked out of her job for not taking part in a forced medical intervention. The next it will be about Kyrie Irving being unable to play home games for the Brooklyn Nets because of discriminatory medical mandates against him playing, but he'll be able to watch the game from the stands.

All for a product that is ineffective and carries with it far more risk than reward.

Throughout will be stories of doctors being threatened with the revocation of their license for sharing medical information that works, but doesn't follow The System's currently agreed upon science.

This is where being polite gets us. For too long our culture has allowed lies to exist unchecked and those telling the lies have grown more powerful, more brazen.

As Covid fades into the background, we will get a full-court press by the corporate and political establishment attempting to convince us that boys can be girls and girls can be boys. Scott Newgent of TRe-Voices found that every child that undergoes a medical transition generates roughly $1.3 million for pharmaceutical companies.

With all of this, the end goal of the Covid hysteria comes into focus.

The goal of much of mainstream programming has been to destabilize our understanding of reality, making us more easily confused and more prone to manipulation as a populace. It is run by an establishment class hell-bent on pulling the ladder up behind them, safeguarding their resources and position in society, while rendering as many people as possible into a constant state of confusion, anxiety, depression, loneliness, and whatever other negative emotion they can inflict on someone to potentially make them a more compliant consumer.

Drugs. Consumerism. Materialism. Anything to numb them out.

The culture and The System have purposefully stunted our citizenry's development. As people age out or opt out of the education system, they then must spend time and resources working to undo all of the negative programming that's been put into them, if they can undo it at all. To do so, they must actively reject the programming that's been hitting them since they were kids, a reasonably difficult task.

Most people have signed up for this system without their knowledge. We take the path we're told from public school K through 12, then the university, and then the corporate job to pay back the debt accumulated at the university like the good, well-mannered wage slave we are meant to be.

There is another form of slavery we didn't know that we were buying into. There is the slavery of the debt, then the slavery of the intellect. Opting into a system where your ability to pay bills is predicated on your belief in things that make no sense, or at the least your silence.

Paid for by your compliance or your silence. Those are the only two options.

Letting colleagues know you're a Trump voter might put you on track to needing a new job. These are jobs you won't find, at least not in your field. Not with your opinions. Time to find a new career or start your own thing.

"You don't like that Amazon kicked that website off their platform? That's fine, just build your own Internet."

The whole point of the cancel culture has been to force people into going along with the narrative of the establishment, The System. The goal is to force people to not stand up against things that make no sense and to rid your company of the leaders within it that would have the courage to say something, thus ridding those at the top of their most likely competitors in a truly competitive environment.

Cancel culture rids the company of the leaders who could provide leadership, the people willing to do the hard thing, the right thing. It removes competition and helps more losers win by rigging the game against winners.

A total focus on woke issues can allow a company to deflect from more pressing issues for employees, like collective bargaining.

Black Lives Matter is right. The System is rigged. It's just not rigged against any one race. It's rigged against the people. All of us.

Which is why those in profiting off The System want us drugged, depressed, divided, and demoralized.

The slow and continual creep of more government theft from a "pandemic" that became the biggest transfer of wealth in human history. From March 18 through December 30, 2020, an International Labour Organization report found that the workers of the world lost $3.7 trillion, while an Oxfam report found that billionaires gained $3.9 trillion. They estimate that between two hundred to five hundred million people fell into poverty in 2020.

Workers weren't the ones advocating for the restrictions that took away their wealth. It was the "smart" people who could work from home who did that.

Music has always been a class indicator, a sign of who you were in relation to the culture. Rock and roll was a distinctly working-class endeavor. It wasn't created by the classically trained. It was created by working-class people and, because of that, it had the ethos of the class in it. It was raw and from the soul. It was not polished.

Maybe we're in for a musical revolution in the years ahead of us, at least.

Traditionally, and even today with the live music scene we have in Austin being an example, people listen to what's around them. They hear what's at the local bar and the sounds say something to them about who they are and where they are.

Almost Famous is the classic telling of the rock and roll groupie named Penny Lane, played by Kate Hudson. Our high school-aged male protagonist has an older sister, played by a nineteen-year-old Zooey Deschanel, who leaves to become a flight attendant, anything to get away from their overbearing mother. On her way out the door, she tells her little brother, "Look under the bed. It will set you free." The albums there would lead that fifteen-year-old lead character William Miller to become a writer for *Rolling Stone*. It was loosely based on writer/director Cameron Crowe's own young adulthood working as a music critic.

On that journey, William found that true music chooses you.

Lead singer Jeff Bebe would define rock and roll as a lifestyle and way of thinking that wasn't about money or popularity. "It's a voice that says, 'Here I am—and fuck you if you can't understand me.'"

There was a belief that rock and roll could save the world. This was not fiction.

"What it all comes down to is that thing. That indefinable thing when people catch something in your music," Bebe concluded.

"The buzz."

Throughout the movie, the worry is that this grassroots thing they all believe in would eventually, unfortunately, be overtaken by corporations.

It would.

America is a continuous state of rebellion, but rebels age and many make compromises over time. They can only hope that the next generation picks up the baton because rebellion is necessary. This country was founded and molded on that rebellious rock 'n' roll ethos.

The ethos, the feeling of freedom that rock and roll evoked, is not something to tamper with or disrespect. A betrayal of something grassroots is unforgivable. Selling out is the wholesale betrayal of the art of the genre. When the people the artists are supposed to be saying "fuck you" to end up buying the artists, then there's no more room for those artists to say "fuck you."

Eddie's resolve to stay true to the foundational rebellion in his own metal ethos is a living lesson in how to live as yourself in the face of the pressures of life.

James and I parked near the beach and got out of the car. He reminded me of his needing to stay out of the sun. His skin can't take it. We took a walk into the promenade and found a burger joint. He got his burger without cheese.

When he was down on his luck, early in the years of his pursuit of the rock and roll dream in Los Angeles, he had ninety-eight cents to his name. Having not eaten the night before, he walked to the drive-thru window with those ninety-eight cents in his pocket. When he got there, he asked for the hamburger he knew he had the change for, but the girl working the window said that all they had left were cheeseburgers, which were ninety-nine cents.

"I can't give it to you."

"One cent..."

"Can't give it to you..."

As James told me over his hamburger, "I go to bed starving, oh my God. I can't wait to get up and go to work. That's it. No more cheese. And to this day, I don't eat cheese."

"I'd eventually work at Carl's Jr., so I could guarantee at least one meal a day. That's what rock bottom is. When you're working the dead-end job just so that you can know you'll have some free food every day."

He spent the next hour showing me old photos from his Little Rock childhood, through the years making music alongside Eddie. When the music stopped for them, James, the lover of satanic metal in his youth, found his way to God.

It has been an interesting path. One of the first songs Eddie played for me during the weekend visit was a song they made together about abortion on their first demo with his and James's first project together, their band Resistance. While we listened, Eddie and James couldn't tell if they were pro- or anti-abortion. They didn't recall the emotion behind the message, but it was definitely raw.

It's a song about the screams of the baby as it's sucked out of the womb, limb-by-limb. Whatever the take, they were brutally honest.

We naturally made our way to the conversation of religion through a discussion about what some would call a split and others the duality of science and religion.

The duality is the story of what we are collectively going through right now, the clashing of fundamental ways of viewing the world. There has begun to be some widespread cultural recognition that we were told to rebel against things that might not have been bad for us. Religion has its issues, but the spiritual aspects and the lessons of the stories we can use to light our way weren't something the society should have thrown out.

A lot of people might not be religious today, but they're making their best attempt by pursuing "spirituality."

James has had past health issues and in those trying times, both science and God saved him. He's deeply religious now—not

Early studio sessions with the band Resistance, Eddie on the left, James facing away.

necessarily a believer in the organized religion part, but a believer in the teachers he has found, those preaching the word of God and capable of backing up those words with information and wisdom when questioned.

In speaking of his own path, he mentioned that he doesn't discriminate against someone who doesn't believe the same thing he does. He knows that we all have our own lives, our own experiences. We just need a similar goal and vision for how we can make the world around us better.

Our understanding of shared goals and reasonable differences runs counter to the various forces that want to keep us from being the America we can be together. Our differences aren't the problem. The established political and corporate system's desire to amplify, magnify, and exacerbate those differences are the problem.

To have taken the path that James has taken towards God is to rebel. It is the new rebellion, rebelling against the culture that's been made up and pushed on us by those with money and power. These are cultural beliefs that we're told we must believe in by the largest number of voices and all the ones you're supposed to listen to. Believe and comply, or else you will be called an -ist, -ism, or -phobe. The message is spread from everything on your television to everyone in your movies to every singer you might listen to. The repeated messages that aim to promote degradation within the culture are infinite. To be capable of stepping outside of that culture is to begin a path towards freedom.

Having come from a family with a religious mother, James rebelled back to the original message, but a rebellion of his own way. He wasn't getting re-involved in a religion that believed in institutions, but rather a belief in a story.

A pastor named Fred Price at the Crenshaw Christian Center was his sensei on this journey back to the Word of God by explaining to James the truth behind the stories, helping him realize that the stories happened in real places with real people at actual times in history.

James had gone to church periodically during his early twenties, but he was still chasing the rock star lifestyle, still making decisions and choosing to live in a way that might not have been entirely aligned with what a higher power would want for him. This relationship with Fred Price transitioned James towards the recognition of something greater than the glory that could come through music, and it would deeply impact Eddie.

And if there was ever a time where James would have a question for Pastor Fred Price, the pastor would tell him to look into it for himself, to do his research.

With this, James's faith only became more resolute as he proved to himself that the stories were true. The stories he was reading about happened in real places at real moments in time.

It's easy to be turned off by religion. There are plenty of examples of people using religion for deceptive means, the same way we see the modern "woke" religion being used. Plenty of people are saying one thing and doing another. Generation after generation have watched people use religion and ideology to profit for themselves through actively harming others.

When James asked me about where I stood on the subject of religion, being the writer who grew up outside of New York City during the 1990s and 2000s without a religious family, I told him my perspective was that of a belief in the power of the stories. A belief that the stories themselves have been one of the best vehicles for helping people behave in a manner that was better than the way they were behaving or better than the way they might behave.

The power of stories is undeniable. This is what role models are, a representation of who we're capable of being through the living representation that is their lives. Stories regarding the people around us, their triumphs and their proof of who they're capable of being, help provide us the confidence to become who we might become.

It's easier to become a better person if you have a bunch of good examples around you. It's easier to know what to do if you're reading things that are teaching you the right lessons.

A world without the Bible or other religious texts, especially at earlier stages in our humanity, would be a dark world. Even today, we live in a place where many, many humans are prone to behaving on their most basic human instincts. We are prone to taking the short-term gain over the long-term picture, putting our own needs over the needs of others or the community. People need a purpose that ties them together. We need a belief in something bigger than ourselves.

Fred Price didn't just start one church. He started one in Baltimore as well. He was an apostle when he was alive, a Christian missionary spreading the word. James says Eddie is an apostle as well, which is why Eddie is the only man that James will ever call "Master," as Eddie has facilitated the creation of one hundred plus 10th Planet Jiu Jitsu facilities in communities that spread something positive and life changing to so many.

Master Eddie Bravo.

I told James that 10th Planet and Jiu Jitsu have become a form of religion for many people, like myself, providing many of the benefits of church that he's speaking of. It's what drew me to the sport—being surrounded by community, people moving in the right direction with their minds focused on the right things. People who are trying to do the right thing.

That's the benefit of a church community—at the very least the people at church are trying to make an effort. They're getting up and out early on a Sunday to do something positive. That's a worthwhile commitment.

There is this misconstrued and false belief of the need for perfection to be a "good Christian" that we see in our culture's negative messaging around Christianity. We've been made to believe that religion, and the religious, want you to be perfect. That you must be perfect or else. Jesus did not die for the perfect person. He died for our sins because no one is without sin. We are all guilty of something we shouldn't have done. No human is perfect. No one is without sin.

Jesus came to earth as God's son and took on all the sins of the world, all of them. Then when Jesus died, He said, "It's done." We have a tendency to be sinful. That's in our nature, our very human nature, so his death took on our punishment, rather than the eternity of damnation that may have otherwise been reserved for us.

Feels like some New Testament versus Old Testament philosophy.

To James, he sees admittance to heaven as if there was a scenario where he had a ticket to meet Jesus with whatever amount of that ticket was left after a lifetime of sinning had slowly eroded it. To know that Jesus died for your sins is to gain admittance, no matter how small the ticket, because the person who knows Jesus died for our sins is the kind of person who isn't going to go out and do something truly heinous and evil. They know the word of God enough to spend their lives in pursuit of doing things the right way. And with the understanding of how to do the right thing, you'll have enough of an understanding that who are we to judge another?

The pursuit is what is important. The focus on the process.

MASTERING THE METAL

Three hours of conversation later, we were back at James's front door, dropping him off with a hug and a goodbye.

I saw him again on Sunday, this time with Eddie.

CHAPTER 6

EDGAR CANO
(JAMES)

My eventual migration from Little Rock to Los Angeles in 1985 was not out of the ordinary. The city and state have grown rapidly since it became a part of the union in 1850. It's a place made up of migrants from America and elsewhere.

New York City is the same: dreamers pack up their bags, hop on a flight, and chase their dream.

That's what I did. I left Arkansas for my dreams.

At the time of California's statehood, there were just under 93,000 citizens. Los Angeles County had 3,500 of those residents within its borders.

Statehood caused a 310.4 percent increase in population by 1860 to 379,994, then it just kept growing.

We're still talking about Oregon Trail days. Those who came to California for the gold rush in 1849 came by wagon, horse, and feet over untamed land.

Per Erin Blakemore with the History Channel, the first transcontinental railroad was completed in 1869 with magnificent train cars, velvet cushions, and gold-framed mirrors. There were feasts of antelope, trout, berries, and champagne. That railroad stretched nearly 2,000 miles between Iowa, Nebraska, and California, reducing travel time from about six months by wagon or twenty-five days by stagecoach over incomplete dirt roads to just four days on the smooth rails.[6]

That railroad connected California with the rest of the country, but a first-class ticket cost $135—almost $3,000 in today's inflated currency.

By 1880, California had 865,000 citizens and Los Angeles County had just over 11,200. Then, in 1885, the Atchison, Topeka, and Santa Fe Railroad Company charted its own course across the continent, choosing Los Angeles to end the route. This fractured the near total monopoly on rail transportation in the state, resulting in the price of a ticket from Kansas City, Missouri to Los Angeles decreasing over the course of five months from $125 to $15, then all the way to $1 by March 6, 1887.

Other rail companies would follow suit, resulting in a free-for-all of land speculation.

Remember, the Oregon Trail has its name because there was free land in places like Oregon to get people to move there under nearly impossible conditions. Settlers arriving after 1850, but before 1854, were given 320 acres if single and 640 acres if married, with half in the wife's name.

In 1862, Congress passed the Homestead Act to encourage settling of the Great Plains, kind of a "you can keep it, if you can keep it" policy considering that many natives were ready and willing to fight for the land they had already laid claim to, along with the many diseases or other potential issues that could kill settlers. The act applied to Oregon as well.

Any head of family of any age, or a single person over twenty-one who was or who intended to become a US citizen, could claim 160 acres of public land by paying a thirty-four dollar fee, then residing on and cultivating the property for five years.

After five years, they would receive a legal title to that land, but they could also purchase it for just $1.25 per acre after six months of occupation.

Many would leave the main path of the Oregon Trail to settle in Wyoming, Idaho, California, and Utah.

Per Evan Andrews with the History Channel, some 250,000 people traveled the California Trail, mostly gold prospectors looking to get rich. The Utah route helped 70,000 Mormons settle around Salt Lake City. The last wagon trains would cross the trails in the 1880s.

The railroad meant that now there were even more people looking to settle. "Boom towns" sprang up overnight. Agriculture, oil, land, and tourism, California had it all and with perfect weather.

By 1910, there were 2.4 million people in the state. This would kick off a sixty-year period known as the Great Migration as African Americans escaped Jim Crow laws and racial violence while in pursuit of the economic and educational opportunities that could come with more freedom.

The first half of this migration saw black southerners relocate to mostly northern and midwestern cities like New York, Chicago, Detroit, and Pittsburgh. The war effort for the First World War left many industrial jobs vacant and the labor supply was further strained by a decline in immigration, so black migrants were able to find work in industries that may not have otherwise been open to employing them.

Between the two world wars, two million black people left the south for other locales, then the expansion of the nation's defense industry during the war led to more migration, which remained active until the 1970s and even through to today. During this second phase, black Americans eyed Oakland, Los Angeles, San Francisco, Portland, and Seattle. Within twenty years of the second world war, another three million black people migrated throughout the US.

Black Americans found that moving north wasn't always an escape from racism as they were segregated into ghettos in an urban lifestyle that introduced entirely new obstacles, while established blacks in the north tended to look down on them.

My best friend was born in Santa Ana, California at the end of this Great Migration period, and the state's population had ballooned to twenty million citizens. This was ten times the population of the state sixty years earlier, and the state has doubled in population since then!

Before Edgar, who would become famous with the name Eddie, was born, his mother, Maria Gonzalez, was married to a man named Alfonso Bravo. Alfonso was a Porsche mechanic, so he had a good job and a bit of money. Together, they had Alfonso Bravo, Jr., who would be my friend's older brother.

Alcohol, domestic violence, cheating, and constant fighting were a part of this bad partnership. Alfonso would beat the shit out of Maria Gonzalez one final time, then they would divorce, putting Eddie's mom back at her parent's house in the same neighborhood of Santa Ana.

A few years later, Maria would start messing around with Eddie's dad, Pedro Cano.

She wanted to sing mariachi. That was her thing. Anytime there was mariachi music at a Mexican restaurant or some party, she was always there to sing lead, and they loved her. Eddie's mom was hot.

She had crazy dreams of being a singer, but she had no idea how to make it happen business-wise. She'd belt out songs in the shower when Eddie was a kid—people could have heard her down the block.

At a party in Santa Ana one night, she met Pedro. He's married with five kids, but that never stopped him.

During the day, he'd drive a box truck delivering giant-sized food products for restaurants, things like vats of mayonnaise or ketchup. He would drive all over Southern California, from Los Angeles down to San Diego, during the day. At night, he was a concert promoter bringing Mexican bands to downtown Los Angeles and downtown Santa Ana where all the Mexicans were.

As Mexicans immigrated to Los Angeles, white people moved themselves down to Orange County, to places like Huntington Beach, El Toro, and Laguna Niguel. But they forgot they needed Mexicans for manual labor, so Santa Ana was designated as a Mexican city with a little white section.

That's how Eddie's grandfather got to the area. He'd get into construction and support ten kids through that.

Pedro and Maria met at a club one night, some concert he was promoting. He sees her and brings her into VIP. He's married and making moves. Pedro knew Vicente Fernández, Mexico's version of Elvis Presley, and he introduced him to Maria that night.

On May 15, 1970, just a month after my eighth birthday, Edgar Cano was born. Edgar wouldn't be known as Eddie until his late teens.

When Eddie was born, Maria was living in an apartment in downtown Los Angeles that Pedro was paying for, telling her that he was going to leave his family for her. It was an empty promise to keep the fling going for himself.

Living in that apartment, Eddie would discover KC and the Sunshine Band through the song "That's the Way (I Like It)." His mom had bought him the 45. That was his first record and the song freaked him out, drove him crazy.

With two boys and the fling with Pedro ending, Mama Bear would have to move back in with her parents, which was a great time in Eddie's childhood. There were eight people altogether in the four bedroom, but a few years later, his mom would start dating Alfonso Bravo again. Then she got pregnant with Eddie's younger half sister, Marlene.

Alfonso coming back into the picture from years five to ten for Eddie would represent the dark years of his childhood. He had an older brother and younger sister from the same dad, and Eddie is the stepchild in between that. To Alfonso, Eddie represented the years Alfonso wasn't around. Eddie represented another man with a woman he, as the kind of man who put hands on a woman, likely took possession, ownership over.

This time period was when Eddie's last name would become Bravo, not by choice, but by his mother telling him it was Bravo. Neither she nor Alfonso wanted to answer questions about the side baby, so everyone became a Bravo.

Didn't matter much to Eddie. Cano was never around anyway.

Those years were so bad that Eddie became an altar boy at the neighborhood church. He needed to figure out how to get to heaven, since he was going through hell on earth.

Alfonso wouldn't beat Eddie but showed him zero attention or affection. When they were alone, Alfonso would just stare at Eddie and try to fuck with his head.

Around eleven, shortly after his stepdad left, Eddie would lose faith in religion, as he found out that there were other religions, other ways of thinking, and the Catholic Church was trying to convince him that there was only one way. The feeling of being lied to turned him into an atheist.

When Alfonso left again, the family was broke. They went back to grandpa and grandma's house, back to a neighborhood that was filled with single moms as father after father left their families via divorce or other means.

Maria worked hard, but single motherhood isn't easy. It means long hours at work and, potentially, having no one to watch your kids. Working hard doesn't always translate to a lot of money either. She worked at computer factories, putting computer chips together and lower-level stuff on a factory line. It was enough to get by.

There was no extra money for candy or video games, so Eddie, his older brother Junior, and his friends would steal candy and those video games. There was no stealing credit card information, nothing high level, but they wanted enough for the things kids are still addicted to today: sugar and screens.

The crew would go as far as smashing nickels into quarter slugs to try and get five plays out of the Ms. Pac-Man machine rather than just the one play a nickel was worth. Every morning they'd wake up smashing nickels, shaping them, then grinding them down, but around twelve, Eddie, the non-believing altar boy, and his best friend Matt, another cynical altar boy, realized they could steal the collection plate money.

Eddie and Matt would hide in the closet between the robes as the church was closing. When the priests would leave, they would come out of that closet, go to the drawer where they knew the plate was stashed, and take five bucks, seven bucks, just to get the sugar and video game fix.

The boys wouldn't take much, but they would do it all the time, so the church noticed money was missing. It was to the point that the church staff put a note in the tray begging whoever the thief was to please stop stealing.

Eventually, they'd try to steal one too many times. As they heard a priest ruffling through the closets, looking for someone staying behind, Eddie was standing there having an "oh shit" moment. As the priest opened up the closet Eddie was in, he jumped out, yelling "BOO! We scared you! We scared you!"

He and Matt would run out of the church, never to return.

Twelve years old and Eddie had already felt let down by everyone and everything a kid might think he can rely on.

Eddie wouldn't see Pedro very frequently. There was the time he came by school once and gave him a one hundred dollar bill. Then there was the other time he took him to Montgomery Ward, a department store chain that closed in 2001. Eddie was around eight years old and was told he could get anything in the store. Eddie could have gotten a bike, anything, but he decided on an Evel Knievel Stunt Cycle that revved up and went on its own little motor.

It was during the dark years with Alfonso around, at eight years old, that Eddie tried to commit suicide on Theragran and a whole bottle of vitamins.

The only good thing about the years around his stepdad is that those years would get him deeper into rock. Alfonso was a Mexican

that was way into classic rock. He and the family would go camping all the time with the trips' soundtracks being Fleetwood Mac, the *Saturday Night Fever* soundtrack, the Beatles, the Pretenders, Supertramp, Pat Benatar, and on and on.

Eddie would get into what Alfonso would listen to and Alfonso was really into Bad Company, Led Zeppelin, and Ted Nugent. The Porsche mechanic had all the albums and a nice Fisher stereo system in the living room.

Little Eddie wasn't allowed to touch that stereo system. His music listening was relegated to the shitty record player in his room with one speaker. Listening with that, he had no idea that the songs he was listening to in his room had so much more to them as he was listening to just one side—he had no understanding of the concept of stereo.

One day, when Alfonso was at work, Eddie went into the living room and played his records. When the sound came out, there were sounds he hadn't heard.

There was a guitar over here and a drum over there. If you turned that one speaker off, you'll never hear the guitar. It's all spread out, surrounding you. To an eight-year-old kid, it was magic.

KISS started in 1973, then, in 1975, they blew up. By 1977, they were global. The biggest band in the world. But in 1978, they jumped the shark. KISS started becoming like New Kids on the Block-ish, which made all the hardcore rockers say, "Fuck KISS."

They looked like clowns. It was like MC Hammer. He was huge for a while, then a joke. KISS started making disco songs like "I Was Made for Lovin' You," and the hardcore people turned their back on them.

Eddie's stepfather hated KISS for this, so he always heard him saying that it was for kids or goofy. So Eddie thought, "Well, I better talk shit on KISS too." He would tell kids on the elementary school playground that he wasn't going to watch the next KISS-themed movie or listen to the next album. He pretended he thought KISS sucked, even though he loved them.

All the kids were doing that because their older brothers and dads were at home talking about KISS selling out.

KISS was indefensible at that time. They went disco, changing their costumes and dressing like Liberace. The band thought the future was about getting polished and being more disco.

Other bands entered the scene and showed that the future was about getting harder. Van Halen came out, and they were hard. Then Ozzy Osbourne left Black Sabbath, and he came out super heavy with *Blizzard of Ozz*.

KISS chose the disco and more polished route thinking that was where the money would be. It was the late 1970s, their corporatization cycle hadn't graduated to doing credit card commercials yet, but there was KISS candy, pinball machines, condoms, and ice cream—whatever you could think of. Money was clearly becoming more important than the art.

Their first manager Bill Aucoin was the brains behind it all. Bill came from the television industry, having produced the team-based quiz show *Supermarket Sweep*, a sort of *The Price is Right*-style show, but for supermarkets. Contestants would throw a bunch of stuff in their cart and then guess the value of those items.

He blew up their merchandising so much that they were bringing in $100 million a year by 1976, illustrating to the entire industry the many ways to make a buck. Bill needed to see his return on his investment, he had found them during their club days and financed their first three tours and records off his credit card.

So it was fitting that a movie, not an album, was the official nail in their coffin for a lot of people. It had gotten to be about something other than the music.

An eight-year-old doesn't know any better when a band is selling out because the band is selling out so they're more popular to a wider audience. A wider audience can generally mean kid friendly and going that route was why all the hardcore fans were leaving.

NBC had a weekly Saturday night movie special, and on October 28, 1978, they played *KISS Meets the Phantom of the Park* as the movie of the week.

It was so bad.

NBC was trying to capitalize on KISS's popularity and instead gave us a date that will be known as the day KISS jumped the shark, complete with horrible acting and an even worse story line. It was the final nail in the coffin for a lot of KISS fans. No one could doubt their selling out after that.

In the movie, KISS went to Six Flags Magic Mountain in Valencia, California. They were staying there because they had two or three nights of shows there. Abner, the park's engineer, was not happy that KISS overshadowed the work he was doing for the park, so he tried to get them out of there. He eventually got fired for his erratic behavior and his disregard for the safety of the guests, which caused him to swear revenge on the park's owner, the park, and KISS—all of whom he blamed for his troubles.

Abner had created a series of animatronic attractions for the park, so after their first performance at the park, he used those skills to create KISS clones to mess things up at Magic Mountain and get in fights with the guests. Abner was trying to sabotage everything, his own false flag operation.

He captured KISS and put the fake KISS out on stage. They played out of tune and everyone booed.

I'll never forget the commercial. Paul Stanley was in it with this big cut to him saying, "We've got to get out of here." It was time to save the day.

It was so corny.

KISS got out, and they fought the cloned KISS. Drummer Ace Frehley was a black guy in KISS makeup and you could tell. It was hilarious.

Eddie and his twelve-year-old brother thought it was the greatest thing they'd ever seen. They couldn't sit on the couch, that was too far away. Both of them were sitting on pillows three feet away from the screen.

That's what changed everything for Eddie. Watching that movie and watching all these people scream for them had Eddie saying, "I want people to scream for me too. I want that."

He would write down: "Am I going to be a rock star or a football player?" That was it. Eddie already had football dreams, but now it was one or the other, whichever one comes first, whichever one paid him more. He had dreams to chase, despite the depressing life around him.

His family always went to Gemco on Sundays, which was the Walmart back then. The next day was a Sunday, and his grandmother took Eddie, Alfonso Jr, and two aunts who were around the boys' age because his grandmother and mother had kids at the same time.

It was like that *South Park* episode where there's a new Xbox and Cartman drags his mom to the store, focused on a mission. He's in there kicking down shit to get to the Xbox he wants.

Eddie made a beeline for the record section, dragging his aunt with him, obsessed with "Rock and Roll All Nite" after that movie. He found it, but he didn't buy *Dressed to Kill*. It was the live album called *Alive!*

Eddie didn't know what a live album was, but *Alive!* was the album that most would consider their breakthrough as it captured the energy of the band that they brought with their music, far more so than the way a studio album ever could have.

The album starts with a loud audience, making him wonder why the crowd at a football game was on the album. Then he heard what sounded like a promoter shouting, "You wanted the best and you got it. The hottest band in the land...KISS!!!"

From that point on, it was over. He was all in on rock. It was probably Paul Stanley's long hair that made Eddie think he had to have long hair to be a rock star.

His grandfather would give him $2 a week for mowing his lawn, so now he had three KISS albums to catch up on. He thought to himself, "Shit, I can't get into any other bands. I've gotta get all of these KISS albums."

There were just three albums at the time, but $2 a week doesn't leave you much to save for a record that could cost you $6.99.

Matt Macias from the church was Eddie's best friend from about five until the beginning of their teen years. He would buy one KISS album, then Eddie would buy another. They'd swap them out and trade. If Matt bought a KISS album, then Eddie wouldn't buy it, and vice versa.

That's how it would go. My friends and I were the same way. There was no other way to listen to the music of your own volition. There was either having the album or waiting until it came back on the radio. That was it. There was no thinking of a song, looking it up, and listening to it within the span of thirty seconds. The music streaming platforms of today would seem like magic to us back then.

There was a sense of pride in buying the albums of "your" band. If you owned the "master" copy that all your friends would copy for their own use at home, then that was YOUR band. You could copy the other bands' albums from your friends.

Eddie didn't know what disco was, so he didn't know that "I Was Made For Loving You" was their first disco song. It was just a song to him, and he loved it. But if he was seventeen or eighteen years old, maybe he might have understood what selling out was.

It's going with whatever is popular, molding yourself into what the money wants you to be or where you think the money will be.

The next album that would come out after Eddie bought the 1975 *Alive!* album would be *Dynasty*, this super polished, pop disco album that "I Was Made For Loving You" was on. He got into KISS right as they were selling out. Eddie was really into that one, and even with *Unmasked* he had no idea. Even on the cover, KISS had a cartoon alluding to the fact that people thought they stunk.

KISS was trying to expand into new markets because they were deader than dead in America. So for the *Unmasked* tour there was just one show stateside in New York City, but they went to Australia and were treated like the Beatles. Australia's trends are always two years behind ours. The European leg of their tour did something right as Iron Maiden was the opener.

I wouldn't go along with their sell out route the same way Eddie did. Of course, I was fourteen years old when they jumped the shark with that Magic Mountain movie. I had the benefit of a little bit of wisdom being eight years older. I could see KISS transitioning into something far more corporate and money driven.

For Eddie, liking bands was like supporting a football team, and he would argue with his friends on the block over who was the best. It doesn't matter if they're 0 and 16, you're pissed and depressed, but you're saying, "Alright, we'll do better next year." You're hoping the next album is better. Friends would talk shit about their friend's favorite bands like they would with sports too.

Lead guitarist Ace Frehley and drummer Peter Criss leaving the band had some KISS fans upset as everyone was emotionally attached to the idea of the original band they knew when they first learned about them. That *Unmasked* tour was the last with Frehley and the first without Criss.

For others, they were excited. "Let's get rid of these guys. They're trash." We'd of course never admit that to our friends, but we knew the band could find better, and they did. Eddie was sick of trying to defend KISS against friends who loved bands with great musicians, like Rush. All of these other bands had shredders.

Eddie's cousin, Eric, was a Rush fan, so he could say he had the best drummer and the best bass player. Alfonso Jr. liked Van Halen, and Eddie Van Halen could shred. One time, Eddie had a friend, Alex Galvan, over and had to put Peter Criss's drum solo on double speed to pretend he was better than he was.

It was around the age of thirteen or fourteen that Eddie understood. He was getting into heavier music. Juxtaposed against the music KISS was making, it was easy to see the sellout. The music they were making wasn't the same sound as what made them famous.

Sellout isn't even a term you hear today because you have to sell out to make a living in the music industry on the global scale, same with all forms of entertainment, and most glaringly in journalism. It's no longer taboo; it's the norm.

Junior and Eddie in Eddie's childhood bedroom.

For most, it seems like the only way to make a living doing that thing you love with your own unique set of skills.

Even when we met each other, he would pretend he didn't like KISS just to avoid ridicule. But soon after we had met, I went into his room in Santa Ana and, boom, there's an 8 x 10 KISS poster.

That's my boy.

I still loved KISS too. They meant a lot to me.

We had spent so much time talking shit about KISS because we were into thrash metal music when we met, but once we got closer, we could admit to each other our appreciation for KISS.

I might not have gone along for the journey on the sellout, but I respected the way they helped foster my love of rock and roll. Sellout or not, the music was meaningful to both of us.

Music always gave Eddie something to reach for. Those childhood years were dark and KISS may have let him down, but they also gave him hope for something more. Those screaming fans on that *Alive!* album gave him something to aspire to.

His experience and education in watching them sell out were important too.

CHAPTER 7

JAMES DISCOVERS ROCK 'N' ROLL
(JAMES)

KISS was why I would meet another best friend named William.

William was walking down the street in Little Rock with *Dressed to Kill* under his arm. I rushed to stop him, thinking he was about to throw it out, rather than first thinking that this other black dude in Arkansas was a fan too.

"You love rock music?" I asked, surprised.

"Yeah, I love rock music."

"But what do you mean you love rock music?!"

He went, "You know, the Stones, the Who, KISS."

"WHAT?!?! You love KISS?!"

I come to find out he lives right down the block from me. What are the odds of that?

I went over his house. Posters everywhere.

He came over my house. Posters everywhere.

William lived with his stepdad. We'd close the door to his room, listen to music, and play guitar.

In the 1970s, many music magazines featured tablatures, which would illustrate proper finger placement on the guitar neck, making reading music much easier for people who had some basic knowledge. In my opinion, however, reading tabs doesn't capture the grit and urgency of sight-reading music.

I'd learn to play some songs this way, but I realized that most rock players are playing on guts and feel, making the guitar react to the essence of their tone. Once you grasp the very basic chords and structures, you can ditch reading unless you're in a very restrictive, structured setting. Ripping songs with your friends is about trusting your ears and that feeling you're trying to create when playing.

Reading music does have its place, but it didn't have a place with me. It wouldn't have a place with my friend Eddie either.

Charles had taught me how to play guitar, and we would jam together, him with his guitar, and me with mine. He would teach me a lot of other things too.

During junior high school, Charles had already matured into surviving on his own, despite his age. I was still in the eighth grade.

We were driving around in his Gran Torino. He said, "Let's go by this girl I just started dating." I learned so much from him over the years about approaching girls and making the right moves that would lead to sex.

He pulled up to a house, honked, and out came this cute girl who looked very familiar to me. She looked into the car, saw him, smiled, then saw me. Her eyes bulged because she was also my girlfriend.

She turned around and ran back into the house, as shocked as me.

Charles drove away laughing.

We could have cared less. Our friendship remains strong today.

In 1980, the year I graduated high school, William and I went to a Van Halen concert in Little Rock.

I had the nerve to record my cheap ass guitar that Charles had stolen for me on a cheap reel-to-reel tape player I had. The record may have had some singing as well. Somehow I got the guts to think that if I throw this tape on stage, Eddie Van Halen, or someone in their management, would hear it and say, "Wow, this kid is phenomenal!" and then sign me to a record deal.

At least maybe they could play my tape at the beginning of their shows, right?

To this day, I get an embarrassing kick out of that considering how sloppy and bad that little reel tape must have sounded.

I made my way up to the front, threw it on stage, and then was stuck there, crushed against the barrier.

William was sitting back in the seats.

It's the part of the night when David Lee Roth stopped the show and showed why he was the best live front man. The spotlight was on him as he reached in his furry boot to pull out a joint and say something cool to the crowd like, "This one is for you, Little Rock!"

The crowd was screaming and William in the back swore, "Oh my God, he's got James's tape!"

To this day, we still laugh at that story.

It was so rare for someone black to go to rock concerts in the 1970s and 1980s. Whenever my black friends and I would show up, staff would immediately open the doors and say, "Okay, come in." They thought that we obviously must work there. Too bad we were too dumb, not honest, to go in.

We would love for that to happen now, but no such luck.

Charles was a good guitar player, and he would improve, but William was always technically better.

I met William around my sophomore year, but we never went to high school together. Charles and I did, but Charles is a rebel dude. He dropped out of high school. He got a job before all of us. He had that Trans Am.

So, of course, we all started hanging out and going to shows together once he met William. It was unique for three black friends to be so into rock music in Arkansas like we were.

William could read music. We would actually go to college together at the University of Arkansas at Little Rock campus. We took guitar together, but I couldn't read music. Ted Nugent doesn't play from a book. They'd tell me to play Led Zeppelin, but it was all different tunings.

I never tried to read music again. That's it, but I did go to school to learn how to play guitar.

I'd only last about a year and a half, maybe.

William wouldn't make it through college either—too much tripping on women and playing guitar himself.

It didn't matter. He's always had a fantastic job. Always. He lived the dream. When he was in high school, he got a job at a classical music radio station, and he worked at what we would look at as a Tower Records in Little Rock, a store called Discount Records.

When he told me that he was working at Discount Records, I was blown away. We used to go there to get albums like Judas Priest and all the other albums I wanted to buy. That's like working at Mecca to me.

William is still brilliant today, intellectual. Whenever I'm home, I can turn on the radio and there he is, playing something like Chopin.

His dream was to work at an NPR type of place. Now he works at Clear Channel and for a big hospital in Arkansas that is the equivalent of the University of California system out here. He does all of their IT work.

When we got to college, my friend Robert Jenkins said to me, "Dude, we will never be around this many different kinds of chicks again."

In college, I was like "music, music, music," but you add in the girls and it was "girls, girls, girls," like Mötley Crüe would say. I took an art class. There I was, painting and drawing. The teacher would say, "You're amazing." I took art for the girls too.

Where am I gonna see a Jewish girl again? Where am I gonna see an Iranian girl again in my neighborhood? The world was coming to me.

When I was a kid, my neighborhood was 100 percent black except for this older white lady, a grandmama kind of person.

And did I hook up with any of these girls I met in college? Oh, I was a dog. I had a couple of girlfriends in high school, but I was a dog in college.

Once I latched onto music, if there was a concert coming to town, I was there. I took journalism in college, so they had me go watch the concert and then review it for the newspaper. Of course I would do that.

We were all into journalism. William would write a great review about my first band with Eddie one day. He started taking communication and radio classes in high school, which is why he fell into his eventual radio job. He was hardworking, determined, and intelligent—still is. What we've been able to become was because of that vehicle of music, our passion.

In high school, I'd want to take a date to what we called the Rodeo State Fair. There would be bands like REO Speedwagon and Uriah Heep. William and I would go. My friend Larry and I would go. Charles and I would go to concerts everywhere.

Larry could hang with rock music, but when we would really get into it, he barely even liked Van Halen. We connected when it came to Soul and Christian music, but he was not a metal fan at all.

My first real girlfriend was in junior high. All my girlfriends were black in junior high. It was the concerts that first got me dating white girls. A shared love of the same kind of music helped me make my first white friends in a high school that was 80 percent white and 20 percent black. Black kids thought I was a nerd, but I was a safe black friend for white kids.

"Hey, you want to go see AC/DC with me?" I'd ask a black girlfriend.

To which she would reply, "Boy, you crazy. I ain't going to see no white band."

I'm the guy in high school with the Van Halen sticker. You know, Black Sabbath. All the white dudes are like "whoa," and the girls with them looked at me like I was special. They're thinking, "Like, okay, I've dated that and that, but look, this black guy listens to this group. He's cool."

Eddie's first white girl was during the tenth grade. His first three girlfriends were Mexican.

A white girl named June, a name right out of the Brady Bunch, would tell her parents she was going jogging. She was an athlete, so she really would jog over, and he'd have sex with her on his mom's bed when she was at work because "I'm not going to fuck on a twin bed if I don't have to." Ha!

His mom was always wondering to him in the thick accent of her second language, "Why you always date white girls? Why don't you date any Mexicans?"

He would respond with a variation of the same thing I ran into. "Mom, Mexican chicks don't go to Slayer concerts. Just white chicks."

If anything, it's 99.9 percent dudes and like three chicks.

The best thing about the college girls was that they weren't interested in the same things that the high school girls were interested in. They weren't focused on who had the popularity or who were the jocks. There was free love to be had.

I went out for track and football in high school, but I was out there like Rudy. I was struggling, but playing hard enough to have the coach say things like, "If you guys gave it half the hustle that Watson did."

I wasn't the one out there leading the troops. I was always the smallest guy so I didn't play much.

"You're on special teams, Watson."

Charles, William, and I would never form a band. The first one was going to be Roxx. The next one, Lucifer.

We were looking at a band called Nazareth, and there was a band called Exodus years later. For us, we thought, hey, let's look through the Bible to see if there are some cool names in here.

Hey, Lucifer, that's cool. I could draw a long *L* and then put the *U-C-I* of Lucifer in there like so. Oh yeah, that would be cool.

In my high school yearbook, there is a picture of me holding a cheap ass guitar. Underneath it says, "This is James Watson, leader of the band Lucifer."

We had a guy playing drums that had never played drums. It was never a real band. We just talked about it. It was the best we could do. All my friends knew how to do was play guitar. It was the thing we learned together.

My earliest job was in the kitchen at a fish food restaurant called Cajun's Wharf. I was fifteen and lied to the manager, saying I was sixteen as that was the legal age of employment at the time.

Cajun's Wharf was upgraded to a really nice place to eat in Arkansas before shutting down a few years ago. It might have even been nice back then, but I was strictly a fish washer's boy then. I had almost no idea how fancy the place was as I only saw it when I was refilling the salad bar or taking dirty dishes back and forth.

With an intelligent mom who taught me so much herself, my bosses encouraged me to go back and forth with customers at the restaurant as other workers had more "country" or "ghetto" accents than me. I worked there for a little over a year, taking the city bus to and from, which couldn't have been great for the other riders as I smelled like fish and sweat. My parents told me to leave my work boots on the porch.

I got a job with my sister working at KFC and also worked at Franke's Cafeteria during high school, where I'd cut a fingertip off on my right hand, which thankfully had no impact on my guitar playing.

Franke's was a Little Rock staple, closing in 2019, exactly one hundred years after it had opened as a doughnut shop. Cajun's Wharf closed that year too after their own forty-four-year run.

These were the jobs that helped me pay for my early record collection, rock magazines, and concert tickets.

Other friends of mine had started getting interested in buying sharp clothing as high school was coming to an end. Most young men were interested in getting their own cars and clothing.

Me? I was trying to catch up on all of these rock bands that had been going on. I had to figure out what was better: Ritchie Blackmore of Deep Purple's Stratocaster guitar or Mick Box of Uriah Heep's Gibson SG?

I didn't have all the newest threads, so I settled for keeping my Jeri curl moist, plus the addition of a Members Only jacket.

During my time at The Butcher Shop, a higher-end steakhouse in town, a good buddy washing dishes with me would say, "You should buy a van, load up your guitar, and move to start your own band!"

He planted that seed in my mind, the thought that I could really do something like that.

At the time, I was reading every single rock magazine: *Circus, Rock Scene, Creem.*

Looking at the magazines, I would see Angus Young of AC/DC or Matthias Jabs of the Scorpions and think, "He sells millions. He's great. But I don't know how to write music. I don't know how to read music."

I just liked to rock.

I'm just turning magazine pages, seeing all of these dudes. The only black guy in these magazines was Jimi Hendrix, yet I wasn't even much of a Jimi Hendrix fan.

But I was beginning to imagine that this was something I could do.

It was the back of *Circus* magazine that had me pen palling with a girl in Anaheim. It was just like Facebook now, but I was writing to her from the back of *Circus*. People would put their information and the bands they were into in the back of these magazines to create social networks and connections through their love of music.

"If you're into this band and that band, write me."

She lived in Reseda, but she put that she lived in Los Angeles. We were writing back and forth.

She would write, "You should come out here. Bands always come to California to start and then they become huge. There's a band here from Pennsylvania called Poison. They just moved out. These other bands came from these other places. They play at such and such."

Those such and such places would end up being on the Sunset Strip, but she didn't say as much back then.

Rock history was happening in Los Angeles.

She would send me pages from *LA Weekly* and *OC Weekly*. I would look at all of these bands. I bought a porno magazine, and there is Mötley Crüe with dates they're playing at this club in Los Angeles.

I was beginning to think, how many more reasons do I need? Do I need to get struck by lightning to realize that this is the place that I need to go?

Flipping through the pages of that *Circus* a couple years earlier, I'd seen this event called US Festival in Southern California, near San Bernardino—four days of music. To hell with working, everyone was going to take the weekend off.

It was huge, a Woodstock type of thing. The first happened on Labor Day in 1982 and the second, and last, event was Memorial Day weekend in 1983. Steve Wozniak, the cofounder of Apple, was the promoter.

Eddie went to the second one, the one I saw the ad for.

That Saturday had a New Wave Day with A Flock of Seagulls. Heavy Metal Day included Quiet Riot, Mötley Crüe, Ozzy Osbourne, Judas Priest, and Van Halen.

While the Rock Day on Monday and the Country Day that next Saturday didn't interest me the way the other two did, the lineups were impressive. Monday had U2, David Bowie, Stevie Nicks, and Joe Walsh. Country Day had Willie Nelson, Waylon Jennings, Ricky Skaggs, and Hank Williams, Jr.

The total attendance for the first three days alone was reported to have broached 650,000.

After that conversation with my pen pal, I thought, "That's it. I'm going there. I'm going to California."

So I bought my ticket. I told one person, my younger brother. I was twenty-three and he was fifteen, Eddie's age at the time. I didn't see the end of his high school years or anything.

"That's it, I'm going to California. I won't be here in the morning."

No one knew the plan. I didn't tell my parents until I called them from Anaheim.

"Yeah, I'm living in California now. I came out here."

I don't know if they believed it. My dad, who was big on me moving out when I turned eighteen years old, was so shocked by the news that he told me that I always had a place to stay with them.

He and I had our issues too. Those first few years I was out, I wouldn't talk to him on the phone. I was resentful for the years of his drinking and the stress it put on the family. It was only once my mother and sister told me he had quit drinking that we began to repair the damage in our relationship.

Once that was repaired, my parents and I would remain close until their deaths.

I landed in California with my guitar we called "The Destroyer," an imitation Explorer with a spider web design and the stickers of some of my favorite bands. My only luggage was my mom's suitcase, filled with underwear, a couple of T-shirts, some long-sleeve shirts, and a box of cassettes. There were live concert tapes like Iron Maiden from the Los Angeles Forum.

When I bought them, I thought, "Whoa, I'm gonna buy this 'cause I'm never going to see them." I thought that they would never come to Little Rock.

I figured I'd take the tapes, bring them to Los Angeles, and sell them to people. That's how I would make a living, a naïve idea indeed.

The girl I'd been writing to was waiting for me at the bottom of the escalator to baggage claim. I was coming down wearing my brown leather jacket with little pins on it. You know, Black Sabbath, Saxon from Germany, Iron Maiden, a "Heavy Metal Rules" patch, plus a dude with a sword.

She and I had connected over our shared ability to find the best bands early before everyone else. We bonded over Iron Maiden, Motörhead, and a punk hardcore band named Suicidal Tendencies.

I came down that escalator, and she looked at me.

She didn't know I was black.

When I got to her, she said, "I had no idea you were Sound Barrier," an American, all-black, heavy metal band during the time. She might as well have said, "I didn't know you were a nigger." That's what she was thinking.

"Oh, okay. Ha. Ha," I said.

She was a spoiled brat, but she let me stay in her room for how long it was until she went to college, which wasn't long at all. She just told me her dad wasn't going to say anything about me living there because she was constantly manipulating their relationship through her mom. She would always say, "My mom is going to divorce you" if he didn't do what she wanted.

Spoiled brat.

So that was the situation I came into for a short time, then I had to get in her car as she drove me up and down Anaheim looking for an apartment. Reseda is about sixty miles north of where Eddie lived in Santa Ana, which is just south of Anaheim, so my coming down to Anaheim from all the way in Reseda was lucky for us.

I eventually settled at the Katella Motel and stayed there for eighty-eight dollars a week. I figured I could get a job and pay that. The motel was filled with low-level prostitutes and street bums like me.

I could pay. Sometimes. Barely.

My friend Gary would live with me for a short time when he came out to Los Angeles himself, thinking we were going to be cowriters on a book or something. "Bro, I moved here to be in a band." He couldn't handle the lack of cash for food and gave up.

Many times I'd walk around the grocery store, picking grapes off the vine and eating them as I pretended to be a real customer during those early years.

Moving out meant no more guaranteed meals from mom. Those meals I had a hundred times suddenly sounded like something you'd find at a five-star restaurant. An automatic meal of hot cream of wheat with chopped up pieces of fried breakfast sausage still makes my mouth water today.

The only breakfast meal I could master was bacon and eggs, so the ability to cook breakfast was always a test for potential girlfriends.

The things I took for granted as a kid were now missed. No mom on bathroom clean up meant my showers became a virtual greenhouse.

These are the years that inspired my distaste for cheese. The times I wouldn't have that extra cent to spend for a cheeseburger, so I'd have to get the hamburger. Some nights all the place had left was cheeseburgers, so I was out of luck. One cent too short.

I tell everybody now: do not come to California unless you have two or three thousand dollars in your pocket and a job lined up. My nieces and nephews wanted to come out behind me. I said, do not even consider it if you don't have three thousand dollars. Well, that's not even enough now when you think about it!

When I went out there, I was a phone call away, but the world wasn't as connected as it is today. Being 1,700 miles away from family might as well have been a world away.

First, I'd get that job at Carl's Jr.

I met a nice woman when I was working at Carl's Jr. She was beautiful. An older man would come in one day and we'd call back to her, letting her know her dad was here to see her.

It wasn't her dad. It was her husband.

She was married.

I didn't know.

A short while later, she'd offer me a place to stay in the apartment above their garage, saving me from that eighty-eight-dollar-a-week hotel.

Sometimes he would go out to work, so she'd be home alone and would invite me over to watch some TV.

"He's gone, and I'm lonely over here."

That television watching would frequently devolve into a sinful class of behavior, but that was a marriage of convenience and resources anyway. My conscious wasn't too, too guilty. He was twice her age; he knew what he signed up for. She did too.

I met Trudy during these years, a real girlfriend. Now, her mother was a saint, an angel. When it would get close to a holiday, Trudy would say, "Come home and have dinner with us."

I asked, "Does your mom know I'm black?"

She said, "Believe me. My mom doesn't care."

So she took me to her house, and her mom has black, white, Mexican, Asian—every kind of kid you know. Some had like half arms. Some were developmentally disabled.

Her mom was a nurse. She took care of everybody and didn't care who or what you were.

I became like the polite son she always wanted, helping her carry in her groceries, and always calling her "ma'am." It's because where I'm from you only call an older person by their first name if you work together. She was the person who could get me to call home during my early years in California, those times when I was mad at my father for being the angry drunk he was during my childhood.

Now, the grandmother...

One day, Trudy's grandmother came to me with a plate of Brazil nuts and she asked, "Oh, would you like nigger toes?" Everyone at the table shouted, "GRANDMAMA!"

I just said, "No, thank you."

On the television there would be whatever dating show was on at the time. I'd be on the couch, my girlfriend Trudy next to me. Her grandmother would say, "Oh, Trudy, when are you going to get on that show?"

That grandmother was a mess.

But her mother Andrea? That was my true mother out here. That's my "West Coast Mom."

"Oh, I need some money to pay my rent."

"Oh, well, here you go, son."

"Thank you."

She gave me a car. Trudy and her sister went off to college, so "Here, James, you can have this car."

I found family. We're still close, and it never mattered that Trudy and I broke up.

There was just one attempt at a musical project during this time for me. It was with this guy I met at Carl's Jr. His name was Edgar too, but he went by Gar.

He had come into work with an Anthrax shirt on one day, so we connected. Gar told me to come to a practice, so I went.

Gar's like, "Oh, do you know...Rush?"

Me: "Well, yeah. I know Rush."

Gar: "Okay, let's do Rush."

Next song.

Gar: "Let's do Exodus!"

Me: "Okay, let's do Exodus."

Aerosmith too.

Then I'd go and ask him, "Do you know Cirith Ungol?" They are a doom, power metal group known for lyrics based on fantasy, like swords and sorcery, taking their name from a mountain pass in the *Lord of the Rings*. That was their hook. They were supposed to be warriors and Vikings.

He went, "Hmmmm nope."

In Gar's defense, Eddie doesn't like them either. Bringing them up around him elicits a response of laughter.

But it was that experience with Gar that inspired me to put the ad out that eventually found my musical partner. Gar was good, and he was close to my age, so I thought we would be into the same stuff, but he didn't know any Mercyful Fate or Venom, bands from a newer wave of speed metal that I was getting into.

While I was in Los Angeles making my own "young man goes west" American dream come true, Eddie was starting to figure out what was to become of him.

CHAPTER 8

SANTA ANA HIGH SCHOOL
(JAMES)

Eddie's football dreams were ended by the dominant talents of a freshman football team at Santa Ana High School that blew everyone out. Their grace and abilities illustrated to Eddie what he wasn't and would never get the chance to be in football.

Those dreams probably should have been over before then.

In middle school, the schools played flag football. In sixth grade, at his first middle school, he was cut from that team.

He would soon have to transfer himself out of the mostly black and Mexican middle school he started at. Since his two aunts in seventh and eighth grade were popular, he was popular enough to go out with seventh grader Sabrina. He broke up with her, then started dating a sixth grader named Margaret, so all of the older kids who already didn't like him found their reason to torment him.

While claiming a gang meant almost nothing other than making the claim, middle schoolers were supposed to claim a gang at this school. You just have to pretend you're in it and then you go home. You do whatever you want back in your neighborhood.

Eddie was already in a situation where some black kids would say, "Why do you try to act white?" He always felt like these older kids were going to beat him up, but they didn't have a reason until he broke up with Sabrina, and she called the goons on him.

They took him behind the building, so Eddie started crying, which made them feel bad enough to let him go. At that point he knew he needed to transfer schools, so he did, putting the transfer in himself by using the address of another aunt in the area. He later told his mom, "I'm going to the white school. It's a better school."

When he came to the new middle school, he'd get cut from the flag football team again.

Those were tough years for Eddie—more tough years after the already tough years living with Alfonso Bravo Sr. He had one friend at the new school called Lee Mays.

Not having friends when you're a kid is okay when you're going from class to class, but being in recess and lunch on days that Lee didn't make it to school were torture. Early every school day Eddie would check the attendance to see if Lee was there.

Teachers kicked the kids out of the school during recess, and you could only come in if you were going to the bathroom. Eddie spent those lonely days pretending he was taking a forty-minute dump, desperate to not be outside surrounded by kids.

Eddie knew Lee when they were in first grade. Now that they were in seventh he was his only friend. By the time seventh grade happens, kids have formed cliques and stay within those cliques. He wasn't able to make any inroads with the other kids. Lee was a long-haired stoner who loved metal, and they were two loners together. Eddie only being a loner out of necessity now.

For just a moment there, in sixth grade at his previous school, things were finally going well for him. He was popular, kids liked him, and then that was snatched away too.

Once in high school, Eddie was on the tackle football team for the first time since fifth grade and peewee football. He was wearing helmets and shoulder pads again for the freshman team at Santa Ana High School. Eddie says now that if they would have cut people in high school, they would have cut him then too, but they don't cut anybody.

It was the years without the pads on where Eddie was able to convince himself that things would be different with the pads on again. It was an ultimate "Michael Jordan got cut from his JV basketball team" type of story, considering Eddie's future athletic success.

Cut from the middle school flag football team. Man.

The high school coaches couldn't figure out where to put him because he was too slow, too small. He did have hands though. He could catch, and he had moves.

His wide receiver coach gave him the nickname "Phar Lap" after a horse from New Zealand in the late 1920s and early 1930s that was known for starting slow. In 1983, a movie starring Tom Burlinson was made of the unimpressive colt that would make itself into a champion.

All you had to do was not give up after a decent juke move from Eddie because you could just run him down and drag him to the ground. Whenever he made a move, Eddie was waiting for those footsteps he'd hear behind him. He never outran anyone.

Since he was invested enough in showing up to practice, they put him as second-string receiver. That was second string to Royal Wilbon though, and the coaches were never going to take him out. He was one of those kids that looked like they could have played college football as a freshman in high school. He was a real talent, the kind of guy who could have made it. Any time he touched the ball it seemed like he would be gone.

Every game was 55–0, 48–0, 57–0. That freshman team slaughtered everyone.

They didn't just have Royal. There were three running backs that were unstoppable. Hector Valencia was a super fast Mexican kid, Donovan Mauga was a big half-white, half-Samoan kid, but then they heard that this black kid Robert Lee was coming out of juvenile hall.

Hector and Donovan were sweating that Robert was going to come in and take their spot, but they held their own. They were a three-headed attack in the backfield and an insane group of players for a freshman football team.

The word was that Robert would end up being a crackhead and all of that. Such is many a story of Southern California in the 1980s, unfortunately. But when he played football, no one could tackle him. He would finish his varsity career as Orange County's second all-time leading rusher with 4,388 yards.

The next year, everyone would be stars on the varsity team. When they were seniors, they lost in the conference finals. At the end of the game, they were winning so the opposing quarterback threw a Hail Mary into the end zone. Bobby Joyce, another one of the star players, jumped up in the end zone to knock it down, and he knocked it down into their wide receiver's hands in the end zone. Santa Ana lost. It was like losing the Super Bowl for the high school.

After seeing what these guys were capable of as freshmen, Eddie could cross that football dream out. It wasn't happening.

All that was left was rock, and he was committed to it. But could he find people who were as committed as he was to the dream?

When he started making music and having bands was when he shifted from being called Edgar to Ed. Ed Bravo to music people.

With his mom, it was always "Where's Edgar? Where's Edgar at?"

Kids would say it wrong too. "It's not Agar. It's Edgar," he would correct.

When he started a band, he wanted to kill that embarrassment. He hated the name.

His first band was Execrate with his best friend, Matt, at thirteen or fourteen years old.

Eddie had been playing drums on boxes and writing music at ten years old. Matt had an acoustic guitar then. They called themselves "The Bikers" and had one show in Matt's backyard that no one went to. Eddie had even written a song called "Out of My Mind."

I met you at a party
You're looking so sexy
I thought you were a hooker
Cause you asked for twenty bucks
I was out of my mind
Out of my mind

Eventually, Matt had an electric guitar, and Eddie got real drums. Their friend Guillermo joined, then Willie. And then, in high school, there was this kid John who had long blond hair, makeup, and always had Slayer shirts on. He was half-glam, half-thrasher.

At the time, those two styles were two entirely separate genres on their own. Do you want to work glam? Or do you want to look like Slayer? There were two different kinds of long-haired dudes, two different styles. Back then it was which style do you have? But this guy did all the styles. He would do punk, dress punk, but then he would dress metal. He would dress glam or hardcore, but he would always have face makeup on, always eyeliner.

That was cool then.

John was fourteen years old and had this long hair with older brothers who would drag him out to the Sunset Strip. Eddie was fifteen at the time.

John was the most rocked out kid in the whole school. He was always by himself, a loner type. He was too cool. He went out on weekends with his older brothers, Dave and Grant, who were already out of high school. They had longer hair too.

Dave was always a bigger guy, but they were getting girls every weekend. They'd bring John with them to go see Mötley Crüe at these clubs. No one else that Eddie knew was doing that, so of course John was too cool for anybody.

Eventually, he and Eddie would get to talking. John respected Eddie because Eddie had a drum set and a guitar player for a band. Eddie was getting pretty good at musical trivia too. He always knew his shit, the consummate researcher. There is no way that you're going to be a legit musician if you ain't hunting and looking for new music. You need to keep learning and trying to master it.

Some people don't have the time to look for music, but a real musician has to make that time and do the research. You have to see where it all fits in—see what you can hear and learn.

Even back then, Eddie was all about the music. He knew what was up. He knew all of the latest music.

He led John into seeing his vision. "This is what we're doing. This is the plan. If you want to jump in, let's do it. You can sing, right?"

John wanted to be a singer, but he had never sung before, so Eddie hyped him up anyway. "You don't need to sing. We're just doing screaming and yelling. You know? You can just say yes. Because you want to be a star, right? Right. Come on, you could be."

John and his brothers were already heading to the Strip to see these bands, so how hard could it be to be the guy on stage?

Here they were: Rock Star John with the long hair, plus Eddie, Matt, Guillermo, and Willie. Eddie was playing drums and singing in the beginning, before John, but he felt he couldn't sing anyway, so John couldn't have been much of a downgrade.

As much as Eddie would have loved to sing and be in the front of the band, being the star, he was content back on the drums. At the time, his cardio wasn't together enough to even consider it. He's always been capable of doing this, recognizing the role he's supposed to take, and using his leadership skills as best as he can within that role. He's always in pursuit of the best outcome.

That's what a leader does. It's like a professional football team; there is no bias. There is no "I like him more" or "I want to do this." We have to find out what the best shit is—what the best we can do as a group can be.

Eddie would take a handful of drum lessons, it was something he'd do in another teenager's bedroom once a month. After a couple of these, Eddie came in to find this teacher with an acoustic guitar on his bed, leading Eddie to feel like his teacher was cheating on the

Rock Star John and Eddie in 10th grade.

drums with this guitar. Of course, Eddie asked what he was doing with the guitar.

"Most drummers are at the mercy of the singer in the band, who is generally the guitar player," so he wanted to learn the guitar. Now, Eddie did too.

He didn't want to be the guy looking for the songwriter, he wanted to be the guy who could write those songs, so Eddie would get himself a one-string guitar for song-writing purposes. Being the songwriter meant that Eddie would also become the person putting together the musicians, finding the right guys. He could be the producer.

Eddie felt, or knew, the band would be way better if John sang because with John they had a rockstar. They had a rockstar with long hair, but then he started losing his hair a little bit. Then his brothers went bald.

111

Eddie knew Grant, but Dave was older, and he was getting into a bunch of his own shit. He would see him every now and then as Eddie started hanging out with John. That's when Execrate was coming together, before I came into the picture. Eddie's thinking was, "We've got the baddest motherfucker to sing. He can't even sing, but he doesn't need to sing. He's just got balls and he wears makeup to school. He doesn't give a fuck."

Not giving a fuck is always the key, the maximum of cool. The peak.

John did not care what anybody thought of him. He couldn't fight, but there was nothing you could do to him.

He was a loner, but he and Eddie became really good friends, so he became part of the crew too.

Some of the other guys started getting laid, which led to them getting flaky with the band. Eddie was hardcore with the band: "We're going to practice here at this time." But the other dudes wouldn't show. They're teenagers, getting pussy for the first time with a tenuous commitment to music. What can you do?

"Fuck practice, dog. I'm getting pussy."

Eddie knew he had to make a change if he was going to make this rock and roll dream work out.

Whenever you see a documentary or read a story about how a band comes together, there's always a story of one musician meeting another, always one or two guys who answered an ad that they saw. That's a theme.

When Vinnie Vincent auditioned for KISS, Paul Stanley later wrote that Vincent got on his knees, trying to shred on his guitar, which Stanley wrote was one of the goofiest things he'd ever seen.

That was their way of talking shit about Vincent, as he had fallen out of favor with Stanley and Gene Simmons.

In our case, I was the one who put out an ad in *The Recycler*:

"GUITAR PLAYER LOOKING FOR A BAND INTO
DESTRUCTION, RAZOR, SLAYER."

Eddie looked at the ad and thought, "Perfect, this guy is from Arkansas!" The allure of someone who'd traveled almost two thousand miles to play his music sounded like someone worth talking to—someone committed to the cause.

He gave the phone number on the ad a call.

CHAPTER 9

TRAINING PARTNERS
(ZACK)

Saturday, January 29th

Give me the early morning sun and there's no vibe I'm trying to catch more than what I get out of "You Can't Always Get What You Want" by the Rolling Stones. It's a song I fell in love with because of its use in the show *Californication*.

The song starts off slow with what sounds like a church choir, the London Bach Choir. The lyrics remind you of the simplest lesson of all and one anyone chasing anything worth chasing can take with them. You don't simply or easily get what you want, but if you're in pursuit of it, you'll get what you need.

The song builds towards a crescendo with the right combination of instrumental and vocal energy to put you in the proper mental state to get your day done right.

I was heading down to Malibu to meet my friend Derek for a hike at the Los Leones trail in the Pacific Palisades, just north up the coast from Santa Monica. The high for the day in Santa Monica was just under seventy degrees on the last Saturday of January 2022.

The night before, Eddie was in the Tin Foil Hat comedy show with Sam Tripoli and Xavier Guerrero in Long Beach. It was a tight venue, so I didn't bother asking Eddie for tickets; I didn't want to impose. I'll see him do a show outside Austin in late April 2022 anyway. Their Saturday night show would be an hour and a half away, in Bakersfield.

Last time I was in Los Angeles was from the end of October to the beginning of November in 2018. I'd spent four or five days on the couch at my friend Chance's apartment in Venice, the hometown of the fictional Hank Moody from *Californication*. I was traveling to downtown Los Angeles to train with Eddie.

I repaid Chance for the couch by buying us dinners at the best restaurants in Venice, a town known for its food. Gjelina, Scopa, Gjusta—it was a good visit.

The last time I had seen Santa Monica was on the runs I would take from Venice on that trip, up the coast and towards that picturesque image of the pier with the mountains behind it.

Eddie maintains that in many of the songs you like, you don't know what the artist is even trying to say with the music. Lyrics could mean anything. They could be general, vague. Those lyrics that Mick Jagger wrote with Keith Richards, and belted out himself, are to the point: what you want might not always be what you need.

Whether it's life, God, or fate, whatever you want to call it, you get what you're supposed to get, not what you want. You don't want to be the person who gets everything he wants. Failure and struggle are what shape us by deepening our knowledge of who we are. Through that process, we may, hopefully, get what we want.

You don't want the hard times. You need the hard times. It's the yin and yang of life that guides us through, makes us adjust, improve, and better ourselves. It's the struggle.

Jiu Jitsu simulates that daily struggle, a life-or-death level of struggle. It's the only martial art that you can spar at full speed damn near every day due to the lack of brain trauma associated with the grappling art.

An early 2016 podcast between Sebastian Junger and Tim Ferriss was one of the final straws that convinced me that Jiu Jitsu was the final piece of my process of getting off opioids. It sparked recognition of the need for a tribe in a modern culture that has devolved into something that doesn't serve our primal need for community and connection.

I missed the camaraderie that a football locker room provided me. I needed to find something that could replace it. I needed to find a group of hardworking people aimed in the right direction. I was looking for people that could give me an example to follow because once I got out of those locker rooms, it was harder to find people like me.

Humans need things that challenge us: an idea or vision we're willing to give everything to, people we need to be accountable to, and a mission we are willing to dedicate our lives to, something to give our lives to. We need something worth dying for. When the world shut down, it was the real martial artists who kept training, defiantly reminding the people around us that we had a life worth fighting for. We had something we were willing to die for. We had faith.

People need purpose, quality relationships, and personal progress to earn the kind of deep happiness that we seek. Jiu Jitsu gives you all three; it's good dopamine.

For Eddie, the person who was on the other side of that ad in *The Recycler* would be the person that allowed him to keep chasing that higher aim. James was the person who gave him a challenge to pursue, a quality long-term relationship, and the ability to progress in a way that mattered to him.

We need that higher aim. We need people to share it with.

We need training partners.

Once I admitted to myself that I had a problem with opioids, I realized that I couldn't solve the problem through the conventional method of rehab. A month, two, or three in an expensive rehab wasn't a viable solution for people with the problem I had, considering the failure rate I'd seen in the community around me.

The book and docudrama *Dopesick* communicated the problem I intuited: rehabs were made for people with alcohol issues, not opioid addictions.

Opioid issues, caused over a long-period of time, weren't going to be resolved in a short-term stay in a facility, then being shot back into the same environment.

Moving to Austin in January 2017 was the final piece of conquering my demon, leaving the environment where I knew where to get things and who to get them from. I found myself in a new town with training partners like Adam Fujawa and Luke Perry, two grapplers at 10th Planet Austin who I've been training with since day one there. They gave me an example to look towards since they are two people who had conquered similar problems.

Truth becomes cliché, but it's another real "Jiu Jitsu saved my life" story, my version.

The sport saves my life every day. I would feel suffocated in most of the work environments I see today. Instead, I spend my days working at the gym around people I care about, engaging in something that changed my life for the better and encouraging others to do something that can change their lives for the better.

On one of Dr. Rhonda Patrick's visits with Joe Rogan, she spoke of the fake dopamine that makes up an opiate. The quick-hitting, unearned dopamine the pill produced was creating a dopamine deficiency in my brain, the same way that abusing steroids would dysregulate a man's hormones.

The more unearned dope that you consume, the less real dope you create, creating a cycle of reliance on substances that all dope fiends crave, whether that dope comes from pills, drinks, needles, bets, likes, or video game victories. Once you understand one addiction, you can envision how they all work.

Purdue Pharma's Sackler family, the people that sparked the opioid epidemic, was a family of psychiatrists. They knew how the brain worked, and they created a pharmaceutical product that could hijack the brain named OxyContin. They wanted people to be trapped in a cycle their products created—repeat customers.

In 2021, NPR noted that the patriarch of the family Arthur Sackler got rich doing the same thing with Valium in the 1950s and 1960s. Purdue reused his sales and marketing tactics to launch Oxy-Contin: downplay risk of side effects, downplay threat of addiction, and claim that it could cure a wide range of afflictions, while creating an army of doctors, nurses, and pharmacists who believed their lies, thus were pliant salespeople on the virtues of the drug.[7]

Our war in Afghanistan helped harvest the opium that would then be sent to Chinese labs to be turned into OxyContin or compounds that could later be made into OxyContin. Their long-term objective was to start people slowly on Oxy and ramp it up over time. This has all led to the marketplace we now see with fentanyl deaths on the rise.

Dopesick told the story of Purdue's sales team advising doctors to double the dose if the current dose didn't work for a patient. Salespeople manipulated graphs to help convince any wary doctors that the time released function of the pills fell within a certain dosing range that wouldn't lead to addiction, while making the pills more effective than the alternatives.

In 1995, Janet Woodcock, the then-director of the Center of Drug Evaluation and Research, was part of the process that allowed Purdue Pharma to add a label to OxyContin that said it was nonaddictive. That label changed the way doctors, and thus their patients, perceived opioid-based painkillers. Dosing didn't matter since the drug was deemed nonaddictive.

She failed upwards. Today, she's the Food and Drug Administration's principal deputy commissioner. Since 1999, over a million people have died from drug overdoses (that we know of), a great many surely related to that decision. Many more saw promising lives derailed, their God-given potential snatched away from them.

For me, getting off opioids was a two-and-a-half-year process from my peak of seventy-five milligrams of Roxicodone. An absurd total. They were two and a half little blue pills that packed a punch, taken generally fifteen milligrams at a time between noon and when I'd go to bed as I tried my hardest not to take a pill before the afternoon started.

It seemed important and relevant to have rules when you do bad drugs. The more you stray from those rules, the more the drugs become a problem.

When my neck injury began to worsen once my football playing was over, and I became lazy with my strength and conditioning training, I started breaking the rules more and more.

What had been two half-Roxicodone pills per week during college, one pill split into two fifteen-milligram halves each time, eventually became something else. My general rule was that I wasn't allowed to take one of those half-pills until six o'clock in the evening. It was something for the end of the day, like a drink, something I would actually rationalize to myself. That's how twisted the logic was around pills.

I'd first been prescribed hydrocodone and Percocet as a sixteen-year-old after my first football injury, a broken foot suffered during preparation for the first week of my junior season. This was the same day I earned the starting cornerback job for the Ramapo High School team that had state championship dreams. It was an expectation for a proud program run by Drew Gibbs, a New Jersey high school football legend and Hall of Famer.

Future two-time Super Bowl champion Chris Hogan of New England Patriots fame was a starter at wide receiver and cornerback the year before, and I relished the opportunity to try to replace him, but I wouldn't get the chance that year.

What I wanted wasn't what I got.

Things were meant to be harder than I thought they would be to get the scholarship offer that was my sole focus from the time I started playing football at Ramapo. Sometimes you move a little too fast through life, wishing things away that were the things you had wished for from the beginning. Nearly my whole childhood, ever since I had seen future Texas Longhorn Chris Simms sling the rock for Ramapo when I was seven years old, I wanted to be a Ramapo Raider. Then I spent my high school years chasing the next moment.

Always chasing.

Be present. Stay in the moment.

Those were mottos that a short-lived Rhode Island Rams head coach Darren Rizzi would instill in us—pretty zen.

The scholarship I thought I would get wasn't meant to be, but I'd be set down the path to Rhode Island, living the life and learning the lessons that I was supposed to learn. Those lessons being chosen for us based on experience, whether by God, life, fate, the universe, or chance. Whichever creator you choose, the result is the same.

It was during those times that I got involved in a culture of opioid use that, at the time, was pretty rampant across football locker rooms in the northeast. The pipeline up I-95 from Florida was a real thing with wholesale costs increasing by the dollar based on how far north you were.

It seemed as if you could get it cheaper in Philly than you could in New York City, and cheaper in New York than it was in Boston.

I would know.

Football players were programmed to think painkillers were the cost of doing business like the blue-collar professions who got hit hardest by the epidemic. I even spent two years in college not smoking weed, thinking it was a less acceptable form of pain management.

Even 2010 was early in the opioid epidemic. The problem was fomenting in areas of the country to people that coastal media types didn't speak for. We were all lied to by the institutions we were supposed to trust.

It wasn't until the opioid problem hammered wealthy suburbs that the important people started to notice. It's not like those in power are going to do anything about it though. White-collar criminals don't go to jail.

I wasn't just involved as a consumer. We were all buying and selling it, not recognizing until too late that we were involved with a demon that had the potential to take over our minds.

I'd eventually get arrested, then go through pain management programs to mask my issues through the duration of my probation. I had a problem that had one final destination if I didn't make a change.

The day I got off probation was the day I kicked into drive my plans to get off pills. No longer did I have to worry about pissing hot with weed in a state that would soon legalize it. No longer did I have to deal with the general stress that comes with being under the state's supervision. Time to put that experience behind me.

A friend of mine put me in touch with a source for edibles, which would become my opioid replacement. Over time, I'd naturally, and fairly painlessly, decrease my Roxicodone by 7.5 milligrams per day every couple months, eventually getting off them completely about two years after my probation ended.

It was June 17, 2017, my twenty-seventh birthday.

A lot of rock stars died at twenty-seven years old, so much so there exists the "27 Club" that includes the Rolling Stone's Brian Jones, Jimi Hendrix, Janis Joplin, Jim Morrison, Kurt Cobain, Amy Winehouse, and even Robert Johnson. I got out at a good time too, just prior to the fentanyl crisis reaching its peak.

In that podcast with Ferriss, Junger noted that an individual crosses the threshold into adulthood by facing something that can destroy them. The struggle is the right of passage.

My story isn't unique to this era or this age, but it was an experience I needed to go through to be what I needed to become. It's the driving force behind my skepticism in the Covid narrative and a source of the many similarities between Eddie and my worldviews.

During hikes I would take as a part of my personal rehab, I would become stronger, usually filling my ears and head with whatever was on Joe Rogan's podcast. Sometimes it would be the Jiu Jitsu legend who is now one of my coaches.

Old victories that I could call back on because of my background in sports were the things that told me I was someone capable of accomplishing a seemingly insurmountable task. High aims and achievements teach us how to take on that task. Practice, knowing what progress looks and feels like, helps.

Victories aren't just mine—a lesson you learn along the way. Power resides in the power of the people around you: community.

At some point, I made a list in my notebook of all the people I would be letting down if I carried on the way I was carrying on, a list of people whose investment in me must be repaid forward. That's the point of the ride.

Derek was one of those people. I met him when I was in third grade as the quarterback of the B-team. Derek was a fourth grader who was playing with me on our town's third and fourth grade peewee team as a running back and linebacker, the positions he would play through into high school.

The next year I would meet youth baseball coaches who would help mold me from nine years old through high school. Families would go on trips together and parents like Jeff Brown would always make me feel welcome to be myself. He was always joking around with me, which is important when one is perceived to be a trouble-maker for the crime of not fitting into the school environment. There are plenty of important people along the way for all of us.

It's a label that will propagate its own set of problems for a kid—thinking they're the kind of person who gets in trouble. Making a kid think that's just who they are, someone who makes trouble. Then again, the troublemakers, the people that truly are willing to step out of line, serve a very important purpose, as 2020 taught us. The story of American history is one of good, if sometimes flawed, troublemakers.

When Derek and I got to high school, our bond grew as our goals of winning a state championship and playing football in college aligned with the daily behaviors we both took part in. As he prepared for his senior year, and me for my junior year, we worked to train harder than the teams that came before us after a disappointing previous season; we became closer than ever before.

His senior year would be a disappointment, so would mine. His team, with me sidelined, would go 4–6, missing the playoffs for the first time in years. Ramapo would miss the playoffs the next year, but we finished 6–4 after rattling off six straight wins to end the year after our 0–4 start.

We were the only two teams in the history of Drew Gibbs's twenty-one-year tenure as head coach to not make the playoffs. His career, unfortunately, ended abruptly as Coach Gibbs sadly passed away after experiencing chest pains at the team's Monday night practice in preparation for a November 2021 New Jersey state title game.

Gibbs had already won two state titles by the time we got to high school, then he won five more after we left. He perfected the process of building great teams through the years. Years where the team struggled like our years helped the program adjust and improve. He built a camaraderie around the saying "As One" to represent that we all moved in one direction, together. The program learned how to succeed together.

It's a process, lessons through failure and struggle.

In my freshman year of college, I became friends with Dr. Kevin Elko, Alabama's sports psychologist. I edited a book he wrote, which my dad published, named *Touchdown!: Achieving Your Greatness on the Playing Field of Business (and Life)*. He wanted an athlete's eyes editing the book with him and discussing the topic in a constructive way. It was a humble gesture from a pillar in his field.

Elko is the "Trust the Process" guy, a saying and motto that has spread throughout sports. It's a focus on the long- and short-term actions that will achieve the desired result, rather than a focus on the short-term result.

Once a process is in place, success follows. Alabama head coach Nick Saban has a record-making seven national championships to show for his process.

Derek's senior team's off-season was focused almost entirely on the weight room, recognizing that the team the previous year hadn't taken that area of preparation seriously enough. But Derek's team hadn't focused enough on the conditioning aspect of it.

The next year, we'd attack the weight room the same way, but Coach Joshue Resto would have us run one hundred-yard sprints twice a week to make sure our legs were ready for all four quarters.

You've got to find the right mix. What is necessary to accomplish your objectives? What daily practices will help you do that?

I'd take these lessons with me to martial arts. It's one of my favorite parts of my training today. It's the daily answering of the question of "what are the things I can do around the sport of Jiu Jitsu or fighting that can keep me healthy and moving forward?" with the proper actions.

One day at a time.

I'd have a good senior year and make my way to Rhode Island as a recruited walk on, but the first year would be tough.

I felt like I needed to get bigger than the 185 pounds I was to compete at that level and feel comfortable taking the hits I would need to take going across the middle. But 195 pounds was just too big for my frame, and the weight was put on too quickly.

I wasn't good.

I was slow in spring ball and left for the summer being told that I would need to decide if being on this team was right for me or if I wanted to see if I could hack it with a Division III team.

Not words I wanted to hear, but words I needed to hear.

Derek and I became closer during the spring of my senior year. He decided after his fall semester at Monmouth University that it wasn't the level of football he wanted to play, nor was it the location he wanted to be. Derek wanted more—he just wasn't sure what yet. But he wasn't going to waste time and money during the spring semester at a place he didn't want to be.

He wanted the toughest challenge he could find. It's the same reason I went to Rhode Island. It was a great challenge for me in the

Colonial Athletic Association, the best conference in what was once known as Division I-AA, but is now known as the Football Championship Subdivision.

Returning to our hometown, he'd pick up a job as a personal trainer at a New York Sports Club in the town over from us. I would get a membership there to get back to training with my main training partner. He was someone to work with, but also chase. He was bigger, stronger.

I was preparing to play where I would play, but Derek wasn't sure where he would be yet.

He would eventually decide to walk on at Florida Atlantic University, getting to live out a dream and play special teams at places like Darrell K. Royal Stadium against the Texas Longhorns.

Upon returning from that first year in Rhode Island, I hit Derek up to talk about what we'd do that summer for our training, thinking it would be the same routine as when we were young, but scientific with the processes we thought would give us the best results.

He told me he started to develop a relationship with a local gym owner named Joe DeFranco. DeFranco's Gym was most known for training local Bergen Catholic High School graduate and then-University of Southern California superstar Brian Cushing, a linebacker who had just been drafted by the Houston Texans in the first round.

I was in. I went in on day one and introduced myself to Joe, the guy who would save my idea of what my football career could be and become an important mentor.

I earned a partial scholarship the next spring, after a summer and winter break spent making huge gains because of Joe and becoming a real threat at the wide receiver position.

In a year's time, a coach went from telling me I didn't belong to confirming that I belonged with scholarship dollars.

These are the kinds of victories that you fall back on when you're going through tough times to remind yourself that you have the mettle to push through.

Winning matters. Losing matters. You need to feel it.

You need to find a place to rack up some wins to ensure the confidence to keep moving forward. That's what any kind of consistent training schedule is about, earning victories on a daily basis. Knowing that no matter what else happens during that day, you've pushed yourself and conquered yourself. You've conquered the desire for comfort by recognizing any comfort you're going to find is on the other side of that discomfort you need to make yourself go through.

You need to keep feeling like you're moving forward with something. You need something to prepare yourself for, some goal and vision for your future.

My right hand pushed the shifter in my rental into park, and my left hand swung open the driver's side door. I swung my feet out to begin my first little trek up the hill to meet the crew we were hiking with.

Derek was out here for a work trip as a freelancer in video production, doing projects with big companies and making his way. He's another athlete who figured out a way to push that work ethic into a creative venture.

I got to the gate and saw Derek, a girl he brought from the production team who had to stay an extra day thanks to a New York City snowstorm, and one of his friends that I knew from our high school, Josh.

I gave Derek a hug, introduced myself to the girl, and then reconnected with Josh and meet his cute toddler daughter, who he carried on his back the whole trip.

We waited for Tim, who Derek and I played JV baseball with my junior year. Tim brought a friend named Dean.

Josh and Tim had moved out here, leaving the winters behind for the near perfect weather that we were enjoying.

We began our trip up the mountain, almost 100 floors of elevation according to my Apple Health app count. It's the kind of event that keeps your legs pumping the rest of the day.

Any time I see myself in front of a big-time hike, my mind considers the way that nature and a simple walk, the kind of training I would have thought was useless when I was training for football, got me back into the place I am now. My pursuit of knowledge through this new media of podcasts helped me learn of the efficacy of time spent in nature, plus exercise, and measured improvements for people dealing with addiction or depression. I'd formed my own process.

I took a moment to consider Derek's impact on me from our high school dreams, our training with DeFranco, and turning me onto Rogan's podcast, a symptom of his seeker attitude. My life would be significantly different without him.

This is the value of a training partner. It's the value of the relationship that I would learn about the next afternoon as James and Eddie recounted the journey that made Eddie who he is today.

We become the people we are capable of becoming because we had mentors and peers to compare ourselves to and push us to be better: training partners.

In a roundabout way, Eddie is a big part of why I'm off opioids. He sparked Rogan's interest in weed, which changed the world in many ways, mine included. It was those podcast conversations that educated me on the power of the plant.

Eddie is an embodiment of someone who had used cannabis to become himself.

Driven. Creative. Passionate. Curious. Intelligent. Funny.

His success as a martial artist broke through Joe's old belief system that weed was for lazy people. When Joe was thirty years old, Eddie convinced him to try weed again for the first time since high school. Eddie was sharing how it was helping him with his creativity in Jiu Jitsu and music, so Joe was thinking, "What the fuck is this guy talking about? Marijuana just makes you stupid." That was the old propaganda that most believed.

Once Joe got high for the first time with Eddie, he realized, "Oh, this is what it is. I did not know. I can't believe it."

127

Joe then had an ice cream cone that was the best he ever had. His comedy got more creative. His Jiu Jitsu got better. He couldn't believe how zoned in and focused it made him.

Getting the musical fame and everything that would have come with it, everything Eddie wanted, would have set him on a path that he wouldn't want to be on today. Same for me with my old dreams. Making those music dreams happen would have made Eddie become someone who he wouldn't want to be today.

By cultivating the right mentors through these academies, Eddie has instead helped a lot of people. We are only as brave as we're allowed to be, gaining courage to aspire through the strength of those around us. Good, strong people create more good, strong people and the world needs that.

That's the result of any good leader in martial arts, the creation of strong, confident, decent people.

James showed up as Eddie's life moved from one disappointment to the next, just in time to keep Eddie's musical dreams intact. He allowed him to put together a real band with real musicians, not just kid friends who think they want to make music, but don't want or know how to do the work.

I talked with Tim's friend Dean for what must have amounted to an hour-long conversation on a two-hour walk.

When we reached the peak, the city sprawled out to our left, becoming less dense as it reached the beaches that people from around the world see on their televisions and dream of.

Dean is from Honduras, native to a town where the installation of the first traffic light warranted a day off from school. He has the kind of positive attitude you come to expect from a successful personal trainer. You need a ton of energy for the job, preparing people to push themselves just past where their current limit is on a regular basis to force improvement. A session goes faster the more energy you use. Clients feed off it. And you better be friendly, like Dean is.

As is usual with people in an industry that was made political for a time just by the very nature of engaging in our passion and profession, we get around to discussing where we work, what we do, and some conversation about how the Covid event impacted us.

It will be our generation's version of the natural story of war or oppression that seemingly cycles through societies, no matter how much we hope it won't or convince ourselves that things will be different this time.

Struggling together bonds people closer. It makes them trust each other. The benefit of a Jiu Jitsu gym is that it becomes very clear who people are through a multi-year relationship in a place where the struggle is that real, that constant. You know that the guy who you see training every day, having that level of consistency and taking care of things on and off the mat, is the kind of person you can trust to get a task accomplished.

A good gym is a place where people are judged on actions and effort, not words or titles. Ideas are judged on their merit, efficacy, and outcome.

We reached the bottom of the hill and dispersed. I'd be seeing Derek in Austin a few months later.

I pointed the rental in the direction of Laurel Canyon, wanting to check out the place I'd heard so much about. It was a nexus of perceived countercultural activity in the mid-to-late1960s and the early 1970s, but David McGowan's research, covered in his book *Weird Scenes Inside the Canyon: Laurel Canyon, Covert Ops & the Dark Heart of the Hippie Dream,* brings questions about the legitimacy of that movement. It makes you question if it was real at all.

I pulled into the Laurel Canyon Country Store to use the bathroom in the basement the owner used to sleep in, half expecting someone to pop out from behind one of the basement's shelves filled with inventory. The store had a nice porch on a corner at the bottom of the hill. The intersection in front of it was far busier than it would have been in the late 1960s, but it was pleasant, nonetheless.

My rental made it to the top of a considerable hill with streets tight enough to force you to slow down when you encounter a driver moving in the opposing direction.

The Lookout Mountain Laboratory pad on the top of the hill was a strange site. A military building made up of multiple white rectangles, nestled into place on land that looks like it was cut out of the mountain.

In 1947, the US Air Force established a secret film unit, the 1352nd Motion Picture Squadron, which was headquartered in Laurel Canyon until 1969. From this Lookout Mountain Laboratory, which Jared Leto now owns, a staff of more than 250 filmmakers with top-secret clearance would travel the world documenting nuclear bomb blasts from as close as two miles away.

Just prior to Leto's ownership, beginning in 2012, the facility was leased as a rehab center by a company named One80. They charged up to fifty thousand dollars a month but shut it down in 2013 after *The Hollywood Reporter* revealed questionable activity that included the deaths of two residents.

That was the same year that Leto returned to prominence for his role as Rayon in *Dallas Buyers Club*, playing a transgender AIDS patient. Leto got down to 114 pounds at one point for the role.

Two years later, he bought the laboratory, and all the dark energy in it, for $5 million. Parts of the building seem to be in disrepair today.

It's heavily secured and secretive. Gated with a sign warning you of the potentially vicious dogs that an intruder might encounter, or maybe it's just trying to scare you off. Further up the hill, immaculate views of the city sprawl out in front of you.

The romanticization of the city is for good reason. It's an amazing feat of human innovation and conquest over nature. That country store was originally built in the early 1900s as a resting place for hunters in pursuit of the city's once dense deer population. It now sits in the biggest metropolis in our nation, sitting in what amounts to a desert that humans have somehow been able to provide enough water for those millions to survive.

My trip down the hill on Lookout Mountain Avenue had me passing the house of "Our House" fame, the song released in 1970 by Crosby, Stills, Nash, and Young. Graham Nash was the most inspired of the three, writing of the home he was sharing with Joni Mitchell. Her living room was reportedly where the band first met and played together; she still owns the house. It's right next to Frank Zappa's old house.

Weirdly, almost all of these perceived countercultural figures seemed to have familial ties to military intelligence. Most notably, the Laurel Canyon based Jim Morrison's dad was the general at the Gulf of Tonkin incident, a false flag that served as the basis for our government's invasion of Vietnam.

The incident in the Gulf of Tonkin between North Vietnamese and American forces allegedly happened in August 1964. Less than a year after Kennedy's death, President Lyndon B. Johnson brought us to war.

The Doors are said to have formed in July 1965. They'd make a six-song demo that September. On July 29, 1967, "Light My Fire," off their self-titled debut album, would reach #1 on the *Billboard* Hot 100 chart.

President Dwight D. Eisenhower's outgoing speech in 1961 warned of the permanent military-industrial complex that had been built up during World War II and their influence over American politics. At the time of his speech, 3.5 million Americans were directly engaged in the defense establishment.

War is big business, so war must be permanent.

While in Los Angeles, Crosby, Stills, Nash, and Young threaten to remove their music from Spotify if Spotify doesn't remove Joe Rogan from their platform. Mitchell makes the threat as well.

Rogan's crime? Spreading "Covid disinformation."

A few months later, they returned to the platform when they realized that no one gives a fuck what they think. The controlled opposition has become so obvious now. Once-invisible enemies are now visible.

Their fear isn't disinformation; it's information.

Soon the Covid narrative will be dead and these people will move on to cheering for their next war, a war in Ukraine. In May, Graham

Nash will tell *The Guardian* that he would kill Putin if he had the chance, despite being a "peacenik" as he lazily compares Putin to Hitler.

He would also mention his own past "toxic masculinity" in the interview before he came back to the topic to blame Putin's invading Ukraine on "toxic masculinity."

It's a shame. Nash is predictable, boring, and lazy.

Plaster texted back to meet me at Griffith Park. We smoked, walked, and discussed the next day's meeting with Eddie and James, which Plaster planned to film.

As we parted ways, Eddie shot over a text with an address, an address almost directly across the street from Joni Mitchell's house.

It's Danny Lohner's house, the award-winning producer of Nine Inch Nails.

What are the odds?

Sunday morning I woke up with nothing on the schedule until three o'clock to meet at Danny's.

It was my last full day in Pasadena. I traded in the hotel rooms for Plaster's apartment in downtown Los Angeles while he was in Mexico at Ed Clay's CHIPSA Hospital, getting a stem cell procedure for himself and his old injuries, while also interviewing Forrest Griffin on his experience with the treatment.

Wanting to take advantage of the beautiful mountains, I opened the AllTrails app and found the Altadena Crest Trail. I hiked three miles uphill with more than one thousand feet worth of altitude. My headphones played the latest Tin Foil Hat episode with Sam Tripoli, Eddie, and a guest named Drew Weatherhead, a Jiu Jitsu black belt who was forced to move from Canada to find a way to live freely.

Weatherhead discussed his older sister becoming paralyzed from the waist down after one shot of the Pfizer "vaccine." He then watched as the Justin Trudeau led Canadian government made it harder and harder for his family to live their lives in peace without taking the jab that has since been proven to be almost all risk and no reward.

At this point though, we were deep enough into this to know that there was no rational explanation for the general establishment, governmental stance other than to understand it through the prism of malice.

This is all a part of a big lie that we're all trying to unravel together.

It's another beautiful day in Southern California, a little nicer than the last. I headed back to the hotel, showered, and then made my way back to Laurel Canyon.

I arrived before everyone else, parked down the street, then came up on Danny as he came back to his place with some chairs he found at an estate sale. We stood outside for a bit getting to know each other, waiting on the arrival of others.

Plaster parked, then we went inside to wait for Eddie and James. Eddie drove down from his place north of Los Angeles to pick up James, then took another drive from Long Beach up to Laurel. James can no longer drive, hasn't been able to for a while.

The house was a mess. There was dog puke on the floor; the dog had been sick. When I went upstairs later to warm James's Frappuccino, the top floor was covered with clutter.

The home of the rocker bachelor.

We were two-tenths of a mile away from the set for Lew Ashby's house in *Californication* and the interior of the house reminded me of it. The back room, an almost secret hideaway bar, had a cool vibe inside. It's in a nook of the house that is rounded out like a castle.

Eddie pulled up, helped James up the steps, and they walked in. We exchanged greetings, took a few minutes to get Plaster's equipment set up, and started recording.

The band was back together again. We talked nonstop for five hours.

CHAPTER 10

RESISTANCE
(JAMES)

After seeing the ad and us connecting over the phone, Eddie agreed to come out to the house where I was renting a room at the time. This was something I was pretty good at. I could find a cheap place to rent a room, somewhere to get by. These would be places where an owner had a second, third, or fourth apartment to rent out. It was a boarding home kind of scenario.

At this one, everyone was at their jobs during the day. Eddie was driving a moped at the time, so he called a taxi, packed his drum set in, and came over.

Knowing I was from Arkansas, he had a different image in his head of what I might look like, especially considering my Southern twang, which was far more pronounced then than it is now. He expected long hair, someone like the guys from the German trash band Destruction. They were one of the big four in the German thrash metal scene with Kreator, Sodom, and Tankard.

Eddie knocked. I opened the door. He sees me.

Black skin. Short hair.

James with his guitar at that first boarding home situation.

Not what he was expecting.

Metal was all about image, a look. The look seemed to matter as much as the music, something exemplified by the stories in this book. It was foreign to imagine that a black guy from Arkansas could be into the kinds of bands I said I was into in that ad.

Eddie came in, saw my record collection, and we became fast friends. I knew the German, Canadian, and Los Angeles thrash scenes, the main three metal scenes at the time. As we went over our musical taste, what seemed to be a disadvantage quickly became a strength.

We were legit musicians on the hunt and we found the same music. My tastes illustrated my credibility.

Once he heard me play the guitar, he decided my look was something that would make us stand out. Long hair was a necessity in metal music as proof that you had been into the music for a long time and not some poser who just got into it. Bands had to look the part on the album and long hair was part of that.

With my commitment to the music and a unique personal background for the scene, fans would know I couldn't be a poser. I didn't need long hair to prove it.

Eddie would call out a song as he'd play on the drums, and I'd follow on the guitar. Neither of us could read music, so we just played purely by ear, by feel. We were playing based on what we heard, and he always said I had an amazing ear.

Sometimes he would put something on the 8-track, sometimes I just figured it out in my head. We just started jamming.

He called out the middle part of a song called "The Pestilence" by Kreator. I started making noises with my mouth, fiddling around, and then I played it. Eddie then played along on the drums. In his eyes and ears, I nailed it.

We played for another hour—our first jam session.

Major moments in our relationship are remembered with a feeling captured by three words. I reminisce over these moments today and say, "That's my boy." Our connection over music immediately bonded us.

"That's my boy."

At the beginning of what would become our first project together, we practiced in the bedroom Eddie shared with his brother in the two-bedroom apartment they shared with their mother. Eddie's drum set resided in that small bedroom, covered with T-shirts taped on it to dampen the noise a little bit.

Eddie and I got to work putting songs together right away, and we wrote our first five or six songs in that room. We spent endless hours together, falling into a practice schedule of Sunday, Tuesday, and Thursday that we maintained throughout our musical training together. This was the beginning of our quest to master the metal.

We put some songs together, then the rest of that band began to trickle in. It wasn't all at once.

Eddie took the best guys from Execrate, which were the bass player Willie and lead singer John. The two guitar players were gone. They weren't serious enough anyway. They always skipped out on practice for man's favorite distraction, that thing they'd just discovered. Those guys wouldn't start a new band. Eddie was the one who was keeping Execrate together, so now he was on to his next band, leading the charge.

The group we got together was ready to practice, ready to move to Hollywood, ready for the big time.

We would add a second guitar player named Chris Friedman—I don't remember where we found him—but he was a long-haired blond metalhead who played on the first demo we put together. He left after the first demo as he wanted to play more like Primus. We, of course, thought anyone who wanted to leave speed metal was a sellout, so "see ya."

Chris was replaced by Kelly McLaughlin from Delaware. Kelly was an actual fan of the band and came to us saying that Slayer and Resistance were his two favorite bands. He actually knew our songs when he joined our band, a fan of our first ever demo.

Kelly was another "young man goes west" story, a California dreamer with no more than a couple hundred dollars in his pocket. He still plays music today, making it happen.

Left to right: Chris, Eddie, John, James, and Willy.

As we might say now, with the wisdom of time and the self-deprecation that comes with it, he was one of the twenty-three fans we would eventually gain, but we did have fans worldwide. Fans found us through the same rock magazines that I spent all my extra money on as a kid.

Kelly knew all of our songs.

> *When the Gods possess our minds*
> *And society enforces decorum*
> *When morals battle temptation*
> *A resistance must be formed*

The band was called Resistance. Those lyrics came from the first demo tape we put together, the bridge from a song called "Presence of Resistance."

Rock Star John was our lead singer, but he ran into a problem: genetics.

Around seventeen or eighteen years old, John was already losing his hair. His older brother Grant was twenty with a bald horseshoe on his dome. But the hair Grant had left was still long, at least. This made him think he could get away with wearing a wig on top of that, telling himself, "Well, a lot of it is mine."

Grant was a few years older, so John was stuck staring at his future as his hair began to thin.

In the thick of John realizing he had a hair problem and worrying about a potential solution, we went to a party with Grant. At this point, we thought Grant's wig might be John's solution.

And he needed a solution. The hair was becoming a problem.

"Dude, what are we going to do? John is losing his hair. Grant already has and that wig looks like shit."

During photo sessions, John had to start combing his hair forward a bit to hide the growing bald spot and receding hairline. He started wearing a headband, a good trick to buy him some time. Headband? Boom. You're good. Always wear it, hide that hairline.

So Grant ended up in a fight with some dude at this party. The guy grabbed Grant's wig and pulled it off right there in the middle of the party. He threw it to the ground and started kicking it in the dirt.

John and Eddie felt their jaws hit the floor.

Once the fight was over, they got right in the car and drove home in silence. A wig was no longer an option. You never want to go through something like that.

Nobody was more rock star than John, Superstar Rock Star John. He didn't care about the hair for the hair's sake or for his sake, but it mattered for the music. It mattered at that moment in time. All those photo shoots we did wouldn't hit the same without it. Our future album covers had to look legit.

In high school, John and Eddie would hang out on the outskirts of the stoner crowd. They didn't smoke weed at the time and didn't even really like stoners. Our bass player Willie was the friend in the group that had the connection; he loved that stuff. John and Eddie had rock stardom on their mind, fitting in or finding the right crowd during the moment didn't matter as much.

But what was John going to do about his hair?

The band with Chris Friedman before Kelly.

"That headband is not going to work forever...."

By this time, they graduated high school and were nineteen years old. It was 1989, the height of long hair, a part of the almost three years where long hair was king. During the height of heavy metal in the mid-1980s, long hair meant that you could only get metal chicks. Poison and Mötley Crüe were huge at the time, but it wasn't mainstream with girls.

Guns N' Roses changed all of that.

Their debut studio album, *Appetite for Destruction*, was released in July 1987. It hit number one in America, with eighteen million sold domestically and thirty million worldwide. By January 1988, it blew up. Later that year, they released *G N' R Lies*, which hit number two in America, selling ten million worldwide. This changed the game and brought the scene away from hair metal and into a more dirty, manly rock with long hair included.

They broke a hair barrier that remained open until late 1991. It was like *The Twilight Zone*—all normal chicks wanted long-haired dudes. It was *Revenge of the Nerds*.

Guys like John and Eddie went from long-haired scumbags to sought-after commodities. They'd have nightmares during these years of their hair getting cut. Once you took away the scumbag tag, there was suddenly no competition. John and Eddie were kings of the night.

After high school, Eddie often went to clubs by himself because he couldn't have you needing a ride home if you didn't pick up a girl. But he knew if he took John with him, he'd make it work. They worked well together at clubs. They'd separate, work the room. Every now and then they'd reconvene to discuss what they were working on. There was very little stopping and talking, though; they were working, so much so that they would walk away in the middle of a conversation with a friend who wasn't in pursuit of the same objective.

Some friends might think they were being dicks, but such is the way of the young man, especially the young rocker. Rock star dreams are filled with excess.

"How are you going to get home? Cause you ain't riding with me."

Movie Star, Rock Star John was the only dude Eddie would drive to the club with because they both knew they were going to get laid.

But 1991 was when that pussy faucet turned off. We might even be able to pinpoint the date that it all ended for the long-haired dudes as September 24, 1991. That was the day that *Nevermind* came out from Nirvana and suddenly long hair stopped being wholly associated with the coolest rock bands of the time. It was now associated with a grunge scene that was a bit too depressive, sensitive, and emotional—a bit too heroin. The wrong kind of heavy.

"You hear the new Nirvana shit?"

"Fuck you, don't bring that shit up! Nirvana is killing the pussy!"

Nevermind hit *Billboard*'s number one by January 1992 during a big time for rock.

The year 1991 saw Metallica's self-titled album hit number one, Pearl Jam's *Ten* hit number two on the charts, and Soundgarden saw its first commercial success with *Badmotorfinger*. Guns N' Roses saw *Use Your Illusion*, a two-disk release, hit number one and two after a September release and Red Hot Chili Peppers resided at number three with *Blood Sugar Sex Magik* only because they released their biggest album to date the week after the Guns N' Roses release.

But the era of long-haired dudes being in the spotlight was gone. By 1992, long hair was a curse. Even so, Eddie would hang onto his long hair until 1997, always able to find a metal chick who was into it because of a future job in the DJ booth of a strip club.

We'll get to that.

I wasn't ready to move out financially yet by 1990. I had to figure out the job and living situation in Orange County, so John and Eddie would do me the solid of traveling back to Orange County to rehearse until I moved out myself.

John's solution to the hair problem was this new method where you could sew this permanent wig into your existing hair. It would work perfectly for John because, like his brother, he had that bald horseshoe dome coming in.

They were like high-level extensions, sewn in, so it can't get pulled off. All fake in the front, all real in the back.

John would have to get "The Unit" adjusted and tightened up at periodic appointments. Once we eventually lived together, we'd see the routine he would go through with his hair every other night, pulling up the flap where the fake hair resided to put on fresh glue.

It all ended the first gig we did together.

John didn't quit. We didn't fire him.

All we needed to hear was some dude in the audience yell, "Take that fucking wig off, faggot."

That was that. He's out.

No one needed to say anything to him. He didn't need to say anything to us. That was just his last performance ever. We went through the motions, finished the set, and that was it.

Eddie was crushed. John was the most superstar, rock star guy that he'd ever met. "Most rocker motherfucker" he knew. He was "more metal than everybody." He just had a gene problem.

Rock Star John and Chris before they left the band.

Thankfully, we found another singer—a real singer. John was never technical, but none of us were great then, at least in our opinions now. You wouldn't have been able to convince us we sucked back then, but now with the wisdom of time and mastery in other domains, Eddie especially takes a more pessimistic view towards his own past skills and talents in music.

He was a drummer, and a damn good drummer, in my opinion. It's just like how he thought my guitar playing was great, even if I might have those same self-judgmental feelings about myself today. We all do with our growth of humility in older age.

Now that he knows what real, elite levels of practice look like, Eddie will tell you that he never practiced, real practice, at least. Largely this is also a personality trait of his. His desire to actually not be the person playing the instrument because he saw that his best skill was being the leader who finds the right guys with the right talents to put together the best team.

Eddie thinks he was "a good faker," but I disagree with his assessment. People who aren't as technical in their knowledge of what constitutes music don't know that they don't know what is or is not good.

We might not have been the best, but we were in pursuit, trying to create great speed metal just like our favorite bands. We were making eight- or nine-minute songs like Metallica, trying to show off everything that we knew and everything we were capable of. We were doing it. We had people coming to shows and moshing, people who genuinely liked what we did. We created something.

Eddie's goal was to find the people who could shred the best, then he played the role of putting the song together. He listened to the various bits and pieces the musicians brought, then organized those various inputs into something meaningful.

He wanted everyone doing the best shit. He felt the song would suffer if he was on it because he wanted to find someone more

passionate about playing their instrument to give him a reason and an ability to sit back to do what he wanted to do: produce the song.

Take what works, discard what doesn't, and make what works best.

Who he was then is who he has become today. He wants to compose and organize the various parts that make up a song or a submission into what it can be, whatever the objective.

Kent, our next singer, helped us level up. Whereas John was there with us through our first demo tape mostly because he projected the image of a rock star, Kent actually had vocal talent. His hair ended just above his shoulders, not optimal hang time, but he still had long hair. He looked like Glenn Danzig, but he wore a headband because he looked like he was losing his hair on top a little bit too.

Kent had three different voices he used, voices that sounded like metal legends. There was his far-reaching falsetto tone that was like a King Diamond voice and a Rob Halford voice from Judas Priest, reaching the levels of the throaty growl. But like both artists, Kent was unique for his wide-ranging vocals from the most piercing of highs to the lowest of lows. And like Bruce Dickinson, he could oscillate his tone, making it move and alter itself between various pitches.

It was exciting. We had a real singer.

We brought Kent to some gigs. He was front and center crushing it.

One day, Eddie was on his drum, fucking around. I was on the guitar. Kent walked in the door, didn't look anyone in the eye, just grabbed his voice pedals, got his cables, and started plugging things in.

We looked at each other. We looked at him.

We looked at each other. We looked at him.

Oh shit.

His hair was now down to his mid-back.

Kent was bald the entire time, but his last wig was short enough, and he had the headband, so no one suspected anything. Then he got

Kent, Willy, and Kelly, with James and Eddie.

greedy. He was wearing an obvious wig now. It was too long—long enough for people to start questioning us, his friends.

Eventually, we had a band meeting, but the only conclusion we had was that we'd just see how it went when the gig came.

We'd joke back then that if you had short hair, then you better own a PA system or maybe own a van or your dad owns a club or something. Kent was committed to the wig.

Meanwhile, Kelly had grown into a real asset for the band. Not only was he great on the guitar, but he could also write songs. He put together this one song called "Utter Darkness" which was basically all him, created entirely by him.

Kelly and Kent had become fast friends, super tight. So much so that Kelly and his girlfriend let Kent move into the apartment they shared, sleeping on the couch. Something happened where Kent was up in the middle of the night, taking a piss with the door open, completely naked, and Kelly's girlfriend ran into him.

Kelly was furious.

And we still had the band going.

Kent had the short wig for about six months prior to the hair coming halfway down his back. We played a few gigs, he had the short-haired wig, and no one gave a shit. No one noticed. No one said anything.

But, again, he got greedy.

Sometime after the longer wig came into the picture and the day after Kent, naked, ran into Kelly's girlfriend in the middle of the night, we had practice. We had a month or two between the new wig and our next gig.

"Okay, let's see how this fucking gig goes. Hopefully it doesn't go like that last time with John...."

But before that, at this practice, I was on my guitar. Eddie was behind his drums, and Kent was on the ground, adjusting the electrical cords for his vocals.

Kelly just walked in, reared back his leg, and punted Kent's face like he was trying to make a forty-five-yard field goal in the snow with two seconds left in the Super Bowl. It was that level of focus and eye-foot coordination.

Kent's lip split all the way to his nose. The busted lip flapped when he talked. Kelly just kept saying, "Fuck you, fuck you, fuck you."

Kent was crying, "I don't know what I did. I don't know!"

Kent went to the emergency room where they sewed up his lip.

They hated each other and never got over it.

Then the gig didn't work out. It went exactly the same.

"Take that wig off, faggot."

Kent was out.

CHAPTER 11

. . . .

THE RAP GAME
(ZACK)

Sunday, January 30th

Back to 2022: Eddie, James, and I sat on the couch of Danny's back room bar. It was a circular room with seated cushions along the wall and a bar towards the inside of the house, with windows behind the cushions.

We started off the conversation with a cassette player, listening to one of the earliest songs that James and Eddie made together.

Danny had two masks on and discussed how badly he didn't want to get anyone sick. He tested positive for Covid about ten days prior. Something he alerted us to when we all showed up.

Eddie busted his balls, which, of course, just got Danny worked up. He prodded Danny with comments like, "You know the tests are fake, right?"

"Eddie, I know three people who have died of Covid!" Danny retorted.

"It's the flu, dog!" Eddie laughed back.

The tests serve their purpose, just like the masks do.

Danny was terrified of getting James sick because of James's health history. Understandable, but it was shocking to see how much it impacted Danny.

Eddie speaks of it often. People's good will has been taken advantage of by those who wish to do us harm under the guise of nice-sounding plans or programs that never seem to work out for the actual citizens they claim they intend to help.

When I went upstairs to warm up James's Starbucks Frappuccino, Danny was at the top of the stairs. He had tears in his eyes over the worry of potentially getting James sick.

You could see the amount of care in his eyes; they were a little watery. He was genuinely worried.

That humanity and decency is what has been taken advantage of. Designed to stress people out, make them fearful, and manipulate them into changing their lives, acknowledging and fearing the existence of something they don't quite understand.

How could he? How could anyone really? It was hard for me to stay on top of what the real story is throughout the Covid event, and I took excessive notes and had endless conversations about the topic, for the primary purpose of trying to keep track, knowing that goal posts would be moved and the establishment's lies would be memory-holed.

I gave Danny a big hug and a smile saying, "It's okay, man. I know you care. Everything will be alright."

Those moments are important for me. I've been angry about what happened in those almost two years since lockdowns started, and I needed to be reminded that most of those who disagree with me just don't fully understand. Their fear has been manipulated. Our very human fears of death, economic instability, and social consequence have been used against us.

Like James said, not everyone has the same experiences as you. Not everyone who disagrees with you is a bad person.

Remember.

We should do something about the people who did the manipulating, though. You know, just to make sure that something like this never happens again.

Crimes against humanity must have consequences. Treason must have consequences.

Nuremberg 2.0.

I made my way through his kitchen to his microwave, climbing over the clutter.

His albums are in a good spot and well organized.

The internal is the external. It's a chaotic mind, but a brilliant one.

Trent Reznor brought Danny into Nine Inch Nails in 1994 to play guitar, bass, and keyboards for the band live. He stayed with the band through the tour for *The Downward Spiral*, the recording and touring for the album *The Fragile*, the live album and DVD titled *And All That Could Have Been*, and the recording of the *Still* EP.

In 2020, he was inducted into the Rock and Roll Hall of Fame as a member of Nine Inch Nails.

He was featured on Marilyn Manson's breakthrough album *Antichrist Superstar* playing the acoustic guitar on "The Reflecting God" and lead guitar on "Angel With the Scabbed Wings." Through Manson, he worked with Eminem on a remix to "The Way I Am."

His résumé is deep. Danny worked with Puscifer, Thirty Seconds to Mars, Angels & Airwaves, and more. He can engineer, produce, remix, and fill in on various instruments.

Mastery.

Thirty Seconds to Mars' Jared Leto let Danny borrow his dress shoes once for, as Danny describes it, "this one time I got married."

When I got back downstairs, Eddie had gone back to the demos.

We listened to the first demo, a song called "Without Recovery" about rich people and an army of corpses. Eddie explained the lyrics. "There is an economic collapse and now the rich are down with the poor people, the scum. They're down with 'us.'"

There are two or three songs where Eddie wrote the whole thing and two or three where James wrote the whole song. Typically, there would be a mix—first verse, then second verse, on and off, but this one was written by Eddie.

This first demo was done when Eddie was eighteen years old. We listened to a small piece of the song. While I wouldn't consider myself a music expert out of respect to people who are, I know that this speed metal sounds the way it's supposed to sound. It has the right pacing, the right energy, and the right riffs. James can shred on the guitar.

Being the one who arranged the songs, Eddie sees the insecurity he had in himself through those nine-minute songs with seventeen different parts from almost thirty-five years ago.

Eddie explained the insecurity as being unsure of his own skills. "Yeah, I might not be a virtuoso with an instrument, but damn, look what I'm putting together, dog. I'm putting this together."

So he made the arrangements complex with different time changes and all these different parts.

"Look. Look! Look what I can do! Look what I can do!"

Instead of being comfortable with what they were making by keeping it simple with three or four minutes songs like everyone else, Eddie felt compelled to go the nine-minute route to prove to himself and everyone else that he was worthy of these rock and roll dreams. But he now knows that trying to maintain someone's attention for nine minutes when they're generally used to songs that are less than half the time takes a mastery level of skill. In lieu of the skill, they just made songs fast and crazy.

Eddie explained the desire to reinvent the wheel, the attempt to be like Metallica and make the eight- or nine-minute song. We listened to a song that Resistance never got around to playing at the club. Eddie pointed out that the song goes on for eight minutes, but there's a ton of unnecessary stuff involved that could have been edited out, shortened down, and turned into a solid three minutes.

Eddie would have the song go this way, then that way, this tempo, then there, and by the end of it, the audience would leave confused.

He tried to blow the listeners' minds over and over with things that were unnecessarily insane.

James felt like the long, multi-part songs reminded him of his favorite band Dream Theater, a band Eddie happens to not enjoy, but it's the highest compliment that he can give Eddie.

Eddie shrugged him off. Embarrassed at his youthful desire to create the most complex and complicated song possible, he reiterated that simple music is always the best. Embarrassed the way any artist is with their earliest work. Of course there is so much to improve on, that's the point. You have to strive.

Desires to reinvent the wheel aren't realistic. Music is not even necessarily about being original. It's about taking what already exists and making it unique. You're bringing the audience something familiar but all its own with its own message and tone. You take what exists and make it your own.

Sentiments around most of the stuff on the radio being shit aren't inaccurate, but there's a reason why that music on a large scale has the same relative sound.

The game is to remove the ego, not try to impress anyone, and create magic for yourself, musically. "Shredding is all the different layers interwoven," Eddie explained as he moved his hands together with his fingers spread wide as a way of signifying this joining of layers. It's not one guy shredding out and making a show of himself, it's not the producer overcomplicating things, it's the group creating something that blends and molds together nicely, something organized. Familiar, yet different.

Another Danny, Eddie's cousin and James's good friend to this day, was a bass player throughout these years, sometimes working with their various musical projects. If you ask him, Danny says that James's lyrics stand the test of time—very complex, rich, high-level lyricism.

Eddie played another song on the cassette player, this time with Kent as the lead singer because we just had to hear his voice.

They weren't kidding. Kent's voice is incredible. It's right in line with what I'm used to hearing from the best heavy metal bands of this era. If the hair wasn't a problem, and Kelly's eventually hatred of Kent, then there might have been something.

A third singer would enter the picture: Ernie, a Mexican kid from Wilmington, California. They would play a few parties with Ernie, but Resistance soon broke up.

The first day that Eddie met Ernie, he walked up to him and did a quick pull on the hair on his head—just had to make sure his hair was real.

By now, in the timeline of their relationship, both James and Eddie were ready to move on from playing speed metal. It had been four years of the same thing, four years of making generally angry music. The way Eddie tells it, they'd grown tired of it. To me, part of it sounds like he'd worked through a lot of the anger and insecurity he had in those years through the music. Like, primal scream therapy is an actual thing, so too might be the idea that a lot of young anger could be worked out through the making of this more generally mad music.

The end of Resistance came as Eddie and John were moving to Hollywood, finding a place that used to be a hotel in the 1800s, back when horses were the mode of transportation, not cars. In 1991, they were being rented out as apartments, but they weren't really apartments, but small, little hotel rooms. Elevators were so small that three people could barely fit in them.

They were renting singles, and that's all the boys could afford, $495 a month.

When Eddie and John spoke to the landlords, it was an old Mexican couple. The wife sat there the whole time talking shit in Spanish to her husband, thinking they were two white guys who were going to be nothing but trouble with loud music all night.

Eddie stopped her and said, "I'm Mexican, and I just heard everything you said."

They got the apartment.

To split the room, they took a black curtain and stapled it to the ceiling.

"That's your half."

Eddie's half was the one closer to the bathroom, closer to the door. John's was closer to a little kitchen.

Walk to the bathroom or kitchen and you're walking through someone's "room."

John was in Hollywood to be a movie star. With his blond wig.

It didn't work out.

Eddie was moving into a new phase of his musical journey with James, making what they now describe as a weird, non-metal rap.

It took a while for Eddie and James to find out that the other liked rap. Liking any kind of music other than metal within the metal community could earn the label of sellout by some. The early years of the relationship were so focused on rock that they didn't move into other things, but the admittance of their appreciation of rap to each other was a sign of trust.

Eddie loved rap, but he didn't love the funky, jazzy, James Brown type of music that it was coming from. Rap represented a new horizon for them. Where rock had to be poetic and Shakespearean, rap could be straight out. You could do whatever you wanted.

You could do anything.

You could be super dirty. Violent. Funny.

Try to be funny in a rock song. "What are you? 'Weird Al' Yankovic?"

Eddie went on, "In rap, you could be fun. You could always throw in some funny shit. If it's clever and sophisticated, you could do it. Rap represented no limits. You can do anything you want on this motherfucker."

Rap was a blank canvas, something Eddie brought with him to martial arts.

James turned him onto Run-DMC, which he saw as an AC/DC style of rap, a band Eddie was never into, but at least it was rock-ish.

"Rock Box" was the song that got Eddie thinking of what he and James could do together.

To me, rap has always been the most metal thing I could have found as a kid from the suburbs. It was "Parental Advisory." It was made by people who would have been considered lower-class. It was hard, it was tough, it was so many things that a suburban lifestyle might neglect to foster.

But that music fostered something in me. Listening to that kind of music gets you fired up, gives you courage, and puts you in the mindset to go hit that lift, do those sprints, or win that game. Listening to the words of an experience that was foreign to me provided me with perspective, a different kind of education.

Their first venture into rap wasn't metal at all, calling it Brav-Watts, a combination of their last names. At the time of the first demo, they were trying to assuage the fears of their bandmates in Resistance that they weren't moving on to a new project without them. So their first rap demo said that it was a "Resistance Production." It even had the Resistance logo.

Eddie wanted to make sure the band saw that they were still giving it up to Resistance, but Kelly, Kent, and Willie didn't like the new project. It made them all uneasy, but it never mattered as the band eventually blew up on itself.

The idea behind the rap venture was that Eddie and James could create an Eric B. & Rakim thing where Eddie was the DJ like Eric and James, the MC, like Rakim.

BravWatts was short-lived. It was a short hiatus from heavy before they brought the heaviness back.

Blackened Kill Symphony would be the name of the next project, a combination of rap, metal, EDM, goth, and industrial.

Eddie had been learning how to play the keyboard on a Yamaha DX7 synthesizer when they were still in Resistance, always open to learning something that might enrich his skill set. He'd gotten into Depeche Mode and the Cure. Making metal music had become old and boring to him.

Both of them were "burnt the fuck out."

This new Blackened Kill Symphony project was intended to take some of that heaviness from Resistance and add the keyboard. Eddie wanted to do some weird shit, Halloween music stuff. He wanted to have the artistic freedom that rap provided while maintaining some of what he loved from metal. He wanted the hard-powered music with just a little bit of keyboard underneath for the uniqueness of that rap experience.

Their first song together as BravWatts sucked in their eyes. They couldn't figure out how to make their premise for the project work with the new style they were trying. Anthrax and Public Enemy's collaboration on "Bring The Noise" showed them what they could create together. It allowed them to bring some of what they had already been doing into what they wanted to do next. They were molding their skills into something unique.

When Eddie heard "Bring The Noise," he told James that he knew what they were going to do next. They should do a whole band like that, but add keyboards, synthetic drums, piano, clean guitar, and have some metal singing, but mostly rap. That's the formula they switched to, hoping to make something epic.

Another change was that Eddie learned how to make a four-track demo as studio time created problems for them. When Resistance would go to the studio to cut a demo, they always found themselves in a hurry because they had no money. Being in a hurry meant that mistakes were being made when they went into the big studios; it wasn't the best they could do. Considering Eddie already had these producing skills, he figured, "Wouldn't it be better if I did it myself?"

Rather than go to these studios that were costly to use and a completely different environment than what they were used to playing in, one where they could barely hear each other, Eddie started doing the entire process from the recording to the producing of the final product. It wasn't digital at that time, everything was on tape, so editing was extremely hard. Sometimes they'd have to just run it all in one tape, but Eddie figured out the task of editing.

Eddie and James didn't just learn how to make music during these years, they worked to master the whole process. When a problem would arise, they'd solve that problem.

If you care about doing something, you'll find a way.

As Joe Rogan will often say, "Fighting is high-level problem-solving with dire physical consequences." Problem-solving is a skill—its use is just a matter of the domain you exist in, the tools you have to utilize, and the objective you're trying to accomplish.

Bruce Lee has always been a big deal. Those of us who decided to start training and immediately found a great school, like I did on two occasions, can forget that there are people all over the world who, to this day, don't have access to good training in generalized fighting or the martial arts that they prefer.

At some level, movies were the closest people could get to learning how to fight. That's probably why martial arts movies were such a big deal.

In 1991, Eddie read a book by Jesse Glover, Bruce Lee's first student and friend. Eddie brags that it's one of four books he's ever read—maybe this book in your hands will be the fifth.

The early 1990s was when Brazilian Jiu Jitsu was beginning to spread around California a little bit. It was still early. Eddie's eventual Jiu Jitsu coach, Jean Jacques Machado, one of the first-generation of Brazilians to bring the art to America, wouldn't arrive in the United States until February 1992.

Jesse mentioned how few places there were to learn martial arts, oftentimes seeing foreign-born, Asian teachers refusing to teach their art to people who weren't of the same race as them. Even if you could find someone to teach you, the student was only able to learn from whatever school was close enough to attend for frequent training, while also being at the behest of someone who could be full of shit and not truly know anything.

McDojos, which are schools that teach nonsense and only exist to siphon money from their students, still exist today in the age of the Internet, so they must have been widespread in previous generations.

Finding a good coach was, and is still, the most important aspect of one's training.

How lucky must any of us be to just have ended up in this or that neighborhood, next to that school with that coach who made that huge impact on us? Whether we're eight, eighteen, or thirty-eight, whether that coach is for the art of fighting or a youth baseball team, the examples that we can model ourselves after matter.

Bruce taught Jesse his Gung Fu and its underlying philosophy, while Jesse helped Bruce learn how to stand up in front of a group to give a speech, a very important skill to be a good instructor.

Bruce wanted to create a super system. He didn't just use what one teacher or sensei taught him in one domain of an art form. He wanted to create a system that could beat any system, a system that took into account all of the various possibilities. It was not a system built on reverence to a form or structure, but something built on practicality and function. It was something that could stand up to any test, something that could objectively measure up well against all other forms of fighting.

Whenever Bruce would meet someone who could beat him, he immediately wanted to become a student to that man, learning whatever he could. He'd study judo, boxing, wrestling, Wing Chun, karate, and other Gung Fu styles, trying to take in anything he could and learn all he could. Fencing was even deemed a necessary course of study just to find out the best way to close the distance on someone.

Being that he was, at one time, the sixth most highly-rated Wing Chun man in the world, he wanted to figure out ways around those who were in front of him in the Southern Chinese Gung Fu style built on quick movements and strong legs. He didn't try to put his head down, grit his teeth, and go through them—he instead tried to outsmart them.

Bruce tried to create an angle, conceptually and physically. You have to learn the conventional so deeply that you understand how to find ways around the conventional to create your own path, speed up progress, and present something to your opponent that he is not prepared to deal with. He was willing to take a look at things that were banned by a style to forge them into new techniques that wouldn't be banned.

In football, this concept is akin to Mike Leach being a pioneer with the spread offense, bringing it to Texas Tech, which had difficulty recruiting against the big dogs in the states of Texas and Oklahoma. He turned Tech into a formidable foe on a yearly basis after being fairly mediocre for about twenty years.

His system was built on spreading the field with four or five receivers, creating holes in defenses that had been constructed to defend two or three receivers each play, rather than four or five. It meant that the opposition didn't have the manpower to defend the kind of athletes Leach would be putting on the field.

Bill Belichick's 2007 Patriots matched up slot receiver Wes Welker against bigger outsider linebackers and safeties who couldn't cover Welker, who was listed at 5'9", 185 pounds, but was definitely shorter. At the time, NFL defenses didn't have the extra cornerback in that same size-and-skill mold as Welker to match the way he moved.

From 2007 through 2012, his last year with the Patriots, he would average 7 catches for 80 yards per game, which adds up to 112 catches for 1,243 yards over 16-games—incredible numbers.

Spreading the field wide wasn't banned when Leach brought it to Texas Tech and Belichick put some of those principles on display in the NFL, but old-school football guys believed the game was built on a kind of toughness they didn't think existed in a style that emphasized passing. These coaches wanted to keep the fullback on the field, put him in front of the tail back in the I-formation, then ram the ball down their opponent's throat three to four yards at a time with that tailback. Throw on third down if you have to.

Their belief that this different philosophy wasn't real football could get in the way of being successful.

It's akin to Joe Maddon in baseball shifting his fielders based on the tendencies of the batter, creating wild-looking diamonds where the shortstop was to the right of second base, almost where the second baseman normally would be. Meanwhile, the second baseman would be in short right field and the third baseman would be just to the left of where the shortstop typically stands before a pitch.

It's all to put players in positions where the data, which the organization collected on them, indicated the batters were more likely to hit the baseball.

The NBA has seen a data-based revolution around the three-point shot, something that didn't exist at the sport's founding, but was introduced in 1979 on a one-year trial basis. Many felt the three-pointer was a gimmick taken from the American Basketball Association (ABA), which ran from 1967 to 1976, so it was disregarded. Now, it's a team building strategy.

With teams getting a certain number of possessions per game, teams want to maximize what they do with those possessions. Just like Billy Beane tried to maximize how the Oakland Athletics could best utilize their twenty-seven outs in a nine-inning game.

The NBA average success rate is around 46 percent on two-point shots, so a team only needs to shoot 31 percent from three to outearn those points. With a league-wide three point success rate of 36 percent, three pointers prove to be far more efficient with the right players, so teams and players are adjusting to that reality with who they sign and how they prepare.

Novices don't come up with new, unconventional ways of doing things, lifers do. These are people who have gathered as much information and learned as much as they could, then created a better way.

Have a problem or question? Take in data. Come up with a solution. Test it. If it fails, test it again. If it succeeds, test it again. Tweak when necessary. Create the right response to accomplish your objective. Do what has the highest probability of success.

Trust the science. No, actually.

When Eddie started training, he thought that was what everyone was doing. That's what Bruce Lee did and he was a legend, so he thought of course everyone would do that. That premise is sturdy. Take the best shit from wherever you can find it and bring it into what you do.

It would only make sense that people would be open to any and all information as the consequences of being wrong are too high to be obtuse.

Eddie was wrong.

CHAPTER 12

······················

JAMES MOVES TO HOLLYWOOD
(JAMES)

During our early years together, like most young men, Eddie and I held a bunch of odd jobs. Every job was just the job we'd be doing until our rock careers took off, a small part of our story.

"Did you hear about Resistance? Their guitar player used to work at Carl's Jr. and their drummer was putting bulletproof windows on cars when they got signed to their record deal. Now they're the biggest band in the world!"

Around twenty, Eddie would meet this guy named Stuart from Movie Star, Rock Star John. Stuart was a thirty-two-year-old white guy bodybuilder hanging out in Venice and always in strip clubs. Never met anybody who liked that guy.

So, at the time, John's older brother, not the guy with the wig that got kicked around in the dirt at that party but his oldest brother Dave, was working with Stuart. His gig was dyeing carpet, which is like cleaning carpet, but instead of cleaning it, a dye is sprayed into the carpet, then manually brushed in.

This process was supposed to make carpets look better. It was an alternative to ripping out all of your carpet. In theory, dyeing a carpet sounded like a good idea or at least it might have in the late 1980s, early 1990s.

Over time, people drop so much shit on their carpet that if you had a special fluorescent lamp, the entire floor would be covered with spots, even spots your eyes don't pick up.

Go in there, dye it, and some parts aren't going to take to the dye like others because people drop all different kinds of things on their carpets, and at different times, so the spots are different. They would spill something six years ago over there and never really clean it up right, so it just kind of dried into a camouflage. Sometimes the dyeing would go right like, "Damn, this carpet is not that bad," but much of the time, it wouldn't. If you were working in the carpet dyeing business, you never knew what might happen that day. There was no consistency to it.

It wasn't a carpet cleaning, it was a dyeing. There was no cleaning involved, really.

Stuart was this big buff dude who was always telling everyone how he did tournament karate. His hustle was that he would put an ad in the *Orange County Register*, which was how everyone would make money back then. Orange County was a big market and the *Orange County Register* was number one. Everyone read the newspaper; that was the number one propaganda back then.

He would put out an ad for, let's say, two hundred dollars, put his number and a slogan like "Don't rip out your carpet. Dye it! Call us at 1-800-DYE-TECH and we'll dye it for you!"

Stuart was always going to strip clubs because one of his best friends owned strip clubs.

English Dave was a big, 6'5" Chippendales-looking dude. He was a shredded, huge monster who was properly roided out with an English accent. I've never seen strippers lose it over someone like they did him. They couldn't believe this Greek god-looking guy existed.

English Dave used to work as a bodyguard. Then he became a half-owner in three strip clubs in Los Angeles.

Stuart and Dave would hang out during the daytime, in pursuit of the goal of banging as many girls as possible. They had girlfriends, but they'd have threesomes with their girlfriends and other women. They'd get crazy. Stuart was a helicopter pilot, so they'd spend a lot of time doing that. His whole life was about one thing: "I'm going to own a strip club one day." That was his goal, but how was he going to do that?

The answer lay in check cashing stores. He was going to open up a bunch of them, then use that money to open up a strip club. That was the plan.

Dyeing carpets was the first step in that plan; that was the mission. Stuart was going to save up that money carpet by carpet, wondering how much he could make with this first gig.

His racket was that the phone number in that ad wasn't to some office in Agoura Hills like he made it look. The phone went to Rock Star John's bedroom. John would make it seem like the caller was contacting the serious office they envisioned in Agoura Hills, while Stuart would show up to the job like he was just a worker. There was this whole operation he put in the head of the consumer, but Stuart was essentially the entire operation.

John would answer the phone, pretending like he was a professional. "Hi, this is Dye Tech. How can I help you?"

"Hey, yeah, I saw the ad in the paper, sounds like it's doable. How much does it cost?"

John would then put every appointment into a book with their addresses and phone numbers. Stuart would show up at John's place around seven or seven-thirty in the morning, and John would give him the schedule.

"Where do I have to go today? Oh shit, I have three today."

"Damn, I only have one? Fuck. Alright. Alright."

Sometimes Stuart would call John to change an appointment to the next day or the day after because he'd get lazy. He was all the way up in Marina del Rey, but John was still down in Garden Grove in Orange County when he started working for him in 1989. So Stuart had a trek that some days he would rather not have to make.

Stuart's job was to get in a person's home and pretend he was just doing his job. He acted like he was just a worker, he didn't act like the owner, and he would start building a rapport with the customer just to figure out how to shake them down later. He was a genius, but no one liked him. You'll like him for a little bit—you might think he's amazing for a little bit, then you're going to discover the real him.

Neither Eddie nor I have ever met anybody like this guy since. Dave, John's older brother Dave, was kind of big too, like 6'3", hair in a ponytail. He was working with Stuart at the time. Stuart would spray the cleaner on the rug while Dave would be the guy scrubbing it and doing all the other miscellaneous things that needed doing around the project.

Get a bucket of water. Connect the tubes. Scrub the carpet.

Stuart's job was to embed himself into a person's life from the outset. While Dave was setting up, Stuart was saying all the right things to the customer, working to make it very hard for her, or him, to want a refund. He got into this person's life, getting to know them, then breaking it off. He was always ready to pull his MK-Ultra deal to get their money—intimidating them a little bit.

"I fought tournament karate for twelve years. How old do you think I am? Guess. Just guess. Oh, twenty-four? I'm thirty-two."

He would say thirty-two one more time, making his mouth into a circle. This was all in the lead-up to the dye job clearly failing.

It was always the same schtick, always working to manipulate the customer, knowing the carpet was unlikely to look like they imagined it would look when the project was over.

"You're still gonna pay me. You're still gonna pay me...."

Stuart was like a mad genius, using his mad genius powers to secure ill-gotten gains.

So what happened was that, one morning, Stuart's heading to John's house, checking out the schedule, and he was supposed to meet John's brother, Dave, there. Dave was always late. He wasn't reliable. There were a lot of drugs involved.

Stuart was on a mission. "I'm going to get a check cashing store up and running, then I'm going to make it into a chain. That's going to be easy. I just need the capital. I'm going to save this money up, that's it, then boom. Next is check cashing stores, then I'm going to open up my own strip club. My best friend knows how to do it. I know what he's doing, and I know what needs to be done. He is a half-owner in three big strip clubs."

Eddie would be at John's house often. This was before they moved to Hollywood, so they were pretty fresh out of high school. Stuart wasn't happy with Dave, so he needed someone else and Eddie was there.

At the time, Eddie was working at UPS, trying to figure his way out of what is still the worst job he ever had, and there Stuart was offering him one as he was looking for a new "apprentice."

So now here Eddie was, Stuart's apprentice, driving around all day with the cigarette-smoking manipulator who spends the entire day talking about his steroids, his stripper girlfriend, and how they fuck other strippers together, which is how they met English Dave. That's their connection.

Stuart was the guy who changed Eddie's name. At the time, Eddie was going by the name Ed, so one day, Stuart goes, "Ed Bravo...dude... that's retarded. You're Eddie."

Eddie never liked the name Edgar, but Eddie Bravo didn't sound much better at the time. It sounded pussified in Eddie's eyes, but at least it wasn't as lame as Eddie felt the name Edgar was. Like many kids, he didn't like the name that his mom used when he was in trouble.

Eddie hated his last name too. Bravo wasn't a name he chose, but Cano wasn't much better either. Both of them were dicks.

So when we started BravWatts, my name was Icy Cool, which came from William, while Eddie's name was Ed B.C. He didn't want to give any power to the Cano or the Bravo names, so he was just Ed B.C.

Stuart changed Eddie's first name for him, the same way Eddie's mom and stepfather changed his last name for him. Stuart was the only one calling him Eddie. For me, even until recently, I'd call him Edgar, not knowing truly how much he didn't like the name. I thought it was just a sweet indicator of how long we'd been friends, long enough to know him as Edgar, rather than by the same name that the rest of the world knows him by.

Now Eddie was along for the ride with Stuart, watching him psychologically mind flip these people just to get that check. He was a shyster.

One thing he did say about Eddie was that he was a hard worker and a quick study. Eddie didn't fuck around. He was getting a percentage for every carpet dyeing job they did, and it was way better than working at UPS, even if he had to spend the day hanging with some asshole who thought he knew everything.

Stuart called him Eddie so much that when Ed moved to Hollywood with John, he decided it was time to make the name change.

He had gone by Eddie B.C. before the move to Hollywood, but it didn't stick. No one called him Eddie until he moved to a new place and made new friends. Once you tell a new group of friends your name is Eddie after making a move, then it's easier. To all of his lifelong friends and family, he was Edgar, even though today they're just now starting to call him Eddie.

To him, Edgar sucked and Ed made him sound like he was seventy-eight, so Eddie was a decent change. His philosophy was "okay, I'm in Hollywood. Fuck it, let's just play the game."

That's the kind of guy Stuart was, though, he just tells you that your name is stupid and decides your name is now something else.

Those years of scrubbing carpets were tough. Eddie scrubbed those carpets hard. He wanted it to work because there were some scary situations there, anxious times. He wanted to get paid his percentage for every job.

Stuart eventually saved himself enough money and got his first check cashing store, so Eddie went with him and, since Stuart wanted no part in actually overseeing the stores, he hired Eddie as a manager. Usually there are two or three cashiers working the front, usually girls, and you'd need employees from Monday to Sunday.

The other manager was Billy, a former bodybuilder who knew Stuart from the bodybuilding scene; they got steroids together in Tijuana. He looks like a retired offensive lineman for the Steelers. Bodybuilders are like MMA fighters: most of them don't have any money. You better hustle.

Billy was living on Stuart's couch at the time, trying to get his life together.

As soon as they started opening up more than one store, Eddie got me a job there, at the location that was on Rosecrans Avenue in Gardena. At its peak, they would be running five stores.

Billy and Eddie would each work six days a week with the five stores. That was when I moved up to Los Angeles proper, right by Laurel Canyon and Sunset Boulevard in West Hollywood. It was a two bedroom with a living room. Eddie had a room, I had a room, and then Rock Star John had the whole, giant living room, plus the dining area to the side.

Eddie and John had moved up to the first apartment in Hollywood once Stuart had graduated from Dye Tech to check cashing. Eddie's job provided him the stability to move.

Eddie already knew from their time together at the first apartment that John was like his mom, a pack rat. Their house was a crazy dump—a crazy, scary, insane dump. John would fluctuate, though. He would let things get crazy, then he would clean it all the way up.

Shit would be piled on top of shit, then the next day it might be spotless. It was either pristine or in complete disarray, no in between.

We were so nervous about the chaos entering our space that we put locks on our doors. Not because we thought he would steal, but because he was that disgusting. He had the whole living room, plus his own bathroom, while we had one room each and a shared bathroom.

There was no way we could share a bathroom with him. He *destroyed* bathrooms. John was a smoker, so he would put the burnt ends in the sink and toilet, clogging them up. Once the sink in the bathroom was destroyed, he moved on to using the kitchen sink as his bathroom sink, disgusting in its own right.

He was brushing his teeth, doing his hair and makeup—everything you wouldn't want in your shared kitchen sink.

It was a bad living situation, but I was finally in Hollywood. I was another step closer to those dreams, miles closer than Orange County and worlds closer than Little Rock.

Stuart wanted no part in running the stores. Eddie and Billy took care of everything that needed taking care of. The boss would come in every now and then, but he didn't give a fuck.

"Let's just make money...make money...you guys do it...I'm doing other shit...I'm gonna go fly a helicopter."

Those managers always had guns on them. I laugh now when I recall the night we ended up in jail. Eddie pulled an illegal U-turn after work and let the cop know he had a gun on him like a responsible citizen might. The cop found the gun, then brought us into jail until Stuart confirmed that we worked for him.

There was good reason to stay strapped. Check cashing stores are never in the nice neighborhoods. The first store was on Crenshaw.

Pretty early in my working there, some gangsters from Gardena came up to the window. I knew them because they had come by frequently with their women to cash their checks. They tell me, "Oh, we know who the man is bringing the money, the brother with the long ponytail and a truck."

I'm all, "I don't know what you're talking about."

I told Eddie, and he started mixing up the time he would transport the money. The cops started coming by at certain times to check on us, just driving through the lot to keep an eye on the situation and potentially deter the gangsters.

At the time, Eddie would never shave. He would always have on big, oversized zipper hoodies, scraggly hair, and he would never have anything in his hands. He didn't want anyone to see him holding anything.

Stuffed inside, underneath his bulletproof vest, would be stacks of money and money orders with a 9 mm handgun strapped in his pants. Oftentimes he would also have a big, puffy jacket.

He knew the risks, so he didn't want to hold anything in his hands. They could never be sure if he had money on him if his hands were always empty, so it kept a level of uncertainty. It wasn't going to be worth it to try to rob someone who might not have anything on him if you can be patient and wait for the right time to make that big hit.

As managers, Billy and Eddie were tasked with making sure all of the stores had money. They were constantly going to and from the bank, making deposits and taking money out.

Twenty thousand dollars here. Forty thousand dollars there.

They were targets.

And here we were, already being staked out and then the riots happened in April 1992.

It all started on April 29, the day the jury acquitted four officers of the Los Angeles Police Department who had been charged with using excessive force in the arrest of Rodney King. This was one of the first of these incidents between police and citizenry that was caught on video and then widely spread, first through television broadcasts like in this case, then through our phones.

Now, the videos are just more widespread. Every questionable scenario can be recorded by anyone with a smartphone, which is basically everyone.

Another incident that contributed to the riots was the death of fifteen-year-old Latasha Harlins at the hands of Soon Ja Du, a woman who owned Empire Liquor at the intersection of West 91st and South Figueroa in Los Angeles. She and Harlins got into an argument over an orange juice, with Du alleging that Harlins was about to steal from her.

Du shot her at point blank range as Harlins turned around to walk away. It was all caught on the security camera footage.

In November of 1991, Du was found guilty of voluntary manslaughter, which carries a maximum prison sentence of sixteen years. Judge Joyce Karlin suspended her ten-year prison sentence and instead decided on five years' probation, four hundred hours of community service, and five hundred dollars for restitution and funeral expenses.

Harlins's death came thirteen days after the Rodney King incident. A state appeals court unanimously upheld Judge Karlin's punishment a week before the jury acquitted all four officers in the King case of assault and three of the four for using excessive force.

Tensions were high.

For six days, the streets of Los Angeles were in chaos. There was looting, assault, and arson. The situation got so bad that the military and law enforcement agencies deployed more than five thousand to assist in quelling the violence and unrest.

The result of the riots had sixty-three dead, over two thousand injured, twelve thousand arrested, and property damage estimated to be north of $1 billion. That's probably why O.J. Simpson was declared innocent. No jury wanted that kind of pressure on them. O.J. was a hero, so no one wanted to believe it, and, hey, the glove didn't fit.

Koreatown was the hardest hit due to the existing tension between Korean and black Americans in Los Angeles. It wasn't just the Du case. Many in the black community were living under the pretense that Korean shop owners moved into their neighborhoods and jacked up prices for profits.

Korean storeowners accused black patrons of shoplifting. Black customers accused Korean storeowners of disrespect.

Cultural differences and language barriers didn't help tensions.

The result in our collective mind today is the cultural meme of "Rooftop Koreans," Korean storeowners on their roofs with guns to protect their businesses. Thankfully, no one was killed by Rooftop Koreans. They only fired warning shots to chase away trouble.

Like Koreatown, the riots came for the places that were perceived to be taking advantage of the black community.

The check cashing business was at its five-store peak during those years, charging "only two percent" per check cashed. Most customers had bad credit, or it was so close to their homes that it felt like the only option until they could do better. There aren't a lot of banks in the hood and losing 2 percent of every check is a hefty tax to pay for the misfortune of being poor.

Around two o'clock, the riots were starting to hit. We were wondering what we were going to do, and Stuart was up in Marina del Rey, per usual. I'm sure he was ready to go out with English Dave and they were going to go hunt for pussy, or whatever, and then the riots were going on. He panicked.

Each store had a gnarly safe underground. You ain't getting in there. It's a part of the foundation of the building. Picture big, long, steel beams fixed deep into the ground, and covered with fake tiles that mimicked the surrounding floor.

He said, "Fuck that. They'll find it. They'll get it. Grab all the money from the stores. Close them. Bring me the money up to Marina del Rey."

So two o'clock, it's all over the news. Rosecrans was blowing up and we were on Rosecrans and Crenshaw.

"Oh shit, we're real close."

We were watching on TV. So was Stuart.

Stuart knew they were going to break in because there were reports that the mobs were hitting up check cashing stores all over the place like it was the Wild West.

So we closed all the stores and sent everyone home, but Eddie and Billy had to figure out how to get the money they collected to Stuart.

This time, there's a bag. They were rushed.

Eddie said to Billy, "Hey, do you want me to take it?"

Billy responded, "No. I'll take it."

Billy jumped in his car and went west on Rosecrans.

174

Eddie wanted to see the riots himself, so he drove up Crenshaw. He had his gun, a bulletproof vest, and tinted windows.

He drove through it, all the way to Hollywood. It was madness.

When he got to our apartment, he got a call from Stuart. "Billy got shot."

Someone was staking out our store that day, taking advantage of the chaos of a bad situation. They decided to follow Billy because he had the bag, while Eddie had left with nothing in his hands.

They pulled up at a red light. Boom. Shot Billy in the stomach. Took the duffel bag. Tried to kill him.

He survived.

English Dave was a huge reason why we grew to five stores as he had invested in his friend's enterprise as a means for washing the money that would come through the strip club business. There was always a lot of unaccounted cash flowing.

Strip clubs are the perfect money laundering business—that and a shoe repair store. Who repairs shoes? Don't most people just throw the shoes away and just get new shoes?

Now Billy was in the hospital. He would live with a colostomy bag for the rest of his life—shot right in the stomach.

English Dave thought he was doing the right thing, reinvesting his money back into business with the check cashing stores. Use your money and invest wisely.

But he just lost twenty-five thousand dollars. And he was very concerned about that money.

Stuart got English Dave wondering, "Did Billy take it? Was it all a set up?"

English Dave was beside himself. "No way. He got shot in the fucking stomach. He's got a colonoscopy bag now. They shot him. How do you fake that?"

"Ah, maybe something went wrong," Stuart prodded.

So there was a lot of talk, but English Dave finally came to the conclusion that Billy would never have set him up, and he was gutted for even believing it. English Dave couldn't believe that Stuart was pushing the idea on him that Billy might have robbed him.

In retrospect, the person who told us to take all the money out of the perfectly good safes during a riot was the most likely candidate to have set anyone up. Something we hadn't considered until years later. Anything is possible in that kind of madness.

With English Dave feeling bad for his distrust of Billy, he decided to bring him into the strip club as a DJ.

English Dave had three locations, each with a distinctly different kind of stripper. Bare Elegance had high-end girls, while Jet Strip had lower end, dirty chicks. Valley Ball, which was also called Odd Ball, was a combination of both: some dirty, some hot chicks.

Bare Elegance's girls were hot, but they weren't dirty.

That's where Billy was the DJ.

English Dave bought him a Harley too.

Three check cashing stores closed after the riots. We only had two left. Eddie was stuck working there, the only manager left. And he was terrified, convinced he was going to get shot and killed.

"My partner just got shot. They know what's up."

Every store had been sprayed with bullets. They broke into all the stores after the riots. Using sledgehammers, they rammed through the steel doors that separated the customer's area and interior of the store, like a bank. It looked like they hit the door seven thousand times. We thought that door was indestructible, but they finally made it through.

They tried to break through the bulletproof glass, but they couldn't break through. It was all cracked, but they never got through.

Everything, everywhere was broken apart, but those fake tiles that covered the safe?

Those were still there. Those looters never found the safes.

Eddie and Billy could have left the money.

CHAPTER 13

BLACKENED KILL SYMPHONY
(JAMES)

While all that chaos was going on in the check cashing business, we were still taking whatever steps forward we could with the music. We were learning the process of doing something every single day to make it closer to our goals.

Consistency. The most important of skills.

Eddie still sees this with the students in his affiliation today. There are the people who fall off their Jiu Jitsu practice, and then those who persevere no matter what life is throwing at them. These are the people who put their improvement on the mats, and their improvement in life, as their highest priority—putting the time in.

During those years, I moved into Hollywood with Eddie and John—with John in that living room situation, creating about as much of a mess as a person can. We were young, trying to figure out how to survive financially, but still moving forward. That's the hard thing about the levels of this life. You're trying to break free from whatever "norm" might be destined for you, but you have to do those things that help you take those steps.

No matter what, we would always practice on Sunday, Tuesday, and Thursday, but when you're just trying to survive, sometimes you lose that discipline. We would go days without working on anything, thinking "Fuck, I work way too much. I'm tired. I just want to watch TV. I want to chill with the chick. You know there's boxing on tonight? Let's watch boxing."

We bonded over boxing. Eddie started to show interest in whatever martial arts were close to our living situation. During those years, we saw legendary metal guitarist Yngwie Malmsteen on stage. He was wearing the same kind of tight-fitting clothing we'd become accustomed to on the scene. But he had gotten fat. Very fat.

"Oh no, we've got to stay in shape," Eddie thought.

He started training some karate and, of course, Kung Fu to stay in shape because of his Bruce Lee fanaticism. He had picked up a regular gym membership, but that lasted for like a month. Lifting or running for the sake of lifting and running doesn't have the same motivational factor that preparing for any kind of one-versus-one interaction does.

We wouldn't spend too much time at the check cashing store after the riots; the business fell apart. We couldn't keep it going. Riots ruined businesses. The stores were cracked. Everyone's trying to cash their checks surrounded by cracked windows.

Stuart didn't care because Dave was bringing him into the strip club business as an assistant manager at the Odd Ball. Those windows weren't getting fixed. He didn't care. It was time to move on. He was ready to make that dream move into the strip club business—another step closer.

Stuart's goal was to learn the ropes, work with English Dave, then open up a club.

"I've got some money saved. We'll open up a club in Orange County. Call it The Fun House, but first I've gotta learn the ropes."

Eddie asked him to bring him along. Stuart replied, "What do you know about strip clubs, dog?"

Here Eddie was, years as an apprentice under Stuart, and he's not going to hire him. The backup plan was to work for West Hollywood Cab. They didn't hire longhairs, so Eddie tied it tight and then put a wig over it for the interview. It wasn't much more than "well, do you have a good driving record? Okay, what days do you want off?"

It was not a big deal, but Eddie needed to keep his hair hidden. He was still committed to the hair.

He got the job and got his Thomas Guide with all of the maps of the city. He drove that taxi for two weeks. He was destitute and he hated it.

I had already gotten a security job at Universal Studios.

One day, Eddie was driving the cab and drove by the apartment in West Hollywood. He parked the cab and just went into the house to lie down in bed and think, "What the fuck am I going to do with my life?"

There were no cell phones back then. That apartment phone went off. It's Billy.

"They got rid of Stuart. He's going to open up his own club with English Dave's backing, The Fun House. Come by. We're going to get you a job here."

Eddie went in and started working as a floater. That's the guy with the clipboard who keeps track of all the girls dancing in the main area and in the dance booth.

"Tiffany brought this guy back for three songs. Amber is back there for two."

Sometimes nobody was there for a song.

You've always got to make sure that you're not counting the same dance twice. You've gotta be focused.

Everything is a system with Eddie, and he eventually created his own system for counting lap dances.

He would eventually go from the floater to DJ shifts, then from shitty DJ shifts to better shifts, and then even better. He was slowly moving up the ladder when people quit or whatever happened,

happened. Sometimes people don't quit for a long time. It's easy money, easy cash with chicks everywhere in thongs. It's a good gig.

Musically we moved from the short-lived BravWatts into Blackened Kill Symphony when I moved out to Hollywood. Eddie wanted to create a name that no one would forget; he hated BravWatts.

At first it was going to be Blackened Symphony, but it sounded like you're just saying "black and symphony," so people might go, "Oh, who is Black and who is Symphony?" Eddie needed to find something in the middle.

One day, Eddie was driving south on Fairfax with the radio on and a Sizzler commercial came on selling blackened Cajun shrimp.

"Oh shit, that sounds good. 'Blackened' and you put a K after 'black,' and it'll separate it."

So we needed a K word between "Blackened" and "Symphony": "Blackened Kill." Okay, that's about as dark and evil as you can get. The name didn't make sense, the concept came from a Sizzler commercial, but it just sounded like "Kill Fuck Death," which was cool with us.

We might be doing rap, but we were still metal.

Eventually, we wouldn't like the name.

We were in Hollywood, trying to do this new rap-metal thing with keyboards, samples, and synth. We decided to make a demo. Eddie sold his drum set. He was ready to just go all in on being the music producer. Maybe he'll play some keyboards on the side, maybe a little guitar, maybe rap a bit, but he didn't want to have to play anything. I was rapping, and he wanted the responsibility of making it happen from production through performance.

Eddie liked the idea of having fewer responsibilities. "I could just stand there and press buttons. Rock, you have responsibilities. You've gotta be playing something." Eventually, he would play a little electric guitar on stage.

We weren't even a band at first. We were just making music off an 8-track. It was me and him, so the only way we could have performed

live would have been a stripped-down, acoustic version. We didn't do that. We weren't into that.

With no band, we made a demo. I would do guitar leads on some songs, but Eddie was doing all the music, producing it, creating it, and I did all the raps. Every now and then, Eddie would sing a little bit, but it was mainly rap.

At the time, Guitar Center had a book with the names and addresses of every record label, so we bought that and sent this four-song demo we had made out to every address. We figured that by the time anyone would respond, we would have put together the band.

The demo was called *Two Minute Warning*.

Blackened Kill Symphony got record label interest right away before we could even put together the band. Rachel Matthews from Hollywood Basic Records called to tell us that she fell in love with it. Rap, metal, keyboards. She was into it.

"When do you play next?"

Eddie told her within the next three weeks we would be playing at the Roxy as we knew that as long as we bought thirty tickets, we'd have a show. It was pay to play.

There was no band, but it's amazing how quickly you can get quality players together. Label interest made that easy.

"I just got a call. We have a showcase. You want in on this?"

It was easy. We got an amazing drummer, an Indian guy named Rich. We got him quick. Eddie's cousin Danny came on as a bass player, then we got a keyboardist. Ernie, the last singer in Resistance, the one with real hair, came on as our guitar player. Eddie would play a little guitar, and I would play a little guitar in later shows. I was the rapper, though, at the front of the band.

The band came together, but three weeks wasn't enough time to be tight. During the first song of the showcase, Rachel Matthews and her associate Steve Jones stood up and walked out.

It was a nightmare.

Eddie was so nervous before the show that he had the runs. We sounded like shit.

We never heard from them again.

At the time we had a manager. He was a fireman during the day, and they would get like four or five days off in a row, so he was pursuing his dream of being a music manager. He managed us and a band called Frontside, another rap-rock group that did a Rage Against the Machine-Led Zeppelin type of rap. It was nothing synthetic, they had natural drums and a live band.

We did more of what Linkin Park ended up doing, but we came out doing rap, rock, metal, EDM, goth, and techno all mixed up. It had the West Coast-rap vibes of the time in there, but we were still doing long songs, and it was rap in odd meter. No one does rap in odd meter. You want music that people are going to be able to dance to, a consistent beat. Odd meter is about there being no easy way to divide sub-beats into equal groups.

The most popular time signature in the world is 4/4 and with four steady beats in each measure, it provides for a very stable rhythm.

The meter of a song can be a good reflection of the emotions you're trying to convey. A song about good times is perfect for an even meter like 4/4, a nice, happy, easy beat. An odd meter like 5/4 can be used for the kind of music we were used to making, songs about the world being a mess, songs about darkness.

For the genre we were in, 99.99 percent of rap is in 4/4, not odd meter. An added benefit of odd meter is that it makes songs more complicated, which always seemed to be our first aim: try to make the most complicated song we could to show off and impress with our skills.

We just couldn't let go of trying to be different and reinvent the wheel. Even though we were working on a concept that was brand new and unique, rap-styled lyrics with the rock instrumentals together, we refused to do anything that we perceived to be selling out, like moving into three-minute songs, rather than the eight-minute epics that we loved to create.

Eventually we realized and we asked ourselves, "What the fuck are we doing, man?"

Songs that people like, the big ones, they're not super simple because they couldn't find players who could make it technical. They purposely make it super simple; it's uncomplicated. Complicated music is a niche for people like me, people who love shredders and all they want to hear are shredders. It's why I love Dream Theater, which Eddie hates, so Eddie hates the kind of music that's the closest to what we were trying to create, the complicated creation. With every album, Dream Theater challenges themselves to write at least two more complex songs than the previous album.

People want music that is simple, predictable, but not too boring. There is a balance between boring and chaos. Boring is too easy to predict. Chaos is unlistenable, which is the line we would often get too close to, especially in our metal days. When a song is catchy, you can almost guess what comes next.

You do need to understand the complex to make it simple. Like a good teacher, the genius is in making the complex simple. In teaching, the genius is being able to take something complex and explain it to a child in a way that makes sense to him. Musical artists who can make simple, quality songs can do so because they've put the time in to learn the craft; they're black belts.

We weren't black belts, but we were on our way. We were learning the necessary lessons, experimenting, trying new things, taking what worked, and getting rid of what didn't.

Scientific. Process focused. Consistent.

Blackened Kill Symphony continued to have gigs, but no one was showing up. The music was too weird, so our manager was telling us that maybe we could just rap and mix it up. He was trying to market it and everyone kept asking how they'd market the music: "As rap or metal?" He'd wonder why we felt the need to make these long songs. He was right to.

Eventually he would tell us he couldn't market us, and we lost him.

BKS then lost its keyboardist, so Eddie just said, "Fuck the keyboardist, we'll put keyboards on tape."

The drummer was down to play with a click track and a tape machine that Eddie set up. Eventually, we would decide the path forward was without a keyboardist at all. We'd just play the click track and use synth. Keyboardists can be a problem regardless. They often get bored playing what they're supposed to play because it becomes so easy for them to play what's required, but they just want to play over everything. A keyboardist isn't thinking about the song. They're thinking about their boredom. Their part is easy to put on tape; it's going to be three notes. We don't need the keyboard player to play three notes, then stand around for three minutes.

The band was shrinking in size.

Rich, the fully Americanized Indian drummer, was a superstar for us. He was super nerdy—got a drum degree from some college.

Rich is the guy who introduced me to Tool. He was down with them before they even blew up. He loved to play, and he could play anything.

Rich's dad owned an oven factory; they made industrial ovens. We would practice in their storeroom. It was giant, probably the size of two football fields, like an airplane hangar, but filled with nothing but ovens, an interesting scene.

For every practice we had an electronic and an acoustic kit. Rich loved the idea of what we were doing. Eddie would tell him in that the same way he sold John on joining his first band, the same excited way he talks today, "We're going to mix everything. Sometimes it's electronic. Sometimes it's industrial and big. Sometimes it's acoustic. There are no limits."

Eddie wanted to master that. He wanted to create something that superseded the concept of a genre and rap represented that to him, a canvas that was limitless.

Now it was about 1994, and we're still doing too much. We were still trying to make every song crazy, complicated, and complex.

We eventually lost Rich. He left. We had a gig in Bakersfield without a drummer. It was just me, Eddie, and Eddie's cousin Danny

on bass. At least we had the drums recorded on tape, so that's what we did without the drummer. Eddie brought the 8-track and played Rich's drum parts.

There was one person at the gig: the cook.

No one was showing up to our gigs. We never rocked the house with Blackened Kill Symphony like we did with Resistance. We had a bunch of gigs with Resistance where fifty people were moshing. They were little clubs, but they were packed!

But with Blackened Kill Symphony, the crowd would be Eddie's girlfriend at the time, an aunt, and no one else.

People were like, "What is this?"

That's what we were going through. We had some juice in the beginning, label interest right away, a manager. Everyone wanted to join, but then everyone was ready to give up. Even Danny gave up.

Right before everyone left, we decided, as a joke, to take each one of our eight-minute songs and make them commercial. Fuck it, we'll have fun, make it commercial, and make joke songs. We made one of our songs sound like a Dr. Dre song. Another was remixed with some Latin flavor like with a Latin or Cuban drumbeat and another might have a techno beat put underneath it.

We had fun with and probably made our best, most digestible stuff.

We simplified it: verse, chorus, verse, chorus, bridge, chorus.

You think the game is to be more original, more complex. You think you can always be more creative, and you think people are selling out by making simple, catchy songs. That's not true. Great musicians come together to create a great song where everyone just shows up and does what they're supposed to do.

People feel like they need to get into complicated music because they feel like they need to show more effort. You think people are selling out because these musicians are making simple stuff, but then you realize that is the hardest thing to do. Take something that is already out there, take something that might seem simplistic, and put together a song where no one is showing off. Make people love it.

Danny, James, Eddie, and Rich.

It's a hard task. Build on what exists to make something new. The reinventing of the wheel that we had been doing was us trying to create something so far outside what the listener had heard that they didn't know how to consume it. They didn't know what to do with it.

Look at Coldplay. People talk shit about them, but they have like 150 songs and 10 of them are amazing. It's good musicianship throughout, nothing too crazy. It's professional, something you can put on repeat.

Music is meant to convey a feeling, not to show off. We hadn't been considering the purpose of what we were doing. We were thinking about what we wanted, but outside-the-box needed to be just inches or feet outside that box, not miles and miles outside the box.

Now it's 1994. The first UFC fight was in November of 1993. Eddie and I watched it together. We didn't watch it live, most people didn't. We got the tape.

Before the show happened, they didn't have any B-roll, so the advertisements for the show looked like WWF fighting, which is now known as the WWE. It looked fake, so we ignored it. One day we went to Guitar Center and the guy behind the counter told me "that UFC, ultimate challenge thing was real."

I told Eddie, who was in disbelief that there really was this Bruce Lee-style, no-holds-barred mixed martial arts fighting in a cage.

"Yeah, he said some Iranian dude choked everybody out. Just grabbing people with two fingers by the trachea."

Eddie, being that he had been training in karate, responded, "What? No way. What about karate, dudes?"

"He beat every style. The Iranian was just grabbing people's throats."

That Iranian was a Brazilian, Royce Gracie.

At first, Eddie hated Royce for beating those karate guys, but he would go on a run at UFC 2, in the promotion's only 16-man tournament in history, that earned Eddie's respect. Royce submitted all four opponents in just over nine minutes of total fight time, winning $60,000 in the process.

"Well, then fuck karate. I've gotta go find some of this Jiu Jitsu shit," Eddie said.

He remembered seeing a Jiu Jitsu sign in the San Fernando Valley and showed up at the school ready to sign up. They weren't doing any groundwork, though, only some kind of standing Kung Fu stuff.

Eddie asked the head instructor, "Why aren't you doing any groundwork? Isn't this Jiu Jitsu?"

He responded, "Oh, you're talking about Gracie Jiu Jitsu."

Eddie wondered aloud, "There's a difference?"

"Yeah, their cousins the Machados are here in the Valley. Do you want their number?"

Eddie looked it up, but he was looking it up spelled "M-i," rather than "M-a," thinking it was "Michado."

He found Carlos Gracie Jr. in the Valley and the Machados were teaching.

Eddie went in and a purple belt named Dave Meyer ran a clinic on him. Our future champion said he got choked thirty-seven times that day. A lot of people run when that happens to them, but the world is a scary place. You might need to protect yourself or your family.

We weren't making much money at the time. Eddie had crappy shifts at the strip club, so the $180 per month for the unlimited membership at Jean Jacques Machado's gym was too much, and so was the $120 a month for two days per week, especially because Eddie was holding onto a $75 per month membership at a Cass Magda Institute. Cass was one of Dan Inosanto's top Jeet Kune Do and Filipino Kali instructors. Inosanto was one of Bruce Lee's most well-known protégés.

Eddie instead settled for the one day per week membership for $80 per month with Jean Jacques, while training with Cass on Tuesdays and Thursdays for $75 a month.

For two and a half years, Eddie trained with Cass Magda and Jean Jacques Machado, but without consistent Jiu Jitsu training, Eddie found that the white belts who were six months in and training five days a week at Machado's were passing him up, tapping him. Around 1996, at twenty-six years old, he got better shifts DJing at the strip

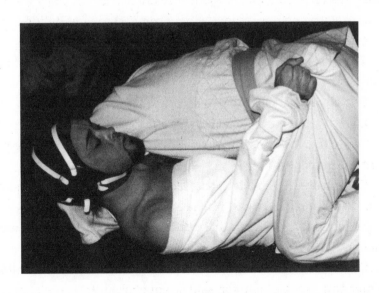

club, so he picked up the unlimited membership with Jean Jacques and dropped the membership with Cass Magda.

The last time we lived with Movie Star, Rock Star John was in 1994. That living situation with him out in the living room wasn't going to work out for us. John had a lifestyle change of sorts.

He got a girl pregnant, and now they had a kid. He was living in the living room with her, the kid, and his girlfriend's brother who was a girl now. We had to walk through all of that every day.

I wouldn't see John again after we left. Eddie would see him once again in 1997. We aren't sure where he has ended up.

CHAPTER 14

....

I'M ALIVE
(JAMES)

When you start at the strip club, you get a speech.

"No fucking the girls."

You say, "Oh shit, okay." You still take the job.

In his head, Eddie's like, "Damn, you're going to be around a bunch of hot girls all day, and you're going to get fired if you have any sexual relationship with any of the girls? Okay. That's going to be a weird one. You're at the club like fuck I don't want to get fired, but damn, I don't want to get fired, but girl. Shit, I don't want to lose my job...."

That didn't last long though. You soon realize that everyone is fucking everyone. There are two reasons they tell you the rule. One, so they can say, "I told you so." Another equally good reason was that it gave you a reason to totally ignore a chick at work. "I don't wanna give it away. I don't want to get fired." It gave you a reason to keep it cool and keep it under wraps, if necessary. If you're single, it works out well for you. The girl shouldn't want you acting like her boyfriend at work either considering she's trying to make money.

With John's new family taking over our space, we knew we had to get out.

Eddie still had his gun from our check cashing days together, so he started helping one of the strippers with security during bachelor parties. Girls have to have a bodyguard for that. They can't just be dropped off anywhere with who knows what on the other side of the door. He'd get like two hundred dollars a night for security, while this girl would go in and do her thing.

That was the first stripper that Eddie had sexual relations with. The second one was this girl, Shay, who was making a lot of money and didn't look that good. She wasn't very attractive, but she was a hustler. She was very smart, very articulate, and very manipulative. She made a lot of money, did like fifty couch dances a night at the strip club, tipping everyone who worked the club twenty dollars. When you're working at the club, you make sure to take care of that one.

The minimum that strippers were allowed to tip the DJ and the floater was five dollars. The good girls were making eight hundred or one thousand dollars per night, so you better give us twenty dollars if you're doing that kind of revenue. We had to take care of each other. That's how you work. That's how you work off the tips and the girls that you're governing. It's a weird conflict of interest. They're paying you, so you better be nice to them.

So Shay and Eddie start dating. She had a kid who they found out is a diabetic as they start dating. She knew she wasn't a ten, but she was smart. She'd buy Eddie chains and jewelry and always pay for things, everything everywhere they went.

A lot of strippers are generous with their money for two reasons. When you make fast money and a lot of it, you're more likely to be generous, as the money doesn't have the same value. But also, if they're the ones out there spending money, then everyone shuts up. You've gotta accept that she's a stripper. You do like the money, right?

We were right in the middle of all this turmoil in our lives and this girl pulled us out of that scenario with John. Eddie was commiserating about the situation to her, so she found a place for all of us to move into for twenty-five hundred dollars a month in 1994.

It was a big house in Hollywood. She knew I could only afford two hundred dollars a month or whatever, so she had me in the guest house, Eddie had his own room, then she had her own room.

We told John about the situation, and he went out on his own.

Of course, the situation with Shay wouldn't work out. We needed a new exit strategy, so we found one with another one of the DJs at the club. He lived in West Hollywood too, in a duplex of sorts. There were four houses on one lot. The other DJ is in one of the front houses, then Eddie and I fit ourselves into one of the two smaller guest houses in the back.

It's a one bedroom. Eddie takes the bedroom, I take the living room, and we did that for a little while.

But that was around the time that I started dating this girl, Jenny. Eddie was twenty-seven, I was thirty-five. It was time for me to do that last little bit of growing up that I needed to do. A similarity between fighters and us musicians, we spend all these years chasing what we love to do with our boys, but eventually, we want to find the right girl, settle down, and move into that next stage of our lives.

Jenny and I decided to move in together. As Eddie will tell you now, he understood how crazy it was that two grown dudes were sharing a one bedroom with a living room, but we were doing this thing together. There was a deep camaraderie there. We were living the dream together. Every time Eddie moved jobs or living arrangements, he made sure he had a place for me to stay too. He brought me along with him to more than one job. He was always looking out, always making sure we were able to stay on the path.

I still call Eddie "the Dream Maker" because he made my Little Rock dreams of playing my guitar on stage in front of people out in California come true.

Now I was leaving him. Just because you understand why someone does something, doesn't mean it doesn't hurt.

Eddie says now, "I thought you left me, man."

And to that I say, "Well, you seem to have done pretty well."

We were still making music, but we just weren't living together anymore. There was one more demo made with us and Danny. Eddie just programmed the drums on a drum machine since we didn't have another drummer. This band wasn't going to be called Blackened Kill Symphony. That was behind us now. There was too much fatty tissue in the music, all this unnecessary shit. We were moving on. Eddie didn't like the name Blackened Kill Symphony at this point anyway.

This was going to be called Victim Kill System. We even made some bumper stickers, but then Eddie realized that's essentially the same name as Rage Against the Machine.

I had moved on to working at Universal Studios on a full-time basis. My job was to walk around and deliver documents to people. I wasn't the mail guy. I was more of a personal assistant kind of guy

Eddie and James the day James moved out.

delivering to people on the property largely from within the property. Sometimes it was like million dollar checks from one office to another.

One day I was at work thinking, "Boy, it's hot today" as I was unusually sweaty, so I called my office, thinking that I'm having a heat stroke. They let me off work. I drove home and did everything I could to stop myself from passing out. Thankfully I lived close.

I spent the rest of the afternoon in bed and the bed was wet with sweat. That feeling I was having wasn't going anywhere. Jenny got a call from me telling her how terrible I was feeling, so she came home from work to drive me to the emergency room.

Someone took my blood and told me that my blood work was terrible.

I was sitting there, not worried about a thing, not afraid of anything. "What does that mean?"

He said, "At worst, that means you could have cancer."

At the time, I wasn't smoking, so I was like, "What do you mean cancer? That's for people that smoke."

So he asked, "Do you do heavy drugs?"

"No."

"Do you work in manufacturing?"

I said, "Well I used to, but now I work at Universal Studios delivering mail and documents."

It was probably from one of those jobs that Eddie and I worked at in my early days in Southern California. I worked at a printing company in Anaheim with all of these resins that would get all over my hands. I'd ask how to wash it off my hands, and then get directed to a bucket with benzene in it, which is now well known to be cancer causing, especially for leukemia and other blood cancers.

With that car bulletproofing company, we would put a couple layers of fiberglass into door panels, and they would be bulletproof. All the fiber dust in the air from us cutting those pieces up couldn't have been good either.

He says, "Well we are going to put you in an ambulance and send you over to UCLA for the main cancer doctor."

Thankfully, being that I was now full-time at Universal, I had just gotten health insurance. I had never felt the need to pay for it before. I never had any health problems, so why pay for health insurance? Any small issues that I had, I'd call my West Coast mom Trudy, and she would get me the occasional antibiotic.

I went to see that doctor.

"It's leukemia."

I think, "Okay, well how do you cure it?"

The vibe I got back from the doctor, in fewer words, was "dude, what are you talking about? How do you cure leukemia? You've got to do this, then that, but people don't really get cured from leukemia. It might go into remission, but cure?"

I thought, "Well, I'm going to get cured." I didn't feel anything. I didn't feel bad other than the heat stroke thing I had going on before, but by then I was fine.

"How do I get cured? Just give me the pills. Tell me what I need to do."

I'm a stubborn, hardheaded guy, but looking back now, I had a lot of faith too. Looking through Christian eyes, one might say that was my faith carrying me through, but I wasn't even thinking about God. I was thinking, "Why would this happen? What is the point of me dying?" All I wanted to do was make sure that my family wasn't sitting around my dead body, looking at me, and crying about me.

I called Eddie, he was driving at the time. "I've got cancer, man."

I wasn't worried about the news I had just gotten, but Eddie was catastrophizing a bit because he cared so much. He thought that was it.

Maybe he knew the odds intuitively or through just hearing about leukemia as it was, and still is, one of the deadliest cancers, although the treatments have gotten more efficient and effective over time.

I'd learn of how scared he was later on a podcast we would do together and, while I knew we were close and I knew that he was my brother, I had no idea how much it affected him. His voice cracked as he recounted my story.

That's definitely my brother.

The next few years would be a blur of medical issues.

The year 1997 was a doozy.

I'd go to UCLA for more tests. It feels like I've been taking tests ever since.

I was in a fragile state already. This was desperate.

I immediately went into radiation, then chemotherapy.

The radiation left my skin burnt like a crisp. I looked like I'd been electrocuted like a gag in a cartoon, third-degree burns all over my body, frayed hair. I was very, very dark. My skin would never grow in properly, and it left me unable to play guitar. The callouses on the tips of my fingers from years of practice on the guitar were gone, and my skin wasn't ever going to grow back strong enough to allow me to build them up again.

As I began my first day of chemotherapy treatment, minutes into it, the nurse asked me how I was doing.

I told her I was sweaty. I wasn't. I was totally dry.

She knew it must be a brain bleed.

Emergency surgery was required to go in, stop the bleeding, and keep me in the fight. The nurse found the doctor that saved my life on the elevator on his way out the door. The doctors were in the middle of a shift change, so without finding that doctor, all might have been lost.

The chemotherapy has still weakened my immune system. My brain aneurysm, a hemorrhagic stroke, resulted in a hole in my skull that still exists, a loss of eyesight on the left side of each eye, and memory loss.

Once I got back on my feet, I'd keep walking into the women's room because I never saw the "Wo" at the front of the word. I can't drive because of this, and many of the memories we put together in this book were things I needed to be reminded of.

I'd be in and out of consciousness for a few days afterward, in and out of a comatose state. They had to keep putting me under because I was having a continual series of seizures when I was awake.

Every time I'd wake from those little comas, I'd ask, "Where's my girlfriend? Where's my girlfriend?"

My mom had flown across the country and was right next to me, but I had to call my girlfriend in.

A few months prior, Jenny had gone in for surgery for cancer that was near her ear, inside her head, and she felt the same towards me.

Her father was next to her bed. "Where's James?"

She'd ask me if I was okay while she was the one in surgery. "Why are you worried about me?! I'm worried about you. You're the one who just had surgery!"

Jenny was by my side through it all and through today.

One day, I had the hardest conversation one has to have in this kind of scenario.

"Jenny, you didn't sign up for no boyfriend with cancer. If you want to get out of here, no one would blame you...."

She didn't.

She signed up to be with me.

To this day, she makes sure I take my medicines. She takes me to every appointment.

Jenny kept my California dream alive, my California life with her.

Together, we're a success.

We had my family test themselves for their bone marrow type back in Arkansas, looking for a donor. Doctors thought it would be my younger brother, but he was missing a few genetic markers they needed to see, so he couldn't do it. It was my older sister Gail and her bone marrow that would save me.

Gail was a mother of two at this point. We were hoping it would be my brother because some of the healing properties of Gail's bone marrow went to her two babies. Had she not had her babies yet, her bone marrow would have been more effective in healing my skin and fingernails from the radiation.

Either way, I made it to as I am today. Alive. All thanks to Gail.

There are new processes to extract bone marrow today, and it's this bone marrow transplant that is decreasing the fatality rate of leukemia, but back then the only way to get the bone marrow out was by sticking a long needle inside the hip bone of the person donating the marrow.

With my immune system weakened by the radiation, Gail's bone marrow was injected into me, and I began my road to remission.

For a time, I had to use a sponge to brush my teeth because any small cut wouldn't stop bleeding as the platelets in my blood were wiped out to destroy those cancer cells. To this day, my fingernails are deformed, and my skin is spotted and dry.

The doctors say, "Everything we did almost killed you."

That's a harsh take. Gail's bone marrow saved my life, the doctors did that, and they still take care of me today.

How could I be resentful of that? How could I be angry or sad? I'm alive.

CHAPTER 15

LAUREL CANYON AND RELIGION
(ZACK)

Sunday, January 30th

Eddie, James, and I I were still sitting in Danny's bar. Plaster was on his second camera battery, recording the whole time, making sure we didn't miss a word.

James's skin was much better than it was right after his cancer treatments. For a time, his skin was so dry and raw that the regular movements we take for granted were impossible. His skin is no longer burnt to a crisp. If humans do regenerate cells every seven to ten years, he's gone through this cycle two or three times, old ailments becoming better with time.

A small piece of his skull is gone, so a couple square inches of his brain can actually be felt through the skin. It's like nothing I've ever seen, but also risky, leaving his brain unprotected in a spot. He hasn't been able to get a nice metal cap on it yet.

Fred Price was the first black televangelist. James found Fred's church right here in Los Angeles at the Crenshaw Christian Center. During the years following his cancer treatments, he had a lot of free time. He is still recovering, now disabled in ways that make life extremely difficult.

A healthy, handsome thirty-five-year-old with a whole life in front of him is now in constant pain and a self-consciousness that has ebbed with time and maturity. His skin has been burnt, his hair is frayed, his fingernails deformed, he can't see well, and he has a hole in his head.

It was a shocking change for him.

Price gave him something positive to focus on, something to fill his head with, something other than that natural, creeping inclination we could develop to feel bad for ourselves.

Now when he's on the church bus that takes disabled members of the community to and from places, the blind person next to him will marvel at his ability to see anything. The person in the wheelchair is amazed that James has the ability to walk.

The pain becomes the purpose, to be worthy of our suffering and to make the most of it was the highest aim of the Stoic philosophers.

"I thought you were dead," Eddie says of the days James was in a coma.

James had his own rebirth in the physical, then the spiritual. Price provided him with a story that he could use to inspire and change him, to give him the mindset that could allow him to make something of the life he had left.

It could always be worse. You could always be dead.

We can say that, but to have lived it internalizes the message.

Nothing was going to be the same for him, no matter how much he wished for it to change, so he had to practice and foster one of the most powerful traits we can foster in ourselves: acceptance.

By learning under Price, James heard stories about the Byzantine Empire, the Middle East, and Israel. These were places he knew about and times that could be confirmed historically. No longer was it the *Wizard of Oz*; it became real to him. He'd start going online and figuring out what this or that really meant, getting the right translations, and cutting away the fat.

James found that some stuff you'll hear is bullshit, but everyone needs to make their own choice and do their own research. You need to take what's useful like Bruce Lee and remember the most important messages of it all.

While he was fighting through that coma, he had two visions.

The first was that he was hot and sweaty in a dark place, surrounded by other black bodies, kind of like the description of a slave boat. It could have been a past memory from a movie or who knows, a trip from an ancestor. He says, "Who can really explain it?"

His second vision was of his friends and family standing around a casket crying. He didn't want to let that happen.

These are the main memories of that entire period. He had faith he would persevere—what he knows now to be a religious kind of faith. It was knowledge that he was meant for more than dying in that hospital bed.

Two or three years were spent with his mother and Jenny by his side, helping to care for him, so he could one day recover enough to live the life he lives now. Surely he was on a cocktail of drugs and in such a fragile state, with such little to occupy his time other than sleep, those years felt like a blur. They would feel like a blur with the stroke, the brain bleed, and the surgery.

As James was recovering, Eddie sent him a track, looking for lyrics to instrumentals he had put together. James sent back lyrics in some weird arrangement that almost looked like he was drawing a picture with the lyrics; it was odd. The lyrics made no sense either.

Eddie wasn't sure if James was out of it or telling him to move on without him, but it was clear he had to move on. James doesn't recall the story. Lost to the holes in his memory.

Without his musical partner on the journey with him, Eddie poured himself into Jiu Jitsu. This was right around the time that he had better shifts at the strip club and elevated his membership from once a week to unlimited at Jean Jacques's, so he had new training partners, a group of guys who would include Todd White and Joe Rogan.

Todd is now a prolific artist after a decade in animation on various TV shows like *Tiny Toons* and *SpongeBob SquarePants*. He now owns Jean Jacques Machado Austin in Dripping Springs, Texas. Rogan is who he has become, world renowned. They've become three of Jean Jacques's most well-known students.

To practice, Eddie just needed to show up to the gym, and there would be bodies. Todd would become Eddie's main training partner as they became two of Jean Jacques' most serious competitors.

Starting in 1997 and 1998, when Todd was at Nickelodeon, Eddie would bring mats to Todd's office and they would drill in a basket-ball gym. During these sessions, they'd create flows to move through. Quietly and diligently working away, learning moves and their counters, stacking repetitions.

No talking. Just an hour of work.

Eddie would come up with names for moves and positions, something he'd be persecuted for by those who felt they knew better

Bud Brutsman, Eddie Bravo, Jean Jacques Machado, Aaron Briley (teammate), and Todd White.

or there was a code to follow. He and Todd would work through these early versions of the flows that would become the 10th Planet system.

Eddie had a great training partner, but finding a new musical partner would be a major project.

Two young men who had started off together making angry, satanic metal are now older, sitting in front of me talking about faith and religion. There were years' worth of atheist songs after both had largely abandoned religion as kids. There were also years of songs with satanic lyrics, not because they believed in Satan, but because through that nonbelief, they didn't believe in the consequences of invoking him. They were writing music with the same energy as a writer of a horror flick.

Today's beliefs for both involve a strong connection to the idea of God and of the religious stories themselves, but a healthy distrust of institutions remains. This is as it should be—what institution hasn't

been used for financial gain, enslavement, and perversion? Especially if people believe in an institution so deeply that they believe it shouldn't be questioned.

As Eddie speaks about his religious beliefs, it reminds me of how much some of his lessons and ideas were incorporated into mine without me knowing it, either through podcasts or our community, a true sign of an educator.

Similar to the way that I believe you create a heaven and hell for yourself on earth, Eddie speaks of the goal of reaching the right frequency where the things that you want start happening for you.

He asked James a question that seemed designed to ask him about the position he himself has. "What do you say to the people that claim to be Christian, and they believe the Bible is truth, but the truth to them means that the Bible is a set of instructions on how to live your life? That it's not necessarily that there is a God in the sun and all of that. That metaphor is just a way to explain to people that to get to heaven, you have to be righteous, you have to do the right things and be in a frequency that allows you to enter heaven. And they say that the Bible is the greatest book ever, but it's instructions on how to live your life, but the entire Jesus story might not be entirely true?"

Eddie is likely referring to the seemingly unexplainable, like Jesus's resurrection, walking on water, or turning water to wine.

James replied, "The first thing that I tell people is that yes, I was exactly where you are. I tell everyone that I was an atheist. I'm not better than you because I did this. I say, dude, I was exactly where you are. I just took the path of trying to learn certain things, clear up certain things. And the number one thing I tell people is that Jesus did not come here for the perfect people, he came here for the sinners. So stop trying to think you can be perfect. Jesus came here for the person who thinks they're messed up, so they know that Jesus has their back."

It was when James woke up, all messed up, struggling through these years wondering when the pain and sickness would subside, that he found this relationship with God. Sometimes it takes us being in that kind of scenario to surrender ourselves to a message that has the power to take us out of that darkness.

A rock bottom that was not of his choosing gave him the humility to accept the teachers that came along on the radio and in his life.

What I take from the story of Jesus is that he was willing to speak the truth no matter the consequence, the truth being that he was the son of God. With a Roman government that saw the state as the religion, Jesus was deemed a political subversive dressed in religious clothing, so a mob was led against him. Jesus was willing to die for the truth because the truth matters that much.

While nailed to the cross, next to two thieves, Jesus refused a sponge soaked in a concoction that was offered as a painkiller.

Jesus would be resurrected and ascend into heaven, a reward for not compromising himself or his principles, no matter the cost. It was a test of faith passed and a reminder of the cruelty man is capable of.

Throughout this time of knowing James, his attitude is infectious. Things aren't easy for him, important things have been taken from him, but he has a superpower: acceptance.

It's the serenity prayer in action, the foundation of Alcoholics Anonymous: "God grant me the serenity to accept the things I cannot change, courage to change the things I can, and the wisdom to know the difference."

There was an "old country preacher dude" who went from Genesis through Revelation on the radio, explaining everything to James as he lay in that bed in the late 1990s. These were the times that made him realize that there was a God, the acceptance that man is not the highest form of intelligence on this plane.

He sits in front of us, alive today. "There was a realization that there is something bigger than me. Medicine, electronics, and all of this around me. I could be dead right now, but obviously something didn't want me dead."

Despite all the medical mishaps and issues along the way, the combination of man and faith kept him alive and thriving as best as he possibly can today. He is maximizing what he has left of his ride, living it with the right attitude, rather than the wrong one. He's uplifting those around him through that behavior, including Eddie.

Eddie went on to say how the Bible and the great ancient stories, many of which included Jesus, are instructions to live a good life, not literally true stories in every way, but they show you the way. He says, "This is the life. This is the truth, but it doesn't matter if the story is real or not. If you follow the story and you believe the story, then this will help you. It's almost like a form of meditation. If you're meditating on this story of doing good and you're doing good, then who cares if it's real or not. As long as you believe it's real, then you're going to stay on the right path."

James replies, "People who have faith that Jesus died for our sins aren't going to move off that path."

Plaster had to leave to prepare for a flight to Mexico the next day. He jumped in with a conclusion that we can all agree on, "Jordan Peterson said, when he was questioned if he believes in God, 'I live as though God exists.'"

"Perfect answer," Eddie said.

If you reach that right frequency or vibration, like a great song, then you'll receive the things you want to receive because you're living right.

We all have different ways we've come to a similar conclusion, but we're all there. James reminded us that the most important commandment is to "love your brother like you love yourself."

People have different experiences that make us all believe certain things, but most of us are all striving for the same thing. Most are trying to be better, some just don't know how, and it's up to us to leave space and patience for them. "He doesn't have the same belief as you because he doesn't have your existence or he hasn't been able to look through your eyes," James says.

I'm, again, reminded that I have to study the Bible, I need to overcome that overwhelming feeling I have of wondering where to start.

We pack up the equipment and smoke one more joint.

It was dark outside, so Eddie lit the way with his iPhone's flashlight, while I held James's hand. We made our way down the steps, helping him into Eddie's pickup truck.

CHAPTER 16

THE DEFINITION OF QUALITY
(ZACK)

Monday, January 31st

Eddie started as a DJ in the Valley at Odd Ball, which had the sort of half-hot chicks, half-dirty chicks, then he moved to the high-end one, Bare Elegance.

James's cancer was around the time Eddie would finally cut his long hair. He was sick of looking like an outdated loser, and he was getting no girls outside of the strip club, but every shift had one or two metal chicks. Long hair was like the black plague. Thanks, Nirvana.

At Bare Elegance, Eddie started hearing about this crazy chick from Kentucky that everyone was talking about at Jet Strip, the dirty club. Her stripper name was Darian, but everyone at Bare Elegance called her Psycho before she got there.

She was super hot, top to bottom, but she was nuts. Being that she was at the lower-end club, she was like the highest-paid player on a bad team, the superstar, making a lot of money.

Darian had to change clubs because she fucked the DJ at Jet Strip, and the DJ was her best friend's boyfriend, so they said, "Fuck it," and sent her to Bare Elegance. You can't let a high earner like that go.

Her older brother was a soccer star who played at Vanderbilt, and she was the younger sister who played soccer in college, but she also liked to party. She had insane legs, soccer legs—the kind you don't forget—and blue eyes with blonde hair.

Lesbians like going to strip clubs like any straight man would. Eddie recalled a black lesbian chick coming in one night while he was DJing, and after seeing Darian dancing on stage, she yelled out, "Ummm hmmm, her body is on POINT!"

Eddie is twenty-eight years old at this point. James has cancer, and Eddie didn't know what he was going to do musically. He and James were writing music together since he was sixteen, a twelve-year span of time.

"I've got to figure it out. What am I gonna do, like a Paul Oakenfold, solo, instrumental thing? What am I gonna do? What can I do? Do I look for another MC?"

His music was in limbo.

One night, while Darian's working at the club, Eddie was at Club Lingerie, which is just a regular club on Sunset. He was on Molly with his boy Scott Redondo.

Eddie called Darian. "Hey, can you get out of work? Come meet us at Club Lingerie."

She got out of work and came by. He was just sitting there watching her walk through the club. She was stunning, and he was rolling on Molly. She found him and immediately asked him for Molly, but they couldn't find any. Upon getting back to Eddie's house, she pulled out a joint that some customer had given her.

At this point, Eddie had smoked weed like once a year his whole life and he always had bad experiences. He'd always freak out. "I'm not smoking that."

"Come on, smoke it with me...." she said.

So they smoked that joint and laughed like mental patients all night, laughing over nothing. Eddie would call the neighbor and just start laughing. She would lay on the bed hugging a pillow in between her arms, then she would sit up, put the pillow down on her lap, then just pull the pillow back over her face and laugh into the pillow.

They ordered Damiano's pizza on Fairfax and got everything, the cheesecake, pizza, everything. He was just having the greatest time of his life. In the beginning, when you first really start smoking weed, that's when the food is the best.

That's how he fell in love with Psycho.

And weed, too.

Being that he was now twenty-eight and a little more secure with himself, four years into training Jiu Jitsu at this point, he woke up the next morning with a new perspective on the plant: weed just enhances who you already are.

He and Darian just became stoners at that point. Every night.

Darian stole Eddie from another girlfriend he had been dating for six months, but he was looking for a reason to leave. She was smart, and she knew she wanted to move into his place. So she would come over and cook, buy something like Hamburger Helper, total stoner food, and she would feed him. She would get in his truck and love every song he put on the radio.

While they'd keep the relationship under wraps at the club, Eddie, now a purple belt, was the guy telling his manager, "Don't you ever call her Psycho again!"

She moved in, and it would be a real problem to eventually try to get her out when that time came.

Weed changed everything for Eddie. It was the first time he realized he truly wasn't being objective about music. "How am I supposed to be writing the best fucking music possible, and I'm like tripping myself?"

Disconnect the emotion and just go for the best shit.

He had hung onto KISS forever. At one point, he hated Soundgarden because a girlfriend thought Chris Cornell was hot, so "Fuck Soundgarden."

Eddie would spend over a decade at the strip club, eight hours a day, exposing himself to more music than just about anyone could possibly be exposed to. He'd pick off the good ones, many of which he would have never found on his own, to create a library of songs. Strippers would play deep cuts that he never would have found, stuff that would have never been on the radio, but they're some of his favorite songs ever.

He kept collecting over the years, and it all became an asset. Rather than saying, "Fuck that style of music," he'd try to understand why it was good. He was learning, becoming a better musician in the process.

Eddie frequently brings up the necessity of lacking emotion to be objective through the prism of it being like running a football team: you need to hire the best guy for each spot. This is why he keeps making music. He wants to see what he can create if he has no bias, if he's completely objective and invested in the process.

Eddie flipping through CDs at his job.

What can he create if he can truly pursue and discover what's best?

All of this would come with him to Jiu Jitsu. He believes it was weed that allowed him to be the creator he would become on the mat. He was able to just ask himself, "Does this work? How does it work? How high percentage is it? What level of risk does this entail?"

There's no trying to win by muscling a move, a battle of the ego. It's a battle of who is the most technical. Eddie is always seeking to be that guy, rather than relying on physical skills. You can be more prepared and more creative intellectually, and everyone can run into someone who is more physically imposing—someone like Royler Gracie.

You can't be biased in terms of where a move might come from. If it comes from someone you don't like or someone who beats you with it, then you better take your emotions out of it and figure out what you can learn from it. You can either study it yourself or be a decent enough person to ask the person who just submitted you.

Football coaches do this. They take things that they have learned from others' successes and incorporate them into their own game. That's how you create the best system. You take what you learned along the way, then you make it your own thing. It's why I compare Eddie to San Francisco 49ers great Bill Walsh, the creator of the West Coast offense.

Walsh would create the system in Cincinnati, under NFL pioneer Paul Brown, when his superstar, big-armed, number one overall draft pick quarterback Greg Cook blew out his shoulder, and he had to be replaced with a mobile, accurate journeyman named Virgil Carter. Walsh created a system built on foundational principles of efficiency, making it easier for a wider number of quarterbacks to perform within the system.

Over the long term, he created a system where quarterbacks didn't have to rely solely on using the passing game to stretch a team out long. They spread the field horizontally, putting pass catchers in different zones and at different levels across the defense. Walsh created hard to defend pictures that overleveraged the defense, moving his quarterback out of the pocket, and making the team less reliant on a quarterback's ability to throw the deep ball, which is, even today, a lower percentage strategy for offensive efficiency. He was creating open spaces and putting people in those open spaces to make things happen.

Eddie created his system under the watchful eye of Jean Jacques Machado, an ADCC (Abu Dhabi Combat Club) champion in 1999 who was known for great overhook and underhook grips. It was a necessity for him considering that amniotic band syndrome had left his left hand with only a thumb and a tiny piece of pinky. Where traditional Gi practitioners would grip the collars, lapels, and sleeves of their opponents, Jean Jacques' style didn't utilize those. His grips were the perfect thing to pass on to who Eddie would become.

Back at the Sheraton, it was Monday morning, I was sitting at that desk, excited that I captured the previous night's conversation and got to bring two best friends together for something like that.

I found myself at a Pasadena restaurant called Mi Piace on Sunday night, engorging myself on Italian food and even a dessert. It's a favorite pastime of mine as a reminder of all the family dinners I've enjoyed with my Malatesta side of the family in New Jersey.

A chicken parmigiana, preferably with vodka sauce, plus spaghetti is my celebration meal of choice.

No alcohol the night before, though, I was on the last day of a dry January.

For almost fifteen years now, I've carried along a "bible" in my backpack. It's a book that I consider to be worth thumbing through if I have the time or at least seeing it will remind me of the lessons in it.

For a time it was Elko's *Touchdown*, and for a few years it was *The Daily Stoic* by Ryan Holiday as I would transcribe the pages to embed them deeper into my subconscious. Four years later, that book sits on my shelf with clear tape around the spine to hold it together, every page marked up and underlined.

My current text is *Zen and the Art of Motorcycle Maintenance* by Robert Pirsig, a book that helped organize and center my own thoughts around the concept of "Quality" when I first read it seven or eight years ago.

Quality is broken into Dynamic and Static. Dynamic Quality is the force of change in the universe, the cutting edge of reality. It's new concepts and ideas that build on what already exists. Static Quality is that current state of Quality: the state of Quality left in the wake of Dynamic advancements—the things we know to be true.

Understanding Quality, understanding goals and objectives, and understanding values are what allows someone to create something new that quickly overtakes the old way of doing things. Value is this leading edge of reality. It's the predecessor of structure. It's what determines what we create.

To Eddie, the focus of fighting through the framework of Jiu Jitsu was to find the path to submission. That was the highest value. His fight promotions today have grown and provided a ruleset that others use, which has become the preferred ruleset moving forward in the submission-only format. All submissions are legal.

If there isn't a submission inside the ten-minute time limit, then overtime is three "innings" where both players have an opportunity to submit the other from one of two offensive positions.

The first position is on the back with two hooks in, plus a seat belt grip around their opponent, generally seeking the rear naked choke. A seat belt grip is when the back, attacking player has one arm, let's say his right arm, over his defensive opponent's right shoulder and his opposing, left arm underneath his opponent's arm. The attacker on the back's left hand grabs his own right wrist.

The second position is a spider web. The attacking player has one hamstring across his opponent's head, the other across his chest, and his head-side arm is hooked in deep against the opposing player's near-side arm. Our attacking player's hip-side arm is resting his hand on the mat.

It's up to the offensive player to choose the position.

The more dominant grappler during regulation will generally get to pick if he wants to go first or second, either taking the top of the inning or the bottom in baseball terms: first dibs or last licks. If there isn't an obviously more dominant grappler during regulation, it may be chosen via coin toss.

Each competitor has a two-minute round from the offensive position, which starts on the referee's command. If there are no submissions over three overtime rounds, then the person with the most "ride time," which is time in a position that threatens a submission, will win the match.

Seeing who can be most effective over these cycles of overtime from these two important positions is the best way that Eddie has found to run an overtime to find out who the best Jiu Jitsu competitor is over the course of one of his sixteen-man tournaments.

Eddie's focus as an athlete wasn't about securing points and then stalling out the rest of the round to win. His game was about finding new ways to get to winning positions, then getting to submissions, no matter where you started from. Positional-based Jiu Jitsu has a huge benefit. It's good to be a strong positional athlete for MMA purposes. It's good to be able to take people down, then maintain top pressure, but adding in the element of being the best submission artist is the sharpest form of a well-rounded Jiu Jitsu athlete. Eddie excelled at finding submissions from everywhere, including his back and he was adept at getting someone who was on top of him, off of him, to then get himself back on top in a more dominant position.

As the sport matures and knowledge becomes increasingly more widespread and cross-pollinated, the person who is likely to submit someone at the highest level is oftentimes going to be the person who displays complete positional Jiu Jitsu as well.

When Eddie beat Royler Gracie, the legend of his time, a three-time ADCC champion, Eddie was nine years into training and just six years into training on a Monday, Wednesday, Friday, and Saturday schedule. Royler had been training nearly all his life.

Eddie closed the gap between himself and the top guys by seeking out the submission, by knowing that was the objective above all else. He didn't care where he started. He just tried to find a path from there to a choke or joint lock.

Early in his development, the "Twister" became an apparent preferred attack and a lesson that would continue to serve him. His little bit of a wrestling background was useful.

His first year of wrestling was in eighth grade at the junior high. It was just practice. There was no competition other than competing within the team. The coach who taught the practice was a big wrestler, so he wanted to prepare kids for high school by giving them a head start on the others heading into high school. California isn't Iowa; wrestling didn't start until ninth grade.

When he got to ninth grade, he'd always dip out of weightlifting and end up back in the wrestling room. In there, a junior named Alex Niccochea and Jesse Barrios, a senior, took him under their wings. They were the only two leg-rider guys on the team who did guillotines, which are wrestling's version of what Eddie would tweak to become the Twister he would be known for.

Alex and Jesse saw a weak freshman with wirelike legs, so they said, "You're going to need this, dog, because you're weak."

He'd Twister a few guys in high school, during that ninth grade year, then he was hitting it day one at Jean Jacques Machado's school. Wrestling gave him something he could maneuver around and try to get to, but the Twister was harder to get to than in wrestling because in wrestling the first thing competitors will do is give up their back. People don't do that in Jiu Jitsu. Wrestlers can become easy to ride and set up Twisters because they'll go to turtle position: their knees and elbows are on the ground, crunching towards each other in an attempt to not allow any of their opponent's offense to gain a hold by inserting their limbs between those knees and elbows to pry them open for an offensive attack.

Being that Jiu Jitsu players are far less likely to give up their back than a wrestler, Eddie had to figure out another way to get to a Twister, so that's how he came up with Twister side control. This version of side control is when your body is past your opponent's guard like in a side control position, but with your upper body, chest, and hips facing the opponent's legs. If the athlete on bottom turns their hips towards you, they've opened themselves up for a samurai roll or truck roll, which is when the top player inserts his bottom leg into a hook on his opponent's top leg. If it's your left leg that's hooked in, then you're rolling over your left shoulder, the shoulder that's already closer to the ground, diving towards an opponent's feet to swing them all the way around to a back control position for that top player.

From there, Eddie would get to complete the Twister without the lockdown. It was just with a hook in on the bottom leg, but the same upper body control of the opponent's top, near and top-side arm wedged behind us below our armpit, then a neck cranking motion with both of our hands locked on the far-side, bottom-side crown of the opponent's head.

Lockdowns came soon after "Judo" Gene LeBell, an actor and professional wrestler who was a tenth-degree red belt in judo and a ninth-degree black belt in Jiu Jitsu, showed it to Eddie at one of the seminars he taught at Machado's school in 1994 or 1995, early in Eddie's Jiu Jitsu training.

At the time, Eddie was doing the truck move, which is the entry to the Twister control, but it didn't have a name yet. Gene saw what he was doing with the Twister and said, "You should put your legs together in this figure-four control, and it will be much stronger." And it was.

That figure-four control was where the top of the ankle on that hooked bottom-side leg would fit right into the "knee pit" inside the attacker's knee. With that locked in, Eddie would learn to extend out the leg with the top of his ankle hooked on his opponent's ankle

With that leg extended long, he was better able to control his opponents, allowing him to more easily achieve the spinal lock submission.

That lockdown became something Eddie would use in a variety of places with its most notable success, outside of the Twister, being that control from half guard.

The comfort that Eddie had from the bottom was what would help facilitate his future success. It became a main strategy, an outside-the-box strategy, like how Bruce Lee learned to move past those Wing Chun men who were in front of him when he was ranked number six in the world.

Quarter guard is the easiest of the guards to get into because it's perceived to be one of the worst of the guards.

If you have an opponent in your full guard that means your opponent is between both of your legs with your legs wrapped around his torso.

A half guard means that one of the top player's knees and legs are past your legs if you're on the bottom, while their other leg is trapped between your legs. Your legs are either squeezing around that trapped, single leg to maintain control or your bottom leg is curled around that contained leg with your top leg shielding against their hips. The shield helps to disallow the top player from getting their hips down and pressuring into you as a means of smashing, then freeing that leg that is caught, and then fully passing those legs of yours. Your upper body is curled on its hip and side in this position, the shoulder might be on its deltoid, while forearms and hands are usually working to create grips and frames against the top player's upper body.

Traditional half guard has the bottom player's inside, bottom-side leg curling around the opponent's leg that is trapped inside the guard. Lockdowns come from a non-traditional half guard where our inside leg stays inside and our outside leg figure-fours around the leg of our opponent that is in half guard, the inside leg extends out, hooking ankle-to-ankle on our opponent. This allows total control over that leg.

Quarter guard is when the bottom player only has control of that top player's shin and calf. It's the least amount of control a bottom player can have and still consider himself to have some control with his guard.

Everyone gets smashed when they're beginning their training in Jiu Jitsu, and we continue to get smashed nearly every day from then on because there's always someone better. So quarter guard is one of the most frequent guards that a player can find themselves in. Whether you know it or not as a white belt, you're grabbing onto that shin for dear life and hand fighting from quarter guard.

Jeff Glover is another contemporary Jiu Jitsu player who plays quarter guard like Eddie does, but his preferred style is about using something called "deep half" to get on top at any cost. It doesn't matter if you pass guard, end up in their guard, or have to stand and try to pass the guard from scratch. He was focused on getting back on top, even if that meant resetting.

Eddie likes for his students to work on sweeps where you're getting past the guard, and you're passing the guard in the sweep. Sweeps are when a player moves from bottom to top by disrupting his opponent's base, then getting past the guard means getting past your opponent's legs and into one of these top pinning positions like side control or mount for example.

A trend in Jiu Jitsu today is people discovering for themselves the concept of wrestling up. Eddie has been doing it since he started, realizing early on that he could use this quarter and half guard game as a means of securing double underhooks with his arms underneath the opponent's armpits, thus disallowing them from re-hooking underneath and smashing him down.

He could then swing his hips from the side, using the double underhooks, which are gripped together behind the opponent's back, to help provide the leverage and momentum to pick himself up off the floor and secure an angle with his hips behind the opponent.

The opponent will respond with an overhook, which we refer to as a "whizzer" in this position, with their near-side arm. If they don't secure the whizzer, the guard player has an easy path to the back. The whizzer is intended to block that but can create its own issues.

If we come up into this position from the bottom with the opponent's whizzer in, it's called a "dogfight." From there, the player who was on the bottom quickly becomes the attacking player.

Eddie would use this position because, with his wrestling experience, he'd end up with an experience and skill advantage in this position. But, if the guy had better wrestling skills than him, then he had to have another option like our "Plan B" sweep that uses our opponent's wrestling or resisting back into us as momentum to send ourselves underneath them and swing them to their back with us on top.

The "Electric Chair" is probably the most well-known and effective of these sweeping, pass innovations of Eddie's.

Similar to Plan B, in the half guard position with a lockdown secured, you use the lockdown-side arm as an underhook across your opponent's lower back and send the bottom-side arm for an underhook behind their hamstring. You can then hoist both of your arms up like you're a referee saying the field goal is good while whipping your lockdown towards the side you're moving your opponent's body, towards the lockdown side. There is a crotch ripping, hamstring pulling Electric Chair submission along the way to that once the bottom player ends up on top.

Eddie manufactured and distributed all of this game from the bottom, creating the defense to protect yourself when an opponent or attacker is on top of you.

Self-defense is self-defense first. It's not some cliché from a karate movie; it's real. The longer and more competently that you can defend yourself, the more likely that the attacker on the street will burn out of gas, and then you can take him into the deep water and drown him. If your defense is hard to defeat, then you are free to create your offense.

Rubber guard is an extension of that guard game.

In the Gi, Eddie's game was what we call high guard, a closed guard that is less around the waist of the torso and more around the chest area, pulling that opponent's posture downward and closer to you. It was the bottom-side, guard variation of high mount versus mount. He would use that high guard to attack the opponent's right arm, never the left, doing everything he could to lock the opponent's right shoulder in with his legs and attack that arm with an arm bar.

This was easier to accomplish in the Gi because of the Gi, but Eddie was having so much trouble playing this game in No Gi that he thought his game wasn't going to translate over, a serious concern.

In the Gi, your opponent's jacket and your pants create a ton of friction that disallows them from squeezing and squirming their way out of the guard to reset in a more comfortable position. Back in the 1990s, when athletes went No-Gi in competition or after practice, no one wore rash guards; it was all skin-to-skin. They'd have Gi pants on or board shorts, but no shirt, and it was almost impossible to properly lock the shoulder from the high guard. Your legs are too greasy, and his shoulder is too, so your leg just keeps slipping down.

"I'm thinking, 'Man, my whole game is not going to work for No Gi.' I was worried," Eddie said to me.

PRIDE Fighting Championships was a huge MMA promotion that started in 1997. It was based in Japan, lasting until 2007, ending amid a scandal that tied the promotion to the yakuza and a UFC deal that resulted in all their top fighters joining that promotion.

In PRIDE 1, Renzo Gracie was fighting Akira Shoji, a fight that finished as a draw after three ten-minute rounds. At one point, Akira was inside Renzo's guard and Renzo brought his right leg up perpendicular, across his opponent's upper back, with Akira's left arm locked in down by Renzo's hip. Renzo then used his left hand as a grip to pull his right ankle and shin towards him.

Renzo wasn't able to do much with it. Because his left hand was being used on a grip against the leg on the left, near the side of Akira's head, it meant that Renzo's right hand or elbow wasn't able to strike Akria as effectively as he would have if he had the left arm gripping that right ankle on the other side of his head. This was something Eddie would improve on as he took Renzo's position and turned it into something called "Mission Control." Renzo did break Akira's posture enough to stop him from connecting on strikes from within Renzo's guard, so there was a clear added benefit worth exploring.

Eddie would like to play guard from his right hip, so his left shin would be the one over the top of his opponent's upper back. People look at the move and think it's predicated on extreme flexibility, but while you need to be flexible enough to be an athlete with it, it's largely built on our bottom-side hip's adherence to the mat. We want to be on our side—our hip—not our glute.

With this left leg up, Eddie would use the left arm, which is over his opponent's right arm, to hug his own left knee to him. Their right arm is pinned closer to his left hip, crunched in by the knee hug.

That left ankle can be grabbed by the right hand in either a grip with your palm facing away or facing your palm towards you in a fist with your wrist hooked in the crook of the bones on your outer ankle.

After seeing Renzo do it, Eddie would immediately start messing with this Mission Control position as described above. Then came the "Meat Hook," which is when the left arm that's hugging that left knee reaches behind your leg and ankle to grab your opponent's pectoral muscle near the armpit with your palm facing away and your thumb pointed down towards the opponent's torso, rather than his shoulder.

Eddie came up with the Meat Hook at Grapplers Quest in Las Vegas. He didn't remember how he did it. He was just free styling, and he would have forgotten what he did if he didn't see it on video. Once he had the Meat Hook, that was when he really started playing with the concept of rubber guard and an objective in mind.

By using the knee hug or Meat Hook, the bottom grappler then has the freedom and control of their opponent's upper body to free his own right arm to now grab control of that far, left wrist of their opponent. This creates the space necessary for the bottom player to maneuver the bottom-side, right leg through the window to set up head and arm triangles with his legs. The Meat Hook replaces the hand that was gripped on the shin, continuing the breaking of an opponent's posture. A foot can replace the hand that's in the Meat Hook and really twist their opponent up.

This foundation of his game was created over the years with the same style of slow build that is required in the sport. It was a daily grind that was measured over months, realizing progress in increments, as the knowledge and skill accumulates. The progress is in seeing yourself as better than you were six months before, not knowing entirely how or why every time, but knowing that you are better, smoother, stronger, more technical, and more capable.

All of that progress would eventually put Eddie in the position to earn that life-changing opportunity to compete at ADCC in 2004, the first time it was held in Brazil.

Many of those innovations were founded out of desperation, putting himself in uncomfortable situations, and figuring a way out.

The goal is to become so good at defense that you're not scared of what your opponent is throwing at you, knowing you'll withstand the storm. This frees you to play offense without hesitation, using the knowledge that you can go for something and not be concerned about being reversed into a disadvantageous position.

Eddie's guard game would be this premise in action: by being comfortable on your back, it makes you comfortable with the most uncomfortable. You know you're capable of sweeping and passing your opponent, so you're confident that you're always just a moment away from changing the dynamic of the match.

Royler was known for his smashing top pressure and his knee slice, a move where the top player works to slide through a seated opponent's open guard with the top player's inside leg. Royler was a smashing style of grappler. He would get on top and pressure you until you broke, then, if you were lucky enough to get on top with him on his butt and back, almost no one could pass his guard.

One of my early introductions to Jiu Jitsu was watching Demian Maia go on the run of six straight wins that led to his title shot against Tyron Woodley, to whom he would lose. Demian was winning almost entirely with grappling in the fights I saw. Some would end in submissions, but he'd end up on this knee slice, side control, path to the back repeatedly. It's the most fundamental, traditional form of Jiu Jitsu, something Royler and Demian each mastered.

Eddie's game would be an attempt at an antidote to this from the bottom-side player. Where others would never want to start in the danger zone of being on the bottom, Eddie saw it as an opportunity to get under his opponent, be the lower man, and use that low-man leverage to get on top and pass that guard in the process of getting on top. This was his strategy of choice rather than attempting to wrestle someone down and pass their guard while wrestling, which is a bigger undertaking from an energy perspective as well. With the little wrestling experience he had, his ability to wrestle up became a valuable skill set for him.

His strategy was to pull guard, then offer his opponent the opportunity to go to his right with no top-leg shield up. That was the deal he was making, and everyone would take that deal.

Eddie would then look to go to his lockdown from quarter guard, which is why he would be willing to be on his back with no leg shield. Quarter guard is turned into lockdown via a "mini-stomp action" where the outside leg goes shin to shin, the inside leg is clamping and curling over the top of that calf, the extension happens to turn that quarter into a half guard, and then the lockdown is secured by moving the inside leg inside, putting that outside leg into that figure four position and extending that inside leg with that ankle-to-ankle pressure on the opponent's leg.

Most people aren't willing to play that game because how are you going to play with the shield, but then also have access to the lockdown from quarter guard? You can't. You have to be comfortable with taking that risk of the quarter guard. He would throw up the shield a little bit, but he would take it away at the right time when he saw an opening. Eddie became a master of using people's energy against them.

Everyone took Eddie's offer of quarter guard in competition, because that seemed like a good deal, but then suddenly Eddie would put people in positions they hadn't been in before.

For Eddie's whole journey, Jean Jacques was encouraging him to be different.

In the early days of Jiu Jitsu in America, there were very few tournaments, so schools would only be able to send one or two representatives at each belt and weight class. During Eddie's white belt days, there was a guy named Simon who would get that spot, but Eddie was always tapping him.

One day, Eddie was rolling with Simon in front of a bunch of the instructors, John, Jean Jacques, and Rigan Machado were all there. And Eddie's pissed, thinking to himself "I'm fucking tapping this guy and they're giving him the spot."

So Eddie put it on him that day. He finished Simon with a toe-hold and put him in a Twister.

After the round, John Machado tells him, "Okay, all this crazy stuff you're doing, it's great, it's great, but now you have to start learning real Jiu Jitsu."

Jean Jacques interrupted him and said, "Johnny, we need someone doing this unorthodox, crazy stuff." Then to Eddie he said, "Keep doing what you're doing, Just keep going."

As Eddie tells it now, "Jean Jacques was always supportive of the path I was taking, which was a lonely path. Everyone was always conspiring against me to try and stop the shit that I was doing."

Eddie's abilities pushed his team forward as his skills would cause his teammates to go to Jean Jacques to learn from him on how to stop Eddie's game.

Years later, at the first PanAms Championship in California, Johnny would help stop a riot by calling out to Eddie to stop yanking on a knee bar as the Brazilians in the stands who believed in the tradition of the sport were against Eddie's use of a completely valid submission.

*Jean Jacques watching
Eddie compete.*

There's a Jean Jacques quote that plays in the main 10th Planet commercial: "Just imagine someone who has no idea how different your game is."

In his first match against Royler, it was a situation of Royler on top for the first few minutes, using that knee slice to try and pass, and Eddie playing on bottom. To this point, Royler had never been scored in ADCC competition. He would use a ton of head and arm pressure to smash through Eddie's guard a few times, but he would constantly get put back into Eddie's quarter guard.

At one point, Eddie swept him, Royler attacked with a triangle, Eddie backed out, and Royler came up with a double-leg takedown from his knees, then Eddie went for a 100 percent grip with his left arm coming under Royler's right armpit. Eddie's right hand then clamped the left hand, the right palm facing towards himself and the left palm facing away with a grip that can help facilitate a sweep via shoulder control. But Royler's shoulder stability was too strong. He was too strong.

The rumors about Royler's shoulders were true, and he went right through one of Eddie's money moves. So something Eddie thought would be a trap Royler would fall into turned into a guard pass for Royler. Eddie jailbroke though and inserted that outside top leg into a butterfly guard that allowed him to pick up Royler's right leg enough to get his bottom-side leg back in between Eddie and Royler.

Eddie then made it all the way to a closed guard before entering into his rubber guard, pulling both legs up into a high guard from his back at first, which quickly became a loose-style Mission Control. At this time, both of Royler's arms were inside by Eddie's torso. Eddie made it a full Mission Control by inserting his left arm inside Royler's right arm, then securing an overhook that allowed him to hug the knee. Achieving this overhook grip from bottom is called Zombie as it looks like a zombie's hand coming out of the dirt.

Royler got up on his feet, smashing down into Eddie, which only allowed Eddie to make his grips deeper, bringing his hands all the way into an *S*-grip behind his shin. He then crossed his right foot over his left to secure further control.

While Eddie was under him, recognizing the power and dexterity of Royler's shoulders, he decided that the *omoplata* that would have been open to him would not work, so the triangle was the only potential option to finish him.

He had to think of something because time was running out and Royler was ahead on points due to the takedown he hit on Eddie. Royler had been known for stalling when he was up on points, so Eddie was going to have to create something on his own.

Then Royler passed his guard again, this time to the left with a knee slice. Eddie jailbroke him back into his guard again, and he got the overhook on Royler's right arm with Eddie's own left arm. He grabbed Royler's left wrist with his right hand. Royler couldn't pull back out of Eddie's guard; he couldn't posture out. That was the key. Both of Eddie's shins were on the inside of Royler's thighs in butterfly guard.

The left arm with the overhook kept Royler tight to him, while Eddie grabbing the wrist allowed him to maneuver his right leg. He moved it through that window between Royler's body and outstretched arm, then up and over his shoulder, briefly crossing his right leg over his left ankle before crossing that right shin across Royler's back and switching his left hamstring into a curl over that right ankle to begin to secure the triangle.

Royler's right arm and head were now being squeezed between Eddie's thighs. Royler had stood up to defend and now fell back onto his ass as Eddie cinched in the triangle.

Eddie knew Royler wasn't going to be able to get out, so the only thing left to worry about was the time, so he squeezed with everything.

Royler came back up, trying to scramble out of it somewhere, looking for a way out of the submission, but he fell to his knees. His outstretched right hand tapped behind Eddie's ear four or five times as Eddie pulled his head down to further inflict pressure on the triangle.

As Eddie would tell you, he raised his hands and walked around the mat like a king, but inside he was thinking, "What the fuck just happened? Did I really just do that?"

After having his hand raised by the referee, Eddie fell to his elbows and knees to cry, his first time experiencing tears of joy.

The translation of what Royler told the Brazilian national broadcast team was that Eddie's win was a fluke. "He just got lucky."

Eddie left the mat to hug Jamie Walsh, who he had submitted at trials and who became his strength coach for the six months leading into ADCC, and a young Joe Rogan with a full head of hair. Eddie was still crying when he spoke to the reporter. "He's a legend...I can't believe I won."

Joe kept yelling, "Oh fuck. Oh fuck. Oh fuck."

On the way to the airport, Joe summarized the weekend as when all of Eddie's hard work culminated in one great moment in time where he showed the world he was a champion, despite what would happen in the next round.

It was like the United States hockey team beating the Soviet Union in the 1980 Olympics. The most noteworthy or famous moment wasn't what happened after, despite the importance of that next game or match.

Eddie lost to Leo Vieira, the eventual champion. Leo had seen Eddie at the ADCC West Coast Trials six months prior. He viewed him as a real potential threat as Eddie came out victorious with a win in the finale against Alan Teo of Renzo Gracie's team in New York City, so Leo designed his training around dealing with Eddie's game.

As Joe said, Eddie had created his own thing and figured out interesting ways to get around problems in Jiu Jitsu. Leo had the one person in Brazil who could help him prepare for Eddie's style, Lucas Leite, the best bottom-half player in the country and a team-mate of his.

Most people naturally pass to their left, which is to their opponent's right, because it's easier for them. It means having your right knee and your right arm as the body-side tools, which, for most people, is going to be your dominant side, the side you gravitate towards. Leo Vieira didn't take Eddie's half guard bait once. Not only that, but Lucas told Eddie that the leg drag, a move where the top player pulls his opponent's leg across his body to pass the guard behind the leg, was created to deal with him.

If Eddie wasn't able to force someone to the side he wanted, he'd stand up and wrestle. If he got taken down, he was going to put you on his good side. He had no such chance.

Eddie got blown out on the scoreboard: 16–0. Points are judged in the sport based on passes, sweeps, mounts, back mounts, and submission attempts. Leo kept on passing Eddie's guard. Eddie re-guarded repeatedly and played a solid defensive game, but time and points were factors. Leo had a submission attempt with a head and arm choke where Eddie had some leg control of one of Leo's legs, but it was a game of passing and re-guarding for most of it. Leo added a feather to his cap by finishing the match in mount.

Leo scouted his opponent, game-planned for him, and came up with new strategies to deal with the problem his opponent presented. Leo acted like a professional.

Eddie's losing score fueled some of the doubters of Eddie's style and his outspoken respect for marijuana's impact on his game in a sport of rigid traditions.

After he returned home to Los Angeles, his disappointment would eventually subside as he realized that he earned a lot of respect from people on The Underground, a legendary forum for Jiu Jitsu and MMA participants and fans in the early 2000s.

There were still doubters, especially with the way Royler commented that it was a fluke, but Eddie had arrived as a known commodity on the scene. More people were talking positively about his win than negatively about his loss.

Eleven years later, he would get a chance to put the idea of it being a fluke to rest.

"Eddie Bravo versus Royler Gracie 2" was one of the most hyped and anticipated matches in the history of the sport, taking place at Metamoris 3, a Ralek Gracie promotion. Of which there were six shows.

It was a twenty-minute, submission-only match. No judges. It was either a submission or a draw.

Like his ADCC preparation, Eddie rededicated himself to a strength and conditioning regimen, this time focusing on Olympic pool swim sprints. It would be a twenty-five-second sprint down, then he'd wait until the clock hit the top of the minute again to swim back. He had to race himself down there because his rest time was however much time he had once he was there. His goal of training to be explosive, then bringing his heart rate down in that rest period, simulated making a move to a preferred position, then settling into that position and taking that moment to control his breath.

Eddie started the match by coming out, briefly faking like he was going to wrestle, before taking his quarter guard. He knew Royler was going to play the same knee slicing game he'd played eleven years before, eager to prove that Eddie wasn't capable of withstanding that pressure twice. He had his left arm attempting to secure and crossface Eddie's head with his shoulder pressure against Eddie's jaw to turn his face away from Royler, while his right arm was positioned in control of Eddie's lower back.

Royler's game was about putting top pressure on you until you break and for the first six and a half minutes, Royler was pressuring down into Eddie.

Eddie turned his hips from his right to his left with Royler's right shin between his thighs to a kind of three-quarter mount variation. In swinging back to the right, Eddie took his left hand, pushed Royler's right knee down, and secured a half guard for himself when he returned to his strong side for his guard. Eddie then locked in his lockdown.

Eddie fought for the double underhooks and thirty seconds later, Eddie had Royler extended in his Electric Chair submission. Royler's right leg was extended out in Eddie's lockdown, while the back of his left shin was curled over Eddie's right shoulder. Eddie had a palm-to-palm Gable grip over Royler's left thigh, securing him in place. On the video you can see Eddie talking to him, smiling and busting his balls, asking Royler if he was okay as he heard his hamstring popping.

Eddie came on top, then Royler pushed him back to the Electric Chair with Eddie on the bottom, which was actually a more uncomfortable position for Royler to be in. It was a symptom of Royler being overwhelmed by the configuration he found himself in. Eddie then got back on top.

On the broadcast, Jean Jacques can be seen yelling to Eddie, "Know your game, Eddie! Know your game!"

Eddie took his own right leg, which was the one inside Royler's leg, and brought it around the outside of Royler's leg. He settled into side control, and while maintaining control of Royler's head with his left arm, Royler's left, bottom-side leg was curled in Eddie's right arm. Royler was turned away, and Eddie's hands were connected, squeezing Royler in a bit of a cradle position.

An announcer took a moment to remind the viewers that few people have ever been able to pass the guard of Royler Gracie. Before his loss to Eddie at ADCC, he had never been scored upon in three title runs at featherweight in 1999, 2000, and 2001.

Eddie passed him via that Electric Chair sweep.

He let go of the cradle and settled into a traditional-side control, which caused Royler to work his frames against Eddie's body so he could turn away into a turtle position with both knees and elbows on the mat.

Eddie went to truck and inserted a lockdown on Royler's left leg, secured a 100 percent grip on his right arm, and then came up on top to secure a brutal neck crack. Royler's head and neck were facing towards the sky and his back to the mat. His head and neck were contorted beneath Eddie's left armpit and chest as Eddie's legs extended, and he ripped on that far, right shoulder. Royler was stuck dealing with it for fifteen to twenty seconds before he shucked Eddie off his back. Eddie transitioned to get his hooks in and assumed a back mount with Royler, again in turtle.

Royler was rolling for his survival. He shucked Eddie off his back.

Eddie landed on his bottom and assumed his open guard. Royler jumped into his half guard, and Eddie put the lockdown in right away. Royler smiled now that he was on top, thinking it was his time to start smashing.

The high pace at which the match was going was a testament to the impressive conditioning and skill of the forty-three-year-old Eddie and forty-eight-year-old Royler.

The announcer mentioned that Eddie's wife and two-year-old son had become a major source of inspiration for him, another sign of the times that had passed since the last match.

After two minutes of Royler on top in Eddie's half guard, Eddie secured another Electric Chair submission attempt. He eventually turned that into a sweep as well, using his right shoulder to keep the leg secured and his right hand reaching behind Royler's shoulder to force him down.

Eddie was on top, but Royler swung it back, and now he was in Eddie's half guard. Eddie reassumed the lockdown.

A minute and a half later, Eddie hit Royler with another Electric Chair sweep, but Royler brought it back. Eddie then got Royler's right leg past his body, sweeping him in the process. Eddie was past Royler's right leg with his own two legs wrapped around Royler's left leg in a lockdown, and Eddie's right arm was underneath Royler's left shoulder, securing the underhook.

The ref separated them to move them towards the center of the ring, looking for a reset in the same position.

Around the mat, the crowd was raucous. Eddie raised his arms in the middle of the mat, acknowledging the support for the match. Both men shook hands and headed back to the mat to assume the position. On that reset, Eddie was trying to communicate to Royler to start in his half guard, then Eddie would get it set up by sweeping him and securing the position.

Either Royler didn't understand the position or he didn't want to understand the position as a means of securing himself more time to rest, but they finally reset, although not completely. Rather than giving Eddie the underhook he earned, the reset happened with Royler's arm framed on Eddie's upper body.

Royler had snuck himself a one hundred-second break.

They went back and forth in this position for a minute: Eddie on top, Royler getting him to fall to his side. But then when Eddie was back on top he got double underhooks, securing an even more dominant position.

With four minutes left on the clock and Royler's top leg cleared to allow for the roll, Eddie shot his left arm towards Royler's right leg, which was secured in Eddie's lockdown. Eddie rolled over that left shoulder and grabbed the top of Royler's right foot with both hands. Eddie pulled it down over his own left leg, which was placed in a figure four with the top of his left ankle secured in his own right knee pit.

Eddie got the "calf slicer," or "kamikaze," so deep that he tucked Royler's right ankle into his right armpit, securing an almost heel hook-looking grip on it.

Eddie was now smiling as he heard Royler's knee popping, again poking him with the fake concern of "are you okay?" To which Royler responded with a Dikembe Mutombo-style finger wag between grimaces.

The rule set and the contract signed had some weird requirements in it. Eddie was required to wear Gi pants for the match, while Royler wore compression shorts. Those Gi pants ended up saving Royler as he grabbed on the cuff for dear life near Eddie's right ankle. This stopped Eddie from using that right foot to stomp on the instep of his left foot, which would have produced more pressure on that knee, likely exploding the ligaments in the process since Royler's pride would have him committed to not tapping.

Eddie yanked on that foot for the entirety of the final four minutes.

With fifty seconds left, the crowd erupted into "EDDIE BRAVO, clap, clap, clap-clap-clap, EDDIE BRAVO..."

With thirty seconds left, Eddie put Royler's toes in his armpit, securing them behind the pec, and he just started torquing the foot the opposite way from its natural anatomy. There was a heel hook, and a toe hold. The match ended with Eddie in control. Everyone knew who won.

Standing ovation.

Rock star.

CHAPTER 17

THE SYSTEM
(ZACK)

Monday, January 31st

I headed out to Santa Monica to grab the key to Plaster's apartment from his new girlfriend.

After grabbing the key, I drove up the Pacific Coast Highway, past Malibu, up to Pepperdine. I drove through Topanga State Park on the way to Laurel Canyon on Saturday; there are some great roads there.

My mind took a mental note to do this with my family. It's worth seeing as much of it as I can, heading north toward Santa Barbara, maybe beyond.

I turned around and headed towards Venice to get out of the car and take a walk along that strip of concrete boardwalk that we all know from a show or movie. My summers in New Jersey had trips down the Jersey Shore to boardwalks like those in Point Pleasant or Seaside Heights.

Manifest destiny. We're on the other coast.

A willingness to leave the things you know for something different is the hero's journey, a jump into the unknown, a risk that becomes a story. James was incredibly talented; he was born to play music. It was those stories of other bands that went out to Los Angeles to try to make it that inspired James. It was James who inspired Eddie, then Eddie who has inspired others.

Many people you meet in Jiu Jitsu in places like Austin, Los Angeles, or New York have stories like this. They're examples worth following, profiles in courage.

They're real stories, not just something you read about someone in another time or place, but people you know, something you see.

The story of James's survival or Charles from 10th Planet Headquarters overcoming his childhood: these examples tell you that you'll make it too. Being around winners helps make you one.

Winning isn't what the television tells you it is. It's not glitz and glamour. It's not shiny. It's taking the hand you have and making the most of it with a smile on your face.

Eric LeGrand is a Rutgers football player who was paralyzed on a kickoff in 2010 as he tackled the Army Black Knights returner. A few years after it happened, I marveled at the way he was able to stay positive despite living through what he would have perceived to be a nightmare as a twenty-year-old super athlete.

He is just three months younger than me. At the time I met him, I was going through my shit that was nowhere near as difficult as what he was faced with, yet he was in a far better head space than I was. He had a goal, and still does, a self-belief that he will walk again.

When asked on a podcast by Joe DeFranco's Industrial Strength Show podcast on how he stays positive in the face of what happened to him, a question I gave Joe to ask him, Eric recounted his days in the hospital and therapy, days where his room was filled with visitors, people willing to uplift his spirit. There were others in the rooms around him who didn't have anyone visiting them, people with whom he would begin to build relationships and work to share some of the positive energy he received from all his visitors.

There's always someone who has it worse than you, someone with less support. There's always someone with a worse prognosis or a longer, tougher road ahead. He looked at what happened to him as something that was unfortunate, but unfortunate compared to what? And that "compared to what" resonated with me.

Sure, things might suck for you right now, but how much worse could they be? And in that, how much do you have to be grateful for?

James is Eddie's version of that story, an embodiment of the proper spirit with which to engage with the world.

Heading back towards Eddie's school, I drove a little further east, towards whatever Google Maps has pinpointed as Skid Row, described as a couple square miles, or four dozen city blocks worth of downtown, that is completely taken over by the homeless. It's a problem that I fear is spreading, and will continue to spread, across the country as the economy continues to be disrupted by the various forces acting against it as well as the various cultural forces acting against the soul.

Skid Row's population is projected to be between four and eight thousand, but how accurate could that be? Who knows.

Veterans make up 10 percent of the population, which is disappointing. They paid for their service with their sanity, yet our politicians that profited off a few generation's worth of questionable wars can't even give them a clean room to do heroin in.

Much of homelessness is a problem that resides in addiction and, yes, people's personal decisions, but it often resides in people not having anyone else they can rely on when they hit a tough time. It's an unfortunate part of any society: those who can't figure out how to make it work and what becomes of them.

It's too bad that it seems like no one is going to fix the problem or even try to.

I pulled up behind the gym; it was time for another hard session. I had that slightly anxious pre-practice feeling that comes from too much coffee and just enough weed, plus the knowledge that I'm about to have a hard ninety minutes of training against some of the best grapplers this city has to offer. Weed is known as the 10th Planet pre-practice supplement, the thing that makes the most fun thing you can do even more fun. It's an amplifier of your ability to be playful, so it's an amplifier of your creativity.

Class started with the basics of our Jiu Jitsu warm-ups: shrimps, cartwheels, hip walks, forward rolls, Granby rolls, backwards rolls.

On the wall of the gym resides our 10th Planet warm-up system, which is divided into eight separate days, *A* through *H* days. These days are cycled through every two weeks with the programming being implemented in Monday through Thursday classes. Weekends might be reserved for open mats or another coaching topic if there is a class. After two weeks, the eight sets will loop back around.

Not all schools are like 10th Planet Austin, with six grappling classes a day on weekdays, plus weekend classes and open mats. Many schools start out with one coach that's coaching one to three classes per day, five days a week. They're working to build up, or recruit, some purple and brown belts over time who can help take the coaching load off them.

Warm-ups are core sequences where both athletes progress through a series of moves and corresponding moves. Eddie's end goal is for it to literally be a fifteen-minute warm-up before his advanced classes get to drilling.

One player is drilling the "offensive" aspect of the drill, while his or her partner is responding with the correct opposing response. Over the course of the sequence, the offensive player can become the defensive player, and then the defensive player can become the offensive one as a reversal may have occurred. They're moving between defense and offense quickly like a turnover in football or basketball.

You're learning how it all feels and where it all goes to build pathways in your nervous system, internalizing it. You're making it a programmed movement for your body, encoding the right responses, creating muscle memory.

Rolling with the experimentation and experience that happens there, the data collecting of what works and what doesn't work for you in a live situation, is some of the most important work that's done in a gym.

To have a coach who can place things in a system, in a proven particular order that is intended to make your training deliberate and efficient, is an extremely valuable tool. It's what decreases the time from novice to expert, providing you with the blueprint of what you need to focus on to progress. This coaching is what athletes need to progress and excel.

A-day focuses on Granby rolls because they are the key to guard recovery. A Granby roll is a movement where you use your upper back on the mat to move your legs through the air to reengage or disengage with your opponent. You create a more dominant position or get out of one.

C-day is pressure passes, D-day is standing passes, and G-day is top half-guard passes.

E-day is quarter guard, F-day is butterfly guard, and H-day is open guard.

Eddie's intention with these days is to cover of the primary guard and passing scenarios an athlete needs to master. By focusing on this, Eddie's athletes will have a strong base even in the guards that aren't his forte but in the ones that he thought were important to add. He's working to build the best system regardless of his personal preferences, recognizing that everyone isn't going to grapple exactly as he does. There are different skills, backgrounds, and body types.

The meathead football player is going to roll differently than the skinny former skater or the hot yoga chick, so you better build a system in which everyone can build the core strategies for their own game.

B-day focuses on Hail Marys, which are where some miscellaneous techniques that didn't fit into the other categories are put, things like shin-to-shin entries or moves from front headlock control.

Each day I train with Eddie is a different warm-up day, a different point of emphasis. He has also added a few things aside from the warm-ups, key additions that we'll switch between each day.

There's Ramey Flow, a series of leg-lock positions and movements that help Eddie's athletes gain a level of comfort and dexterity in the variety of positions they could go to offensively or find themselves in defensively.

Hip-switch passing has become a stand-alone exercise, helping his athletes get used to using the momentum and flow of their hips in a pressure-passing scenario that unbalances their opponent's guard and moves past the legs. There's a flyover pass too.

There's a cartwheel pass to a reverse crab ride back take from the partner's inversion that hits on some explosive, complex movements. We're building those into our DNA.

Homie control against our opponent's head and shoulders is used with a scissor sweep to mount.

Years ago, when I first started, one of these core drills would have been arm bars from guard, something Eddie did a lot coming up in the Gi, but he ditched that—recognizing that No-Gi players ended up in different scenarios than Gi players. He and his coaches are always taking information in and adjusting accordingly.

As we get closer to the drilling period of class, my friend Phill Schwartz walks in, the first-degree black belt and head coach at 10th Planet Portland. He's in town with his soon-to-be wife and their new baby boy. By the time we get to drilling, I get a round with him while he's still warming his late-thirties body up that just spent the day traveling.

After a nice pass by me with continual pressure and responses back and forth between Phill and me, Eddie stops the drilling to go on a five-minute speech using us as an example of how we should be drilling. I'm on my back for the first two minutes, taking the moment as an opportunity to catch my breath, thinking we're about to switch roles and keep drilling, before I sit up realizing he's talking about me. Nice. That's cool.

Effort: the one thing you can control.

That's what Chai Sirisute of 10th Planet Long Beach saw when he gave me the nickname "Go Hard."

Phill is sure to smash me in our eight-minute round after class. He taps me three or four times, reminding me where I am in the food chain.

After the next night's class, Eddie gives me the nicest compliment he could: "You're a beast, dog."

I'm just playing the game he helped program into me through Curtis and the other coaches we have in Austin, plus the many Eddie Bravo-black belts that I've trained under via seminars and their visits to our gym. Friends like Phill.

I combine that education with my knowledge from past experiences as an athlete to maximize that training for myself, attempting to become the best that I'm capable of being.

There's a real benefit to hanging around people who are willing to tell the truth. When they compliment you, you know they're not blowing smoke up your ass. We're all earning each other's respect every day.

One of the most valuable things about my dad when I was a kid playing sports was that I knew he wasn't bullshitting me. He told me what I needed to do to play more or be better, and he told me the standard of effort expected.

James saw Eddie's leadership abilities all those years ago and now he's that kind of person for a lot of people, someone who serves as an example, someone you'd like to leave a good impression on. That's an important person for a man to have, another man whose opinion you actually care about.

For the next two hours, we'll hang out, smoke weed, and talk shit.

The topic of conversation often turns towards "conspiracies," which are whatever is on our minds, and whatever seems to be in the zeitgeist.

Lately, the topic of conversation has been around MK-Ultra, Operation Paperclip, Operation Mockingbird, and the way pharmaceutical companies own our media.

In August 1977, Stansfield Turner, the director of the Central Intelligence Agency, testified that the CIA had supported the human behavior control research program called MK-Ultra at eighty insti-tutions, including forty-four colleges or universities as well as hospitals, prisons, and pharmaceutical companies.

It was a CIA program that ran experiments administrating LSD to mental patients, prisoners, drug addicts, and sex addicts. It was a mind control, brainwashing program where the CIA was trying to learn how to control people's behavior without their knowledge.

The CIA's main goal of the program was to create assassins who could kill on command and have no memory of their programming, nor remember the act of killing, via the use of drugs and hypnotism.

Charles Manson was turned into a killer. The CIA hoped his behavior would cause hippies to no longer be seen in a positive light. He was taught how to use LSD to manipulate others, even into com-mitting murder. He was so important to the cause and well connected that every time he would be arrested, the arresting sheriff would be forced to let him go with an excuse of "it's above my pay grade."

Manson, a competent, aspiring musician, even hung around Laurel Canyon and became good friends with the Beach Boys.

Operation Midnight Climax was a subproject of MK-Ultra in San Francisco. The CIA would lure men into brothels, dose them up with LSD without their knowledge, and then study their behavior through a one-way mirror.

Whitey Bulger was an unwitting participant in CIA experiments with LSD in the late 1950s. He was dosed more than fifty times and asked leading questions like, "Would you ever kill anyone?"

He would.

Ted Kaczynski, also known as the "Unabomber," was a part of the Harvard LSD experiments.

Mobster Jack Ruby was visited by Dr. Louis Jolyon "Jolly" West shortly after he was placed in jail for the act of shooting Lee Harvey Oswald, the man who allegedly killed President John F. Kennedy with a magic bullet. Jolly was a CIA asset in MK-Ultra. In letters to Sidney Gottleib, the chemist who was at the head of the program in the 1950s and 1960s, Jolly proposed experiments in using psychotropic drugs and hypnosis to induce specific mental disorders.

About twenty-four hours after the doctor's visit, Jack Ruby went insane and his testimony in court was ruled out because he was incoherent.

Per The History Channel, Jack would die of cancer in January 1967, shortly after the Texas Court of Appeals overturned his death sentence for the murder of Oswald and was scheduled to grant him a new trial.

The end stage of these experiments feels like the constant news cycle filled with young, drugged-up males shooting up schools, parades, and movie theaters. The end goal was to create adults so bad at handling freedom that there's no choice but to accept more government control.

"We just aren't responsible enough to handle a gun or make decisions about our health. Let's all listen to Jeffrey Epstein's friends instead; they would know best."

For Eddie, the July 1969 moon landing is one of the most important moments in terms of unraveling the grand conspiracy. The United States claimed to conquer the moon, a win over the Soviet Union during the Cold War.

The *Saturn V* rocket was developed by the Marshall Space Flight Center in Huntsville, Alabama, a program led by former Nazi scientist Werner von Braun.

Von Braun came to America as a part of Operation Paperclip, a fourteen-year period following World War II during which more than 1,600 Nazi German scientists, engineers, and technicians were brought to America for government employment. The operation brought 34,000 Nazis to America.

The Soviet Union had a similar operation to get all the Nazi scientists they could for the Space Race.

Apollo program director Sam Phillips was quoted as saying that he didn't think the United States would have reached the moon without von Braun's help as he would play a key role in all six alleged successful moon missions.

Going back to the moon would be too expensive for our prudent and responsible elected officials to allocate a budget for today though. But soon, we will go to Mars as our world's wonderful, kind billionaires have promised us. Soon Richard Branson will make space travel affordable—he swears!

In Bill Clinton's 2004 autobiography *My Life*, he wrote:

> *Just a month before, Apollo 11 astronauts Buzz Aldrin and Neil Armstrong had left their colleague, Michael Collins, aboard spaceship Columbia and walked on the moon.... The old carpenter asked me if I really believed it had happened. I said sure, I saw it on television. He disagreed; he said that he didn't believe it for a minute, that "them television fellers" could make things look real that weren't. Back then, I thought he was a crank. During my eight years in Washington, I saw some things on TV that made me wonder if he wasn't ahead of his time.*

The fuckery around NASA is the foundation of all of Eddie's flat earth stuff with the flat earth stuff being a basic troll. It works to get you in a place where you'd consider the most definitively unquestionable thing in the eyes of the kind of people who believe in The Science.

If we're basing almost all of our knowledge of space off of what an obviously corrupt institution says, then we should question it.

"Space is the biggest Covid of all," Eddie joked.

The next "Covid," meaning a crisis, problem, or project with the only goal being to make those connected to the government more wealthy and powerful rather than solve any actual problem, is climate change.

He's obsessed with the story of NASA. He feels like uncovering the corruption within the found of NASA is one of the keys to unlocking people's understanding of America post-World War II. Von Braun was so comfortable with his position that he never even changed his name, unfazed by the potential of being tried for his crimes during World War II.

Brazen. Like when Bill Gates will inevitably try to sell us on his next "vaccine" project.

Eddie's confidence has grown after seeing the grand conspiracy that he'd been warning us about unfold. He isn't even trying to change the minds of people who don't want to agree with him anymore. He's confident with his ability to see patterns in media, information, and misinformation the same way he sees patterns in music and fighting.

December 7, 1941, was the day the Japanese bombed Pearl Harbor. That same day, five hundred United States Army troops moved into Walt Disney's Burbank studio. The occupation lasted for eight months. The way the army tells it today is that the "importance of the Disney Studios to the war effort is best demonstrated by the fact that the US Army deployed troops to protect the facilities," noting that Disney was "the only Hollywood studio accorded such treatment."

On December 8, 1941, Disney and the US Navy agreed to a contract for twenty war-related animated shorts for $90,000. The $4,500 they were paid for each short was significantly higher than their standard profit for shorts. Their three-month production schedule was apparently set for three times the amount of film they would normally produce in an entire year.

At least that's what the public has been told of the deal. Who knows what else Disney got or gave up.

Disney's work caught the attention of the Army Air Force, the Department of Agriculture, and the Treasury Department.

Propaganda, especially the wartime kind, is a profitable business.

Heading into that winter of 1941, Disney was in a financial crisis. Walt would routinely take all the profits from a previous movie and dump them into his next project. *Fantasia*, released in 1940, was met with low attendance and poor reviews, while it cost the studio four times the initial planned budget. *Pinocchio* failed to bring in profits as the war that had started in Europe in 1939 prevented many European moviegoers from seeing the film, minimizing foreign revenue.

Disney was already a well-known company with mass appeal. It was just facing financial difficulties due to the risk-it-all entrepreneurial style of Walt.

Snow White and the Seven Dwarfs premiered in December 1937, became the most successful motion picture of 1938, and by May 1939 had a total gross of $6.5 million, which, at the time, made it the most successful sound film ever made. It was those next investments, those next bets, and the circumstances they created that threatened the company.

But the war that had first threatened them then saved them. It pulled the entire country out of the Great Depression.

Problem, reaction, solution. The government is here to help, and war is good business.

Democrats failed in the previous mid-term election, but the oncoming threat of war in Europe convinced Franklin Delano Roosevelt to run for a third term, citing that only he had the necessary experience and skills to see the nation safely through the Nazi threat. He was then aided by the party as they feared that no Democrat except Roosevelt could defeat Wendell Willkie, the popular Republican nominee.

Breaking with the tradition set forth by George Washington, Roosevelt ran for a third and then fourth term, replacing his vice president who disagreed with his leftist economic policies with a "yes man" in former Republican Henry Wallace of Iowa.

Roosevelt won the 1940 election with 55 percent of the popular vote, the winner in thirty-eight of forty-eight states, promising that he would keep the nation out of war, something he didn't do.

Per *Smithsonian Magazine*, by 1943, over 90 percent of Disney's employees were devoted to the production of training and propaganda films. Production surged tenfold from 30,000 feet of film per year to 300,000. Disney would make millions.

An anti-Nazi propaganda short film they produced named *Der Fuehrer's Face*, featuring Donald Duck, won the 1943 Oscar for best animated film.

Despite Disney's success during the wartime period, it's a time period within the company that they would rather not revisit. *Smithsonian Magazine* noted that a Disney spokesperson initially offered an interview for them with a Disney archivist, but then the company decided to decline to comment on the article.

In 1993, the *New York Times* revealed that Disney was made a "full Special Agent in Charge Contact" in 1954. He passed secret information to the FBI from 1940 until his death in 1966.

1940. The year before his deal with the military.

Disney was allegedly one of those filmmakers who would go into Laurel Canyon's top-secret Lookout Mountain studio to produce films. Hollywood has had a long history with our government. Now, clearly, Hollywood will work at the behest of other governments as well, like the CCP—whoever can provide them with a bag of money is a friend of theirs.

Propaganda didn't end when the war ended. In 1955, Disney was involved in an episode of the *Disneyland* series titled "Man in Space." This was made in collaboration with von Braun, helping set the idea for the country that we would soon conquer space.

Today, Disney, and its subsidiaries like ESPN, will parrot whatever woke propaganda the establishment government class is promoting at the time, almost as an arm of that government class. They're that reliable.

Operation Mockingbird was a CIA propaganda program that began in the early years of the Cold War with the goal to manipulate news media.

MK-Ultra and Operation Mockingbird are clearly in conjunction after what we've seen during the Covid event, as we watched Americans fall into mass formation psychosis based on what their screens and trusted sources were telling them to believe.

The Wrecking Crew in Laurel Canyon were session musicians who were used by record companies to create false idols and rock stars who had a price and could be used to push an agenda. This is illustrative of much of the game. Selling out used to be frowned upon, and now it's the cost of making "art" or commentary in the corporate space where all the money is. Taking part in the lie is the game.

Lights. Camera. Action.

If you have a price, you have a price.

News wasn't the only area that intelligence agencies were looking to control. They wanted entertainment, sports, schools, corporations—they want it all.

By molding the minds of the populace, you control the culture and can push it towards what you want, which is an easily controllable and unaware populace from whom you can extract resources via political and economic means.

You want weak, helpless people you can scare into giving you more money and power.

Eddie's perception of television and movies is that both industries were made to propagandize people with flashing lights and well-edited content. Where music was taken over by corporations that had originally ignored rock and roll as it came up, television only had three channels for a long time. How easy was that to control?

How easy are the producers to control if you're already paying them? It doesn't matter to them who is paying them either. They just need to get paid, and they'll do what they're told.

The *Oxford Dictionary* defines prostitution as "the corrupt use of one's talents for the sake of personal or financial gain."

You can see it with the newscasters they put on the screens, the personalities the screens made famous, and the rock stars created by the shows run by these personalities.

If it is this easy with entertainment, how easy is it with social media corporations? These last two years of censorship weren't an aberration, they are the norm, we just didn't know it. We actually thought we had a say in what is "trending." The algorithms are designed to produce the desired outcome within national and international debates around competing political, social, and economic narratives.

Some, if not all, of these big tech corporations have sizeable contracts with the United States government. Some of those contracts are with the intelligence agencies that have proven to be unquestionably corrupt. And what kind of contracts might they have overseas?

These CIA projects couldn't have envisioned an environment more designed for their purposes than what we see in front of us today.

Fierce Pharma, a news, analysis, and data outlet covering drugs and the companies that made them, publishes a yearly study analyzing pharmaceutical advertising. In 2020, while the rest of US advertising spending dropped 13 percent, the total pharmaceutical advertising increased from $6.56 billion to $6.58 billion.

Of that, $4.58 billion was spent on television ads, which is 75 percent of all ad spend in a dying industry. It's estimated they spend an even higher percentage of the television news ad spend pie, making their money's hold over the corporate television news outlets even more powerful. Pharma increased their spending on digital video by 43 percent, while they were able to decrease print and out-of-home channels by 16 percent and 81 percent, respectively.

The top five spending pharma firms spent $125 million on Facebook, Twitter, and Instagram advertising. Pfizer spent $55 million themselves.

With people at home and on their screens, their dollars were more targeted, helping those dollars go even further than they already went.

After a very profitable year during a tumultuous economic time, the industry would increase advertising spending to $7 billion the next year, a 6.4 percent increase in spending. Pfizer earned $41.2

billion in revenue in 2019, $41.9 billion in 2020, and then in 2021 they made $36.8 billion on "vaccines" alone, so $81.3 billion total.

A lot of success for an industry that's legally allowed to advertise products that could carry side effects that include suicidal thoughts, violence, and general madness. Products that may exacerbate problems that already exist in the subject.

And here we are, sitting in a city where we can't go to restaurants or weed shops without a non-functioning mask and a fake vaccine passport.

Hanging out with Eddie is exactly as you'd imagine it on the podcast. He is always excited. He rattles off the latest thing he's thinking about, and everyone workshops these ideas, adding in knowledge, creating the real narrative for the world as we see it together. These are the core narratives Eddie continues to come back to, summed up as only he could. These nightly hangs that happen at Jiu Jitsu gyms are like our own podcasts, just for us.

These conversations represent the underlying ethos of what originally got us listening to Eddie on podcasts. This search for truth is what we crave.

It's a good group of guys. Phil hung around for a little before heading off to the family. The younger, single guys stay longer. A real men's club of sorts. These hangs are some of the most important moments of our training, a kind of therapy, normalcy in a sea of abnormal, especially these last two years.

We stayed until after 12:30 a.m., passing at least three different joints around, staying so late that I skipped the meal I was hoping to have.

Eddie was the last one out, closing the metal gate outside the door behind him, and jumping in his truck for the half-hour drive home.

I headed over to Plaster's, ready to pass out after a hard night of training and a great night of hanging with what feels like family. No matter where we may go, we can find normal people like us. It's an amazing blessing.

CHAPTER 18

THE MASTER
(ZACK)

Tuesday, February 1st

Waking up at Plaster's was anxiety inducing. It reminded me of a dorm room. A very clean, well organized dorm room, but the same claustrophobia. The six-hundred-square-foot studio apartment was in an old building. The kitchen was just big enough to fit one person between the sink and a stove-oven combo that's about as small as I've ever seen. The fridge sat next to it.

There were no closets. The side of the room had some boxed shelves for storage, and the bathroom was a little nook on the inside of the room. The back wall of the bathroom was against the kitchen. Plaster's bed, a king, took up about 40 percent of the core room space with a desk next to it.

The view was the brick wall of the parking garage next door. Again, it was less than half a mile from Skid Row.

Rent? $1,300 a month.

Austin's rents are creeping up, but they're definitely not where they are here yet.

I helped him do some laundry, considering his travel had been crazy, as a thanks to him for providing me the room, but the dryers didn't work and neither does the phone app that was used for payment.

It was further anxiety inducing as I spent my whole morning dealing with it, and then had to leave the clothes in the dryer for another cycle when I headed out to Long Beach to see our man James one more time.

About six months before Eddie had left for ADCC, the Bomb Squad—a half boxing, half Muay Thai gym—offered him a job to teach Jiu Jitsu. He'd just won ADCC trials, but seeing that it was before his big win against Royler, Eddie's self-deprecating humility came out. "Who is going to want to learn Jiu Jitsu from some Mexican? There are Brazilian legends everywhere. All of the Machado brothers, Rickson is teaching. Who would want to learn from a brown belt Mexican in Hollywood?" Eddie actually had two wins at ADCC. He beat Gustavo Dantas in the first round, then the match with Royler was the quarterfinal and his loss to Vieira was in the semifinals. He was now, arguably, one of the four best 145-pound grapplers in the world.

Right after the ADCC trials, Eddie and Joe started working on *The Man Show*, even working into their contracts that they both could go to Brazil for ADCC. When Eddie earned the spot at trials, he felt like he won a game show for a free trip. Being a brown belt, he didn't really think he could win anything. He was just happy to go.

Doing *The Man Show* was a great opportunity. Joe and Eddie had been writing together for a long time, so they'd been jotting down ideas for years. On day one, they came in with thirty sketches, fully written, and just about ready to shoot.

Joe was at the height of his *Fear Factor* fame, and Comedy Central was scrambling to replace Adam Carolla and Jimmy Kimmel to keep the high-earning show on the air. While Joe was shopping around a sketch comedy show, Comedy Central called and boom, problem solved. Joe got his sketch comedy show, and Comedy Central filled the void.

Joe called Eddie up, psyched to tell him *The Man Show* wanted to use him. He also brought their friend and fellow comedian Joey Diaz along for the ride.

But five minutes into the first day it was clear the show was destined to be a disaster. Those thirty sketches might as well have been thrown out the window. The writing staff wanted nothing to do with them. If Joe and Eddie had already written all of these sketches, then what was their job going to be?

Comedy Central's management lied to get them involved, promised things they wouldn't do, and convinced them that they would have a level of creative control that they didn't have. There was a lot of Joey Diaz drama as the suits didn't like him. All of the producers and writers were scumbags, but it was good for Eddie, he knows he needed to see that. He needed to see that the Hollywood dream wasn't what he thought it might be.

Before ADCC, Eddie felt like it would be a waste of time to open a Jiu Jitsu school, but six months later, after ADCC, with the old online message boards showing him love and him hating the job on *The Man Show*, he wondered if the job offer with the Bomb Squad was still good.

Larry, a friend of his, knowing how depressed Eddie was working at *The Man Show*, offered him a five thousand dollar loan for mats, telling him, "You've got to strike while the iron is hot."

Joe not only got him *The Man Show* gig, but also a job with the UFC as a part of the broadcast team. Here, Eddie would give his own opinion on who won a round based on his own scoring system that took into account a far greater number of variables than the traditional judges using boxing's 10-Point Must scoring system of giving ten points to the winner of a round and, generally, nine to the loser. They might get eight points if they really get their ass kicked.

Eddie called Joe, told him how much he appreciated him, and the he wanted Joe's blessing to quit the show. "Joe, you know how depressed I am. You know how much I hate that fucking job. I'm just going to teach Jiu Jitsu."

Joe said, "Fuck yeah, do that shit." He hated the show too. They lied to get him involved, so fuck them.

On the first Thursday in June, June 5, 2003, Eddie had his first class.

Eighteen people showed up.

It was the first time Eddie thought to himself that he could really make a living as a Jiu Jitsu coach.

"Then there were thirty students signed up to train, then forty-one, then sixty-two, seventy-five...oh shit, I can really do this thing...."

The rock star dreams never went away. Every job was just until he made millions on music. All of his instructional books would include musical stuff because he never wanted people to know him as an athlete first. People were never going to accept his music if they saw him as an athlete first.

While he never stopped writing down ideas, comedy was put on the back burner for about fifteen years. He'd come back later after years of coaching and have the public speaking skills he didn't have in 2003. The public speaking skills he knew would take years to develop at open mics were instead developed at Jiu Jitsu.

Years of bombing in front of his students as he joked between drills when they wanted to train Jiu Jitsu prepared him for a room full of drunk people who want to laugh, the mic in his hand feeling powerful. The joking around between drills isn't meant to be a distraction either. Keeping things fun is the underlying tone of the affiliation. You can't see progress if you're not having fun or enjoying it.

Every good team I've ever been on had fun and liked each other.

A few months after the trip, I met Eddie at a gig in Gause, Texas with Tin Foil Hat. It was a cryptocurrency kind of event, with a bunch of off-the-grid types in RVs, even some with kids. Sam apologized to Eddie for the gig, but Eddie was making good money for thirty minutes of work and had no complaints. Eddie is grateful for these opportunities to make money just by talking, something he's as good as it gets at. A show like this is nothing compared to all the open mics he got to bypass through his learning the trade the way he has.

On the car ride back to Austin that night, he told me about the world-renowned Russell Peters planning to bring Eddie to open for him after seeing one of his best sets.

"Music gets into the soul quicker. It's a vehicle," he said. "It's like how Quercetin pushes zinc into the center of the cell, so the zinc can stop a virus from reproducing. Music gets in your soul, then they drop off the words."

There is bad brainwashing and good brainwashing. That Coach Rizzi of mine in college would have us read a poem with Spencer W. Kimball's main message that "any excuse for non-performance, no matter how valid, weakens the character."

Good brainwashing is a lot of what 10th Planet is, using Jiu Jitsu as a means of becoming more scientific with your thinking, more reasonable, more rational, and more objective. All that "conspiracy" talk has the underlying lesson of only believing what you know to be true, what you've researched, and what you've seen or discovered for yourself. It's a philosophy built around a self-belief and self-trust formed through intense physical and mental training.

Eddie teaches what he used most as a competitor, builds onto that with all that he believes is most effective, and gives his students the full picture so they have a complete understanding of each and every move that could possibly happen in a match. But it's also so that if they have a differing style, they can find something that works for them. And differing styles can be very, very different.

Alex Magala is a 10th Planet HQ brown belt on his way to black under Eddie and the owner of 10th Planet Krasnodar and 10th Planet St. Petersburg in Russia. He has this unique style of crouching low with his right leg out in front of him, sometimes almost with his back angled towards his opponent. The position begs a wrestler to come in for a single leg, which allows him to dive into a leg entry to attack their legs. Oftentimes, he will end up in kind of a backwards open guard, with his head facing their legs and his arms ready to hug on to a leg and attack. That front leg is always ready to reinsert and guard his upper body against an opponent jumping into an attempt at a pass.

It's called the "Mantis Style," and the first time you see it, you have no idea what to do, something that's hugely beneficial in submission-based competitions. That's what we train for, the person who can get the submission and end the fight is what matters. Entirely new styles can be created if your main concern is bringing people into places they don't understand as well as you do, then submitting them. Presenting problems people don't understand is a good premise for sport or self-defense.

Everyone has their own style, but after years of going through the system as a student, then countless hours of drilling and rolling, a black belt should have the capability to teach the complete system.

Eddie explained, "I don't have a reputation for being the most articulate, well-spoken public speaker. I realized, shit, as long as I'm talking about something that I know deeply, it should be easy with any subject. Oh, you can do this with anything. You just have to know it well. The more you go through it in your head, the more you write it down, the more you know it. Writing it out, the act of writing, it ingrains it in your brain much stronger. You have to write it down, then write it down again. Put it in your head. You have to be able to see it."

Jiu Jitsu athletes can teach because all they have to do is explain what they're doing when they're rolling. You do the same things so many times, have the same kinds of successes so many times, that you embed it in yourself, so you just start talking as you're doing it, explaining it to the students. Always stick to your favorite stuff first, but the warm-up system helps coaches with new schools get a group of beginners up to speed on the whole game and provides them with a set curriculum to inspire their daily classes, rather than having to come up with your own special sauce every day.

With anything that works, there are plenty of details to get into in regards to how and why it works, or how or why it might not work based on how your opponent responds, then what you should do to counter that.

Eddie went on, "Then you ask yourself, what's the best way to learn the sequence and therefore teach the sequence? Maybe a little bit at a time. Sometimes you start at the end first and work your way back. Sometimes you start at the beginning. What's best? What's the most efficient way to explain it?"

Eddie's style provides students with the foundational skill of playing off their backs, the next steps are to learn how to play a great top game, but you built that top game that from drilling against a teammate that is playing that 10th Planet bottom-side game. The sport is still the same as traditional, points-based grappling in many respects. You do want to be able to get on top to be the guy smashing, especially if this were an MMA fight or a self-defense scenario.

Take down your opponent, whether from standing or from guard with a wrestle up. Get past the legs and control their hips. You're past most of their power now. Get to various pinning positions with value predicated on an ability to submit the opponent via chokehold, joint lock, knockout, or technical knockout.

The goal is to create an athlete who can play from their back with that ability to sweep, pass, and smash. It's that constant reminder during his class to pass in the sweep, rather than wait to get on top and then pass from scratch. You must make everything towards that end.

You go to "leg-lock college," put your hours in studying there, and learn the leg-lock game, so you can win or defend on your way up the rankings.

"You need to know it all," Eddie told me, "but eventually you have to smash through things, get on top. Under jack their arm." This is when the top player's arm is beneath the same-side arm of his opponent, above the elbow, between the elbow and shoulder, and working to take the power from that arm as it's jacked above the opponent's head as they're flat on their back.

"That's the end game. People have to be talking about your pressure. 'That dude, his pressure comes too heavy, he smashes and crushes.' If they're not saying this, then you're not done yet.

You have got to master how to be super heavy. If you haven't mastered how to smash dudes between you and the ground, you're not there yet.

"What do you have to do to physically or scientifically make that happen? Your body has to maximize the push from the balls of your feet. Pushing. Pressing forward on the balls of your feet and smashing chest to chest. Find that perfect sweet spot where ultimate control is achieved. People need to be tripping on your pressure.

"Turn their chin. Crossface. You want people to feel like that mini-tap. You want to control people and they can do nothing. Nothing will happen.

"You want to pass and never go backwards. Once you beat the legs, you're good. *Never reset yourself once you're past the legs.*" He dragged the words of this final sentence out to add emphasis, changing the tones along the way.

"A lot of people will do that, they'll go backwards. They don't understand.

"Let's play on top, you're top passing. You should feel like you're winning, crushing, smashing. If you're in top half guard, then eventually you're going to get that other leg out and pass. You should be happy. Now you don't have to pass their knee shield. You're onto the next thing."

It doesn't always start with you on top either. Playing well off your back is about self-defense and preservation. We might be seeking out submission only in the format of competition, but being of capable skill, strength, and cardio means being able to withstand long enough for you to turn the tide. Staying alive.

Good Jiu Jitsu is complete: one of the singular martial arts whose mastery will place you in good standing on the feet and expert levels on the ground. It's versatile, it's defensive, it's offensive.

Eddie's competition game was an antidote to the smashing top game that Royler played, the traditional ways, but his dialogue right now is an ode to that same principled style of game he was taught by

Jean Jacques Machado, which he learned through his cousin, Carlos Gracie Jr.

Our end goal is the basics of what he was taught, what we're all taught the first day at a Gracie gym, but the basics are what you'll use the most in a typical street scenario against an untrained attacker. That's good, but you can't just have the basics in a fast-evolving fight game. You need to take it further, which is what the entire sport continues to do, buoyed by minds like Eddie's in gyms across the world, creating things now that we will soon see in competition. New trends, new Dynamic Quality.

To get to that end stage, elite game, to be able to do it against the best, to be able to keep it simple, you need to learn the complex. You need to learn everything. You need to know how to shut it down for yourself.

Only once you understand the truth of what you're looking at can you make it simple for yourself, and then you will have the skill to pass it on to others.

After picking James up, he and I head towards a place called the Long Beach Exchange, a nice food court of eight or nine different spots.

We discussed how Eddie's religious philosophy is closely aligned with what mine is, and then I realized how closely it is that ours align with James's. I see the way that my similar outlook, which has been shaped through my time in Eddie's affiliation, has been influenced by the man who was walking behind me, keeping me in front of his good eye, so he can be as engaged as possible with me. I walked backwards in front of him, doing my best to engage with him where he's at as we talk.

James was present. He was positive. He was content. He was thankful.

He knows what a bad day looks like. He knows what struggle looks like. He knows was triumph looks like, no matter how small that triumph might feel to some. Waking up every morning is a triumph once you've struggled hard enough. "Thank God I've woken up to another day."

James was an outsider in the world of heavy metal, an outsider to Los Angeles, and an inspiration to Eddie as he aspired to his goals as that Mexican American advocating for marijuana use in the rigid world of Brazilian Jiu Jitsu. Eddie went against convention; he was unafraid.

He knew that if he was well researched, like James was, he could contend with anyone. It didn't matter what his background was.

It's important for men to have other examples of men whose approval they're seeking. James was a superstar to Eddie, still is: the man and artist he built himself into before cancer, and then the man he's proven to be since. James has achieved the highest honor of the Stoics, to be worthy of your suffering.

The people of our affiliation have become a reflection of James, people who put in the work daily, working towards being worthy of the challenge of the day. Triumphant in our pursuit of our progress on the mat and all the things it impacts off the mat.

James hasn't been able to get home to Arkansas for two years because of Covid travel being such a hassle and fears of his weakened immune system, but a few months later, he makes it back.

Sharing his excitement for the various ways he was getting to relive these moments he spent with his friend Eddie, James gushed about him in a way that's a cross between a father and big brother. He's got such an old Southern charm about him that you can feel the joy that's vibrating through the sound of his voice.

By 2000, about three years after James was first diagnosed with cancer, a thirty-year-old Eddie realized he needed to get back into the music and keep his chops up.

Every stripper at the club has their own little kind of imprint on the club.

That girl is stripping and making her way through real estate school. That girl is from New Hampshire, and she came out here to be an actress.

This one girl had been stripping since she was eighteen because she had kids, so she had to get that money.

Every chick has a different story.

Nikki was stripping until she became a rock star. She was half Korean, half Italian and from New York. Her mom didn't want her, so she was sent to live with her dad, his new wife, and their two kids.

Her dad went to jail. He was a criminal. Now it's Nikki, the stepmom, and her two kids. The stepmom sent her off to her grandma. She just kept getting passed around.

She had been stripping since she was seventeen, a tough New York chick, and cute. She was super dominant at the club, an alpha chick, now twenty-three years old with the eighteen- and nineteen-year-olds following her wherever she went at the club. She was crazy though—drugs.

Nikki's husband is her music manager, and they just had a baby.

At the time when Eddie came in, she was jamming with this guitar player named Jason. They had a bunch of songs and a producer looking at them.

When Eddie saw the drugs and the crazy, he shied away from the situation, but at that point, he had gone years without someone to make music with.

After James went down, Eddie tried singing himself for a little bit, but he didn't like his voice. He wanted a real vocalist, and he started to wonder what music with chick singers might sound like.

Nikki was the first woman he worked with. The door guy had told him that they had the same taste in music, so Eddie couldn't help it, and they set up a jam session.

Eddie went to her house. Jason was there in the garage studio talking about how producers were going to put it all together, but they wanted Eddie to join up and add to what they were doing.

Sitting and watching, he realized really quickly that the songs had no structure. Nikki had no idea how to structure a song. She was just going randomly. She was good at freestyle, she could freestyle anything, but it was never focused. "Where is the chorus?" Eddie wondered.

Sometimes she would be off key, but the tone was so good. Eddie thought "If we could get her in a legit studio, we could fix up her voice, take out some of the bad spots, and polish it up." Once that was done, then she could hear what it was supposed to sound like, then go back and hit it perfect.

After listening to like six of the eighteen songs Nikki and her husband were putting together to try and sell, Eddie stopped them. She had a great voice, so he saw the potential of helping her focus her talent into something that resembled a song, something that resembled the three-to-four-minute formula he and James realized they should be pursuing just before cancer hit.

Nikki was born to be a rock star, but everything was improvised. Like L. Ron Hubbard, everything was a first draft. She didn't know how to get her ideas together, take her time, and make it right. She was just churning stuff out, always on to the next new lyrics.

There's no way to come up with a song that you've improvised. There are going to be pieces here and there, but the odds of having one jam session and something being done are next to zero.

A nugget over here, a nugget over there, and slowly you put it together.

Very, very rarely it might come out all at once.

He didn't want to join their band, but he had music that he wanted her to sing over, a separate project. "All I need you to do is just sing over this loop for like an hour. Then I will drive around all day listening to it, scrapping, and putting it all together. Then we record it the way I say, and you're going to look back and go, 'Oh shit, that's song structure. Not freestyle shit. You've got to put this shit together.'"

Eddie had her work on one song with him. "Let's see what happens." He was engineering too at the time, and he recorded it. "I'm not an amazing engineer at all. I can do it, but I would rather have someone like Danny Lohner engineer. I just want to produce."

Engineering was a requirement for him too. He was broke, so he had to learn. It's cheaper to do things yourself.

That first song was called "Obsession." Eddie loved it. Nikki loved it.

She started playing it at the strip club, and all of her friends who were already kissing her ass anyway loved it.

They did it again—same thing. Eddie put it together, all her lyrics. He arranged the vocal melodies and decided where the hooks were, maybe suggested some stuff, like "sing like this or do that."

The second song was great too. Eddie was stoked to be working with a chick who could actually sing. She left the guitar player Jason. There was a four-song demo that was distributed among friends, but it got weird and then it didn't work out.

People who don't understand music theory might not understand the difference between the lyrics and the vocal melody. Most people think it's just one thing. She wrote all the lyrics. Eddie might add a word here and there, but she was very prolific.

Nikki and Eddie.

She was on drugs, though, typically something speedy, so she would show up to Eddie's house with five hundred songs. "Nikki, we're working on this one. Stop, relax."

Nikki just never stopped writing. She was really good at it, mad lyrics. She could sing and freestyle over everything. She just didn't know how to arrange it and solidify it into something, how to actually build it into something, rather than the first thing that came off her head.

First draft after first draft. She was never focused.

Eddie loved that she could freestyle, since that meant he didn't have to write any lyrics. There were two other girls he was starting to produce with.

One was doing his lyrics and vocal melodies; she didn't care. She didn't want to write any lyrics. "Just tell me what to say."

Eddie said, "I'd sing it all fucked up and then she would sing it beautiful, and I'd be like, 'Damn, I like that shit.'"

The other girl wrote most of the lyrics, and would play guitar and piano. She wrote her own songs, complete songs. She knew how to structure absolutely perfect; she sang operas, and she was awesome.

Everyone was feeling Nikki's music, and they thought she was doing the vocal melodies. Their praise made her start to get a big head. "Eddie, I want to start arranging the vocal melodies."

She was telling everyone that she wrote the lyrics because she did, but she had no idea where to put them. Everyone was gassing her up.

Eddie tried to get her to just focus on the same process as the last four songs and build on that, explaining to her the importance and value of the role she played and communicating that that structure part is where he came in.

Now the problem was started. Nikki wanted to do everything herself, so Eddie thought to give her some music and have her try to do it herself. Maybe she would get it right, but, more likely, she would realize that she needed to focus on the process they already had in place.

Nikki worked really hard on that song, but it was vanilla. The song wasn't good, but it didn't quell these big ideas she had in her head.

It would eventually get to the point where she had enough steam behind her that it was worth finding a guy who was like an assistant-assistant engineer on Metallica's *Black Album*. He was some scrub on the side, but he was in there. He was at a legit record company in the studio with Sarah McLachlan, stuff like that— small time.

He did a band called Wildside, the last metal band before the record companies pulled the plug on metal. Some bands got signed in those final days of metal, like one band with Capitol Records or someone like that. They went over to sign their deal and were told, "No, you're not signed. It's over."

Long story short, Nikki was too crazy. She had drug addicts coming over to Eddie's house, because that was where they would practice. It got to be where he couldn't have her over because she was always bringing in trash.

This other guy started hanging around. He wanted to fuck her, so he was angling to produce now. He had all these ideas about how the music was going to get arranged, trying to take Eddie's part, and telling her what she wanted to hear.

Nikki decided she wanted to play drums. She didn't know how to play drums.

She wanted to play guitar, but she didn't know how.

Her guitar playing was like a little pattern, one little thing, and then she would just sing loud over it.

The situation was a disaster.

Three weeks from then, Eddie and Nikki had a studio session scheduled with the guy from Wildside, but Eddie was just making up every excuse to not practice because practice just meant she would distract herself with other shit, bring her drug addict friends by, and get more wild ideas about what she could do.

That situation fizzled out. It became a constant cycle of singers for the next few years for Eddie.

I dropped James off at his house, and we watched his favorite band, Dream Theater, on the television for a few minutes. It was the kind of complex, shredder music he and Eddie created when they were kids.

James showed me a folder of old documents. There was a letter from a friend dated September 19, 1988, raving about their second demo and proud of James. There were old flyers made by Eddie, advertising shows for Resistance. Another document was James's mother's biography from October 1993.

After one last hug from my "Uncle James," as I am now his nephew, I headed to the coast.

The car was pointed in the direction of 10th Planet Long Beach. I wanted to see the space that once housed one of our teams before it was burned down on June 1 during the "Summer of the Mob" that was 2020, both online with cancellations and offline with riots.

Controlled opposition across all forms of entertainment and media betrayed the people who supported them as they had the same financial interests as the politicians who were, and are, most obviously abusing the citizenry with an onslaught of divisive and destructive bad ideas.

Covid provided people with the opportunity to do the right thing, the hard thing, the perceived unpopular thing, the metal thing, when the situation got hard. When we needed courageous leaders, so many failed. They chose silence and a paycheck over jumping into the unknown.

Selling out is the cost of doing business for many. Like Eddie saw the underbelly of Hollywood, I saw the underbelly of a corporatized football environment that betrayed the very values the sport taught me.

As the riots started in the last days of May 2020, it was shocking to see NBA athletes who were completely silent when Daryl Morey was reprimanded by China for supporting Hong Kong's sovereignty in October 2019, somehow having the credibility with the media to speak on the issues at the forefront during that May.

LeBron James has a billion dollar lifetime Nike contract. He and his friends couldn't speak up about Hong Kong. They need China's Uighur slave labor to make their shoes as a March 2020 Australian Strategic Policy Institute study reported just before the Covid event kicked off here in America.

I pursued a career as an NFL agent. I know how dirty the intentions are. Successful agents advise young agents that one of the first things you should do for an athlete is create a foundation for "something the athlete cares about" for the good PR and the tax write off.

As riots were happening, the television was telling us that what we saw with our eyes wasn't true, and the CDC was telling us that these gatherings weren't a concern for Covid because racism was the real pandemic.

Everything is fake. It's just a matter of everyone waking up to it together.

A headline comes across my phone: "White House urges Spotify to take further action on Joe Rogan: 'More can be done.'" Getting Apple News headlines via notification is the best way to be aware of all of the top propaganda.

Joe Biden's administration advocated for the silencing of the most reasonable voice in media. We'd soon find out that the White House was pressuring Twitter to ban "anti-vaxxers" like Alex Berenson off the platform in the summer of 2021 and that the FBI told Facebook to suppress the Hunter Biden laptop story. Those two huge news stories would break on Rogan's podcast in 2022, the first via Alex, the other via Mark Zuckerberg.

The following month, the Olympics were in China and not a single one of the dorks in corporate sports media said shit about it, yet they'll advocate for the relocation of meaningless NBA and MLB All Star games from American states that implement laws this corporate-political establishment disagrees with.

A once-invisible enemy became more exposed, an enemy of the people more fully known.

The former Long Beach home of 10th Planet is still boarded up, and so are the stores next door. It looks like no one has rebuilt—it's a developed city block that's now undeveloped. It's next to a clean, newer apartment complex that almost got burned down that night as well.

My television and the smart people on social media told me that these people had insurance, but it doesn't look like it.

I'd lose my last book deal for lashing out at the members of sports media after seeing 10th Planet Long Beach burned down. I was combative with those media members who were publicly supporting these riots via donations to corrupt bail funds and their rhetoric on Twitter.

They would stay employed, of course, despite having the wrong opinion on nearly everything. Their primary function, outside of having a reasonable level of understanding of the sport they cover, is to have the opinions that their corporate masters want. Being wrong is their job. Intellectual prostitution.

The sun was going down. Thirty minutes out from this spot is the Point Vicente Lighthouse in Rancho Palos Verdes. It's a picturesque California scene: the lighthouse at the top of a bluff and waves crashing against a small beach with rock cliffs that must be two hundred feet tall.

The scene evokes a feeling of wonder at what's beyond the horizon, a wonder at the beauty of what's in front of us. We're making our ride uniquely ours, for ourselves. That's a gift, a present worth having.

I headed back to the ugliness of downtown Los Angeles to train one last time at HQ. Austin was expecting another winter snowstorm, and after most of the city was without power for almost a week in February 2021, I moved my flight up a day to make sure my family wasn't left to deal with that alone.

Watching all of the Jiu Jitsu programming Eddie implements in his classes as a function of the warm-up, Eddie embodies the core Bruce Lee philosophy: keep what works, discard what doesn't. Keep adjusting, stay in the pursuit of maximizing your time on the mat, become skilled at all that is necessary.

We finished up the session. It was one of HQ's last Tuesday night practices without a ten-round Tuesday, taking on the tradition we started in Austin.

Sitting on the mat after rolls, Eddie recalled his story as he kept bouncing around with the music, working with different artists, and looking to fill the void left by James.

By 2005, he was auditioning rappers and, with him having notoriety with Jiu Jitsu, they started to act weird. "Oh, you could probably fuck everybody in this room up" type of energy. Eddie could, of course, but nobody talks like that.

He wasn't connecting with those guys.

Eddie was thinking how he needed an MC who does Jiu Jitsu for his rap projects. He wasn't vibing with the guys who didn't train. The next day, Eric Cruz gave him a CD at Bomb Squad. Eddie invited him over and played a track that was a remixed hip-hop beat off "Terrible

Lie" by Nine Inch Nails. He rapped over it, had a verse in the chamber, and that song ended up becoming "Frantic Mind States."

The first song they did together, Eddie loved it thinking this was it—perfect.

Cruz went by the name "Compella" as an artist. He'd eventually grow into one of Eddie's black belts and open 10th Planet Pasadena. He would throw in UFC, Muay Thai, Jiu Jitsu, and MMA references.

Eddie took all the stuff he did with Nikki and turned them into hip-hop beats, having Compella rap over them. It was originally called "Compella and The Twister."

There would be another chick singer named Miranda, who he met at Legends MMA. He wasn't trying to make music with this chick. He was just trying to fuck her. He knew the odds were low that she could actually sing and do it in a way that would facilitate them working together, but she kept asking when they were going to make music.

After hooking up with her five or six times, and her continuing to ask, Eddie took a song with Nikki on his laptop, pulled Nikki's vocals out, and let it play.

Miranda was legit. She was so talented, even the words were good.

Being that Eddie was on the road so much at this time, it ended up working out for a while and they made music together. Eddie was traveling with Joe everywhere, and there were women all over the place, so he set a rule that there were no questions on the weekend. Eddie would get home on a Sunday, so they'd hang out and work on some music.

She was down with it because Eddie was up front with her, and she liked the music they were making. They probably did ten songs together as "Temple of Mir." She was even on tracks four and eleven of Eddie's "MixFlix of Death and Devotion," a YouTube video where every song is spliced up to a movie, representing a compelling and brilliant visual along with the music. Plaster produced the video.

It felt representative of Eddie's old Hollywood goals to sneak his music into movies as a means of bypassing the record companies that wouldn't sign him.

Eddie and Compella changed the name of their duo to "Smoke Serpent" when they added Al, another eventual black belt. Al doesn't run a school today. He's the head of security at some clubs in Hollywood.

Smoke Serpent was where Eddie mastered the metal. He says he can't do any better than the song "Tonight It Ends," the third song on the album. The song is set to the movie *The Crow*, the movie that Bruce Lee's son Brandon died filming, fatally wounded by a prop gun.

"Hook Thieves" has been Eddie's other main project since 2012 where he worked as a producer with a singer or a rapper. It was Eddie's "side shit" where there's no limit, and there's no band. He is collaborating, doing covers, remixes, and originals. "Hook Thieves" is him stealing hooks to songs and making them his own. Eddie said, "Hook Thieves, we're thieves. We're remixing, covering, original, everything, even remixing and stealing from my own self. Going back and rehashing."

Smoke Serpent was the main thing for him until the group dissipated in 2020. To him, "Tonight It Ends" represented him finishing the job that he and James started. He took everything they learned, their years of practice, and kept it simple—all embodied in one four-minute and thirty-second song. It was a masterpiece for him, just like that second match against Royler. It was proof of all the work that went on behind the scenes.

To Eddie, when you look at Smoke Serpent, that's 10th Planet Jiu Jitsu; it's a little bit of everything. You can't put your finger on it. There's metal, new wave, alternative rock. There's rap. He took what worked and accomplished the objective of creating a kind of music that's beyond genres, something all its own.

The goal is to create a kind of music beyond the simplicity of a genre. It's done by taking the best shit from what you like, the wide array of what you like, and making it into something that's both like what you've heard before, but unlike anything you've ever heard. Something familiar and friendly to your tastes and sensibilities, while taking your ear somewhere new. Something similar, but all your own.

Eddie's Jiu Jitsu takes the best from everyone and everywhere, working to make the equivalent of genre-less Jiu Jitsu. It's not top game heavy, it's not bottom game heavy. Bring in everything you can to understand and approach the entire game, know every position and possibility. Provide your students with a complete map of the landscape to see where they want to go with their own, personal style within the art.

He's provided the blueprints for a game that can go anywhere offensively and defensively with an ability to be offensive from anywhere. The end state is the ability to be a constant threat to the person attempting to control and submit you, *to be impossible to control.*

Take what works. Discard what doesn't. Build a complete system.

It's why the 10th Planet affiliation has so many high level coaches and competitors.

We were in the back of the gym. Eddie sat in the middle with Arman on the piano and Charles sat on that cajón of his, finishing up a final song before we headed out for the night.

As he was cleaning up, Eddie joked to me that this is what it all has turned into, his self-deprecating charm coming through when he says that he's jamming and making "Weird Al" songs.

He thinks it's Weird Al, but I can't imagine it could be any other way with Eddie right now. His desire to poke fun at the narrative shines through in these songs.

In late 2022, they came out with an album called "Jar of Lies," a play on Alice in Chains's "Jar of Flies." The cover artwork is complete with the Covid spike protein in the jar, rather than flies.

We headed out of the gym, turned the lights off, and closed the door behind us. I look forward to being there more frequently and

Eddie, Dan Yukhananov (engineer), Charles Rials, and Arman Fathi.

seeing Eddie in Austin more as it continues to become a hub for what we do.

The next day I headed back to Austin and the first entirely No-Gi scene in the sport of Jiu Jitsu. It was something cultivated by Eddie with his choosing Curtis Hembroff to open up 10th Planet Austin at Onnit Gym.

The next evolution of grappling and the style of Jiu Jitsu that's going to come out of Austin is going to be special. It will be complete Jiu Jitsu and MMA, great wrestling, and highly skilled in every phase of the game due to the competitive environment we get to train in.

When we first started, we were a gym full of white belts, but almost seven years later, we've got a gym full of killers and the best come to train with us. It cultivates an environment that makes us better, smarter, and more capable in every phase of our lives.

The seed they planted in 10th Planet Austin has grown into a forest, every major affiliation is coming to town to plant their stake in the ground. It's a fight city now, along with comedians, technologists, and musicians.

Leaving Los Angeles for Austin is a reminder of the opportunity ahead: a great city in a great state with every opportunity to become what the old California dreamers hoped California could be. It's a land of opportunity and a place for a real revolution.

We just have to maintain the right frequency.

Credit: Michael Plaster

ENDNOTES

1 McAlpine, Fraser. "The Unexpected Origins of Music's Most Well-Used Terms." BBC. October 12, 2018. https://www.bbc.co.uk/music/articles/dc64e24d-c4e7-4e34-b2f7-e34a00ea16ad.

2 Menand, Louis. "The Elvic Oracle." *The New Yorker*. November 16, 2015. https://www.newyorker.com/magazine/2015/11/16/the-elvic-oracle.

3 Ibid.

4 Ibid.

5 Reality Check Team, "Afghanistan: How Much Opium is Produced and What's the Taliban's Record?" BBC. August 25, 2021, https://www.bbc.com/news/world-asia-58308494.

6 Blakemore, Erin. "What Was Like to Ride the Transcontinental Railroad?" History.com. October 16, 2020. https://www.history.com/news/transcontinental-railroad-experience.

7 "All Things Considered," NPR. April 13, 2021, https://www.npr.org/2021/04/13/986929541/empire-of-pain-the-secret-history-of-the-sackler-dynasty-profiles-pharma-family.

ACKNOWLEDGMENTS

This book would not have happened without Curtis Hembroff, my coach and most loyal friend, telling me to pursue this as a potential project in January 2021.

This would not have happened without Eddie Bravo being the person that he is and getting to share that with the world through Joe Rogan's podcast. He has helped attract people like myself to his 10th Planet organization who understand what he and his team are about.

This book is a long time in the making—ever since I showed up on a Jiu Jitsu mat thanks to Eddie's inspiration and even before then. Writing any book is a lot of work, it's four notebooks filled with notes, using my notes app on my phone daily, three different styles of pre-writing outlines, and 20+ hours of recordings to sift through. Understanding Eddie the way I do, as a student, made this process as easy as it could possibly be. He would come to me with a vision he has in regards to the story, I'd already be writing it that way.

It's a surreal experience to see how much a great teacher has embedded himself in who you are through his leadership style.

I am humbled he and James trusted me with this project. James didn't know me before Eddie brought this to him. He trusted and shared with me his life story. Thank you for that.

Thank you to Clinton Mikel, our friend and the most gangster lawyer in America, for always having our back.

ACKNOWLEDGMENTS

Thank you to my father Tim Moore for being my editor from day one through to today, even when I sucked. He also served as an agent on this product with Doug Hardy and Gary June. Thank you all for taking the time to work with me. Time is our most valuable of resources, so thanks for thinking I was worth any of yours.

Thank you to my mom for instilling in me the values you have. Thanks to you both for encouraging me to do the right thing.

Thank you to my sweet Jamie, Luca, and Mateo. You have given me a family and purpose.

I've never met a more inspiring group of people than my 10th Planet family. My confidence and courage is largely derived from the love I share with these people.

Thank you to my family, coaches, and teammates, past and present, for the responsibilities you've put in me, it has and will continue to keep me on track.

And, lastly, thank you to our publisher Post Hill Press for trusting us and supporting this endeavor.

I am the most blessed.